D0641078

THE
DAVIS
DYNASTY

Fifty Years of Successful Investing on Wall Street

John Rothchild

John Wiley & Sons, Inc.

New York • Chichester • Weinheim • Brisbane • Singapore • Toronto

Published by John Wiley & Sons, Inc.
Published simultaneously in Canada.

Library of Congress Cataloging-in-Publication Data:

Rothchild, John.
    The Davis dynasty : fifty years of successful investing on Wall Street / John Rothchild.
      p. cm.
    Includes bibliographical references and index.
    ISBN 0-471-33178-3 (cloth : alk. paper)
    1. Capitalists and financiers–United States–Biography. 2. Davis, Shelby Cullom, 1907– 3. Wall Street–History. 4. Investments–United States–History. I. Title.

HG172.A2 R68 2001
332.6′092′273–dc21
[B]   2001035229

Printed in the United States of America.

10 9 8 7 6 5 4 3 2 1

Foreword

BY WEAVING THE FAMILY STORY IN AND AROUND the investing story, John Rothchild has written a lively and inspired account of this great stock-picking family. The narrative moves back and forth from Wall Street to the Davis household, so there's a constant interplay between the latest economic conditions and how the family responds to recessions, inflation, up markets and down. Also, the long-term perspective is a useful antidote to contemporary short-term thinking: Bull phases and bear phases have lasted many years.

On the personal front, we see how the elder Shelby Davis prepared his son (also Shelby Davis) to be frugal and to use stocks to build wealth. (Applying some of his father's techniques, his son ran a successful mutual fund.) On the economic front, the Davises adapted to the same challenges long-term investors will face in the future. No matter how big or small the portfolio, every household portfolio manager can benefit from reading this book.

I'd met the elder Shelby Davis several times during my career as manager of the Fidelity Magellan Fund. We talked at conferences, by telephone, and once or twice in my office, where we kicked around ideas about insurance and financial stocks.

I note with pleasure that the elder Davis followed many maxims I espouse in my own books, although in this case, I can't take any credit. He put these maxims into practice two decades before I did. His son and his grandsons have continued to apply some of the same stock-picking techniques I used at Magellan, and their overall view on investing sounds a lot like a Lynch sermon on the subject.

Rothchild's engaging and informative read may have a calming effect on the impatient household, as the Davises have stretched the time frame for long-term investing from one generation to three. They've been wedded to their portfolios for richer or for poorer, and eventually, the periods when stocks turned them poorer became trivial as compared to the overall enrichment. Moreover, their well-deployed capital has far outdistanced the typical paycheck. By owning insurance shares, the elder Davis did far better than most if not all the career executives who worked in the industry.

The popular and misguided notion that stocks are for the young, bonds for the old, is disproved here: for maximum compounding, stocks can be held indefinitely, while bonds outperform intermittently. Though investing early is preferable to investing late, the elder Davis also proved you don't have to start early to make a success of it. He was 38 when he began his insurance stock-picking adventure in 1947, and still he amassed the nine-digit fortune described in these pages.

I'm a vocal advocate of investing in things you know about, a tactic that is routinely ignored by doctors, engineers, and other professionals and nonprofessionals in the work force. Witness the multitude that saw brown grass in their chosen fields and bought into the lush prognosis for dot.com speculations. The elder Davis, on the other hand, capitalized on information that came across his desk at a New York State agency that regulated insurance. Once he'd figured out how to decipher these corporate reports, he realized he'd stumbled onto a "mother lode," as Rothchild describes it. This was the late 1940s, when many insurance companies were sitting on hidden assets their stock prices didn't begin to reflect. Rather than idly marvel at these bargains, Davis took advantage of them. He quit his job, giving up a secure salary to go into business at his own insurance investment boutique. When he found he couldn't coax clients into buying shares, he took his own advice and bought them himself. Great investing requires an independent spirit, and the courage to acquire assets the crowd disdains. Disdain creates bargains.

For a brief stretch early in my tenure at Magellan, I sunk more than 15 percent of the fund's assets into insurance stocks. Six months later, when the fundamentals deteriorated, I changed my mind and scuttled most of these holdings. Thereafter, I'd occasionally find an insurer I liked (AFLAC, for instance), but I never specialized in any single type of enterprise or sector in the market. I found opportunity in small and large companies, domestic and foreign, fast growers and slower growers, prosperous companies and troubled companies that regained their former prosperity. In this eclectic approach, I differed from the Davises, but in one important area we had something in common. Some of my most rewarding investments came from slow-growth industries where expectations were low and profits lackluster. By looking for the most inspired competitors in uninspiring lines of work, I often found great growth enterprises (Toys "R" Us, La Quinta Motor Inns, and Taco Bell, for example) priced for mediocrity.

Similarly, in the insurance arena and later in the banking arena, Davis and his son bought shares in the best and brightest competitors for much less than they'd pay, say, for the best and the brightest in the hottest high-tech industries, which are always highly competitive and subject to sudden reversals of fortune.

You don't hear too many college kids say it's their dream to enter the property-casualty business, but while insurance may be unappealing to most, it has attracted a few outstanding operators like Hank Greenberg, who turned American

International Group into an on-going bonanza for shareholders since the 1970s. Davis' positions in AIG, and a dozen other companies with exceptional leaders, account for the bulk of his gains.

Davis easily could have afforded new tennis balls, but Rothchild reports he continued to play with ratty, old ones. This book is full of other examples of Davis' extreme frugality, and some readers may dismiss his tightwad tendencies as silly, or quirky, or perhaps annoying. But the wallet hugging impressed his children and his grandchildren that the surest way to build wealth is to spend less than you make and put the balance to work in stocks. With the U.S. savings rate at the lowest ebb in recent history, less spending and more saving would help the country and certainly benefit the savers.

Refusing to keep his wealth in the family by willing it to the next generation, Davis gave his son, also Shelby Davis, a gift that kept on giving: an understanding of the basics of compounding and a primer on how to pick stocks. This was a Wall Street version of teaching a hungry person to fish instead of giving him a filet. Davis decided to ship his filets to the universities, foundations, and think tanks he supported, while teaching his offspring to be a fisherman.

The younger Shelby eventually became a fund manager, and took over the New York Venture in 1969, during the same period I was a rookie employee at Fidelity. We exchanged pleasantries, but never had lengthy exchanges. Shelby struck me as personable, down to earth, and devoted to his work. He didn't share his father's enthusiasm for insurance, but applied the Davis approach to other sectors.

Again, our styles differed: whereas I owned an ample supply of retail and restaurant chains that could grow their earnings at a 15 to 20 percent annual clip. Shelby avoided retail and prospected in the "foothills" with the steady but less spectacular 10 to 15 percent growers. Coming out of the bear markets of the early 1970s, we both avoided the beaten-down Nifty Fifty companies and looked for opportunities elsewhere. Sometimes, we ended up with the same names. We both loaded up on Fannie Mae, a once-troubled company that bought, sold, and packaged mortgages. We didn't buy troubled enterprises just because the stocks were cheap. We bought Fannie after we'd seen evidence it had put its troubles behind it.

We both found opportunity in the banking sector during the savings-and-loan crisis in the late 1980s. At one point, I'd taken stakes in scores of S&Ls—if a thrift was publicly traded, chances are it was in my portfolio. Shelby bought Citicorp when pundits debated its survival. Again, our familiarity with the workings of financial institutions gave us the confidence to buy when the news was bleakest. We knew our target companies were solvent, and the fundamentals were improving.

The elder Shelby Davis died in 1994, and the younger version retired from active fund management three years later. The third generation of Davises (Shelby's sons Chris and Andrew) is now in the process of proving itself with New York Venture and other Davis funds. I'd be surprised if the same approach that worked for their grandfather and their father didn't work for them. Their expectations are neither overly optimistic nor pessimistic, which should keep them in the game.

We've all heard that people who are ignorant of history are doomed to repeat it. On Wall Street, history repeats itself routinely, as corrections and bear markets turn into bull markets sooner or later. Investors who are ignorant of this pattern aren't necessarily doomed, but they are likely to lose money trying to escape stocks at inopportune moments. Rothchild's book has drama, and offers wise counsel between the lines.

PETER S. LYNCH
Vice Chairman
Fidelity Management & Research Company

1906–1909

Shelby Cullom Davis is born in Peoria in 1909. Earthquake and fires ravage San Francisco three years. Wall Street panic drops the Dow 32 percent, to a low of 53. Top-hatted financier J.P. Morgan saves U.S. banking system.

1928–1930

Davis graduates from Princeton; wife-to-be Kathryn Wasserman graduates from Wellesley. Both absorbed in international politics; disinterested in stock market, unaffected by the Crash of 1929; unaware of each other's existence.

1930–1931

Future investor (Shelby Davis) meets future bankroll (Kathryn Wasserman) on French train. Both return to New York to pursue his-and-her graduate degrees at Columbia. At the onset of the Great Depression studious couple isn't depressed.

1932

Studious couple marries in New York civil ceremony. Stock market bottoms, Dow at 41. Newlyweds ship out to Europe; Davis lands CBS radio gig.

1933

Honeymoon over; Davis joins brother-in-law's investment firm—gets his first experience with stocks. Five-year stealth bull market enriches small minority who have cash and courage to buy. This surprise bonanza is often omitted from history of period, which features homeless hordes and unemployment lines.

1937

Davis quits brother-in-law's firm to pursue freelance writing. Bull market upended. As Dow drops from 194 to 98, Davis's son Shelby is born, creating disciple for as-yet-undeveloped Davis investment method.

1938

Davis's daughter Diana is born. Davis's book, *America Faces the Forties,* prepares to hit the bookstores. Satisfied reader Thomas E. Dewey (New York governor and presidential hopeful) hires Davis as economic adviser/speech writer.

1941–1942

Davis can't resist cheap price ($33,000), buys seat on New York Stock exchange. Dow backslides to 92, a price it first reached in 1906. America drawn into World War II.

1944

As a payback for Davis's consulting work, Governor Dewey names him deputy superintendent of insurance for state. Davis meets his mother lode: insurance companies. Wartime rally in stocks lifts Dow to 212.

1947

At age 38, Davis quits state government job to tend portfolio of insurance stocks, bought with $50,000 seed capital from Kathryn. Opens office near Wall Street. Nervous in peacetime, Dow slumps to 161 as investors worry that peacetime is bad for business. Experts advise: Buy bonds! Bonds respond perversely, as 34-year bear bond market begins.

1952

Davis a millionaire on paper. It's taken 23 years, but Dow finally surpasses 1929 high mark of 381 for good.

1957

Davis's son Shelby graduates from Princeton and enters Wall Street workforce as stock analyst at Bank of New York. Stocks gallop ahead, on long march toward Dow 1,000.

1961

Davis's squabble with daughter Diana over $3.8 million trust fund makes front pages of New York papers; tabloid fodder for several days.

1962

In most rewarding trip of his lifetime, Davis flies to Japan, visits insurance companies, buys shares.

1963–1965
Third generation of Davis investors comes to life as Shelby's wife, Wendy, gives birth to Andrew and Chris Davis in Manhattan. Shelby exits Bank of New York to start small investment firm, along with two partners.

1965–1968
Mutual fund mania—not seen since 1920s. Dow flirts with 1,000, a barrier that won't be broken for good for another 17 years. Pundits proclaim "new era" of perpetual prosperity brought on by promising tech sector. Stocks fall in first of three successive bear markets.

1969
Davis named ambassador to Switzerland; he and Kathryn pack up for Bern. Son Shelby and sidekick Jeremy Biggs take manager's job at New York Venture Fund. Second bear market in trilogy rattles investors; promising tech sector gets clobbered.

1970
Venture Fund is top one-year performer, lauded in *Business Week;* soon to become bottom performer.

1973–1974
Third bear market in trilogy, worst decline since 1929 to 1932. Takes Dow on 45 percent plunge from 1,051 to 577. Prestigious Nifty Fifty companies take deeper plunge—down 70 to 90 percent. Original Venture Fund shareholders left with zero profit after five years.

1975
Ambassador Davis returns from Switzerland, is reunited with $20 million portfolio worth $50 million three years earlier. Shelby divorces Wendy, soon marries Gale Lansing. Adopts new stock-pricing methods resulting in string of winning years for Venture Fund.

1981
Wild inflation of 1970s finally corralled. Interest rates begin 20-year fall. Stocks begin 20-year rise, but only optimistic pariahs predict it.

1983
With Shelby as solo manager, Venture Fund beats S&P 500 for seventh straight year.

1987
Stocks crash. Global panic. Davis goes on buying spree.

1988

Davis makes *Forbes* list of 400 richest Americans; he has a $427 million portfolio. Shelby makes *Forbes* honor roll for reliable mutual fund excellence.

1990

Chris takes job in grandfather's office in New York.

1991

Chris installed as manager of Davis Financial Fund. Dow hits 3,000.

1993

Andrew takes charge of Davis convertible and real estate funds (created with him in mind) Moves to Santa Fe.

1994

Davis dies, leaving nearly $900 million in trust for conservative causes. Shelby and Chris sell Davis's holdings and invest the proceeds in Venture and other Davis funds. Davis assets and brain power are finally united in same accounts.

1995

Chris named comanager of the Venture Fund. Andrew happy with a less dramatic role. Dow hits 5,000.

1997

Shelby turns 60, Venture Fund turns 28. Chris named sole manager of Venture, with Shelby consulting from sidelines. Shelby donates $45 million of his own fortune to the United World College scholarship program, a signal to his children that they won't inherit his bundle, just as he didn't inherit Davis's fortune.

1998–2000

Andrew, Chris, and Chris's new partner, Ken Feinberg, cope with a tired bull market.

Acknowledgments

SPECIAL THANKS TO THE DAVIS FAMILY: KATHRYN, Shelby, Gale, Chris, Andrew, and Diana Davis Spencer, for subjecting themselves to long interviews and endless questions. Thanks also to cousin Cullom Davis, whose oral history of the Davises elicited valuable information. Russell Wiese, partner of Davis Selected Advisers, provided useful feedback. Tracey Aberman, a trusted family retainer, helped with follow-up interviews.

On the editorial side, I'm indebted to Myles Thompson, who signed up this project, and Jeanne Glasser, the editor who marshaled it through the editorial department at John Wiley & Sons. The copy editors at Publications Development Company of Texas caught numerous grammatical and syntactical errors.

For agreeing to be pestered with shorter interviews, I'm grateful to Jeremy Biggs, G. Bernard Hamilton, the Very Reverend James Leo, two James Rosenwalds (son and grandson of the Japanese investor described herein), Richard Murray, Francis Haidt, Louis Levy, Arnie Widlitz, Judd Higgins, Irving Kahn, Betty Stager, Dorothy Dunning, and AIG's formidable CEO, Hank Greenberg (with an assist from Mona Benedetto).

David Schiff at Schiff's Insurance Observer provided extensive research help. I also received important assistance from Diana DeSocio, New York Stock Exchange; Polly Walker, Fidelity; Scott Kuldell, Fidelity Research; Robert Hagstrom,

Acknowledgments

Legg Mason; James Grant, editor of Grant's Interest Rate Observer; Sam Stovall, Standard & Poor's; Jennifer Ian, the New York Society of Security Analysts; Connie Pickett, librarian, Philadelphia Inquirer; Lisa Panzer, Ellen Thrower, and Barbie Kaiser, the College of Insurance.

Thanks to Michael Gmitter and Cynthia Miller, Securities Research Company, and to Charlene Christopher, AM Best, for charts and graphs.

J. R.

Contents

Introduction   1

CHAPTER 1
Davis Meets His Bankroll   13

CHAPTER 2
From the Great Depression to the Hitler Crisis   23

CHAPTER 3
Beyond the Rear-View Mirror   39

CHAPTER 4
A Last Hurrah for Bonds   49

CHAPTER 5
A Crib Course in Coverage   63

CHAPTER 6
From Bureaucrat to Investor   75

CHAPTER 7
The Bullish 1950s   91

CHAPTER 8
Davis Shops Abroad   105

CHAPTER 9
Wall Street a Go-Go   117

CHAPTER 10
Shelby Gets Funded   131

CONTENTS

CHAPTER 11
The Inheritance Flap   151

CHAPTER 12
Cool Trio Runs Hot Fund   161

CHAPTER 13
The Worst Decline Since 1929   175

CHAPTER 14
Davis on the Rebound   193

CHAPTER 15
Shelby Buys Banks–Davis Buys Everything   205

CHAPTER 16
The Grandsons Get in the Game   229

CHAPTER 17
The Family Joins Forces   243

CHAPTER 18
Chris Inherits Venture   267

CHAPTER 19
Investing à la Davis   283

Source Notes   296

Index   298

INTRODUCTION

THIS PROJECT BEGAN AS A BOOK ABOUT SHELBY Davis, the fund manager. Without much fanfare, Shelby's New York Venture Fund had given investors a great ride: An investment of $10,000 had turned into $379,000 during his 28-year stewardship. In 22 of those years, he beat the market. This record put him in a league with Peter Lynch at Fidelity with the Magellan Fund. I was curious. How did he do it?

We met for dinner at a seafood place in Palm Beach, Florida. We were surrounded by gray hair and blue blazers. Shelby wore the latter. He had a slight build and a boyish face. He was amusing and modest. He steered the chitchat away from himself and toward the latest quarterly report from Hewlett-Packard. He admired the way Fannie Mae grew its earnings in good markets and bad. He made the merger between Wells Fargo and Norwest banks sound as exciting as a French tryst.

We had a follow-up discussion on the 97th floor of the World Trade Center in New York, where Shelby kept an office. There, at the conference table, he filled in details about his excellent—though not particularly celebrated—career. According to him, the major influence on his savvy stockpicking was another Shelby Davis—his father. (The older Davis had confused the issue by pulling a George Bush and naming a son after himself without a "junior" attached. To keep them straight in the pages that follow, I'm calling the father "Davis" and the son "Shelby" throughout.) "The old man was a better investor than I was," Shelby said, pitching his father as an interesting book subject in itself. "He turned $50,000 into $900 million. Insurance stocks, mostly."

Nine hundred million dollars was an attention grabber. Shelby elaborated. Davis was a former freelance writer, GOP campaign adviser, and Dilbert in the New York State Insurance Department. In 1947, at age 38, with no MBA and no formal economics training, he quit his job to become a full-time prospector in the insurance sector. Friends and relatives were skeptical. This was before the midlife crisis was invented. Otherwise, they would have suspected Davis was having one.

Over the next four and a half decades, Davis skillfully chauffeured his portfolio into one of the great Wall Street fortunes. Basically, he stuck with insurance stocks through booms, busts, bebop, beatniks, and the Beatles. When U.S. insurers got too pricey, he bought Japanese insurance stocks. In the 1960s, his Japanese holdings took off like pigeons near a firecracker. By the time he died, in 1994, he'd multiplied his original stake 18,000 times.

This wasn't a rags-to-riches yarn; it was more like Saks-to-riches. The source of Davis's original stake was his wife, Kathryn Wasserman, daughter of a Philadelphia carpet mogul. Most Americans in 1947 could only dream of spending $50,000 on a stock portfolio. Still, the result was an inspirational and hopeful tale: This former freelance writer started investing in middle age and became a near billionaire in his lifetime. Yet, outside insurance circles, the first Shelby Davis was almost as obscure as the second.

"My father made the *Forbes* list of wealthiest Americans in 1988," Shelby said. "His 15 seconds of fame." The *Forbes* reference reminded me of the lack of so-called "passive investors" on that magazine's wealth parade. Among the numerous Silicon Valley whizzes, corporate raiders, real estate developers, inventors, retailers, manufacturers, media czars, oil barons, bankers, and others who routinely appeared on the list, I could think of only one other person who got there by picking stocks in other people's companies: Warren Buffett.

I asked Shelby if his father and Buffett had ever met. "A few times," he said. "They were acquaintances. They had a lot in common." Shelby elaborated. Both had "grown" their money at an impressive 23 to 24 percent annual rate for decades.[1] Both made their biggest profits from insurance stocks, and Buffett owned two insurance companies outright. Was it mere coincidence that these two shareholding prospectors found buried treasure in the industry that was shunned by Wall Street sophisticates as "stodgy," "boring," and "unrewarding"? The insurance angle was intriguing. Should we all be buying insurance stocks?

Both were notorious tightwads who lived far beneath their means. Davis wore shoes with holes and sweaters that were moth-eaten, and he played endless sets of tennis with the same used balls. Buffett wore frumpy suits and ferociously hoarded trivial sums. According to Buffett's biographer, Roger Lowenstein, Buffett was already a multimillionaire when a traveling companion told him she needed to make a quick call at an airport pay phone. (A dime was the going rate at the time.) Buffett fished a quarter from his pocket, but rather than hand the excessive coin to his anxious friend, he walked a long corridor to find a newspaper stand that made change.

As their fortunes moved into seven, eight, and nine figures, both men continued to live in the modest houses they had bought in the 1940s and 1950s, respectively: Davis in Tarrytown, New York; Buffett in Omaha, Nebraska. When Buffett's wife bought $15,000 worth of furniture for their modest abode, it "just about killed Warren," a family friend was quoted in Lowenstein's biography, *Buffett: The Making of a Capitalist.* "Do you realize," Buffett said, "how much that is if you compound it over 20 years?" Davis gave the identical speech to his grandson when he refused to buy the boy a $1 hot dog.

Once he'd broken through the billionaire barrier, the folksy Buffett suffered a spending lapse and bought a corporate jet. He called it the Indefensible. Davis never bought so much as a Piper Cub.

The Buffett/Davis comparison can be carried too far. Buffett was a billionaire twenty times over; he often headed the *Forbes* roster. Davis's name, although listed many times, was inconspicuous in the middle of the list. Buffett's accomplishments were well lauded. Davis's were all but unknown. I mulled Shelby's suggestion to write only about his father—something along the lines of "Best Investor You Never Heard Of," or "Secrets from the World's Second Greatest Stock Picker."

Davis wasn't around to provide details. He died in 1994, leaving a fortune in paper assets but little in the way of a paper trail. He'd kept no journals or diaries, and he never bothered to preserve back copies of his weekly insurance letter. Innermost thoughts, such as "Buy 100 shares Chubb," he scribbled on old envelopes or ticket stubs, to avoid wasting money on note pads. These scribbles, too, were lost to the trash bin.

Cronies and sidekicks from the early stages of Davis's investing were fading fast. His wife, Kathryn (Shelby's mother and the source of the original $50,000), agreed to reminisce, but the spry nonagenarian drew a blank on her husband's financial maneuvers. Husbands from her generation believed in the separation of commerce and wives.

The most informative source on Davis was his namesake, the fund manager I was interested in writing about in the first place. Born in 1937, Shelby had grown up watching his father analyze companies, tagged along to visit CEOs, learned how money went forth and multiplied, as determined by the Rule of 72.[2] That simple calculation put an exciting spin on the familiar adage penned by the overfed founding father, Ben Franklin. Not only was a penny saved a penny earned—a penny compounded 25 times was $671,000!

People who buy lottery tickets know that the chance of winning a million is less than the chance that O.J. was innocent based on the DNA evidence. If a young person with a $10-a-week lottery habit could forgo the fantasy and invest the weekly $10 in a typical mutual fund that returns an annual 10 percent (modest by Davis's standards), becoming a millionaire in 30 years will be guaranteed. To his son, Davis passed along his infectious passion for owning shares in carefully chosen companies (he called them "compounding machines"), his conviction that owning the best compounding machines would lead to unimagined rewards, his distrust of unnecessary spending (why waste money that could be invested?), and his workaholic tendencies. Shelby readily acknowledged that his success as a fund manager resulted from his childhood training. Not only had Davis devised a winning portfolio that paid off over a half-century of stock market gyrations, the frugal workaholic prepared his son to continue the tradition with the same obsessive verve.

Into early adulthood, Shelby was his father's clone. He prepped at Lawrenceville (Davis's boarding school), graduated from Princeton (Davis's alma mater), worked on the college paper (Davis did, too), and married into a wealthy family (same as Davis). Like his father, Shelby studied history and learned the rudiments of accounting, balance sheet diving, and Security Analysis 101 on the side. Like his father, he valued the intangibles of corporate leadership more than tangibles on spreadsheets. He never let a statistical forest block his view of the trees.

Like his father, he rejected the MBA route. By word and by deed, Davis had persuaded Shelby that Wall Street's most popular degree produced a stupefying conformity, which Davis had profitably avoided. Davis zigged when others zagged. He bought stocks when most experts flogged bonds, and he pocketed insurance shares when others avoided them. Shelby showed similar independence. Like his father, he quit secure employment (his at a bank) to launch his stockpicking career.

In spite of this flattering imitation, the Davis-Shelby relationship was far from chummy. As Shelby recalled it, his influential father was often gruff, distant, distracted, competitive, and frequently absent from home. Behind a superficial cordiality, the two were at loggerheads from Shelby's teenage years through his late adulthood.

Shelby cited examples. Davis had set up trust funds for Shelby and for his sister, Diana, then maneuvered to rescind the money from Diana's trust after his clever investing made her too comfortably rich for Davis's own comfort. His competitive side came out once a year, when he sent Shelby, without comment, the annual tally of his investment gains, as if to say, "Beat this." Shelby responded with passive resistance. Davis wrote didactic letters to Shelby in college, but Shelby never bothered to respond. As Shelby neared graduation from Princeton, Davis hinted at wanting to hire his son. Shelby rebuffed the overture: "He was too cheap to pay me anything." When Shelby started his own money-management firm; Davis didn't invest. These two talented investors from the same gene pool rarely traded ideas or traded compliments. Until his health began to fail, Davis kept the contents of his remarkable portfolio to himself.

On hearing these details, I first thought the family soap opera and the frugal overkill were entertaining sidelights to the story of Davis's remarkable investing. On further reflection, the two were directly related. By keeping his wallet zipped, Davis maximized the capital he then invested for maximum return. He disapproved of excessive corporate spending as much as he disapproved of excessive household spending, and he tended to buy companies whose managers were as frugal with their investors' dollars as he was with family dollars.

His favorite CEOs were flinty kindred spirits—cost-conscious workaholics like AIG's Maurice "Hank" Greenberg. He limited his portfolio to AIG and other insurance stocks because they generally sold at a sizable discount to the typical noninsurance issue, and a huge discount to the latest investment fad—usually, something high-tech that soon became high-wreck. His refusal to overpay for things gave him the discipline to buy frugal enterprises at giveaway prices. Thus, his philosophy for daily life, corporate life, and Wall Street life put him in the growth-at-a-reasonable-price camp, as opposed to the dangerously fashionable growth-at-any-price camp.

Finally, so the compounding and wealth building didn't end with his demise, he taught his children obsessive frugality. The entire family pinched pennies as the millions piled up, although until they reached their twenties, the children were generally unaware the millions existed. Shelby and Diana were raised on farmer's chores: stack wood, rake leaves, gather eggs from chicken coops, shovel snow. They were taught never to order lobster or fresh orange juice in a restaurant. Davis acceded to their request for a backyard swimming pool on one condition: The family had to dig the hole.

His goal was to create self-reliant offspring who didn't depend on family largesse, so his accumulated pile could be spared for the worthiest causes. In keeping with the compounding theme, Davis planned to leave his wealth to organizations like the Heritage Foundation, which promoted free enterprise and opposed political threats to capitalist momentum. Thus, his money would help ensure that the U.S. system continued to allow others to successfully deploy their capital, without overtaxing and overregulating their efforts. With investor-friendly leadership, the nation at large could continue to maximize prosperity.

Through the first two decades of our saga, Davis triumphed with his all-insurance portfolio. By the 1950s, Shelby had reached adulthood. He worked for the Bank of New York for eight years, then left to start an investment boutique with two friends. Soon, their small company took control of the fledgling New York Venture Fund. In his rookie year as manager, Shelby rode hot tech stocks to the top of the performance charts. In his second year, the bear market of 1969 to 1970, he rode those same stocks to the bottom of the performance charts. Like a writer in search of his voice, Shelby tinkered with his portfolio, searching for a strategy that suited him.

After a subsequent bear market, in 1973 to 1974, his Venture Fund was on the upswing. By trial and error, he cobbled his own style, based on but not mimicking his father's approach. Instead of filling Venture's portfolio with insurance stocks exclusively, Shelby branched out and invested in banks, brokerage houses, and other companies that shared key attributes with his father's favorite insurers. He bought "growth companies at a bargain price" and outdistanced all but a handful of rival mutual funds.

Davis returned to the United States in 1975, after serving as ambassador to Switzerland. He'd suffered big losses in the twin bear markets mentioned above, and his net worth had dropped from $50 million to $20 million. But then his insurers rebounded and, by the mid-1980s, his portfolio, too, was compounding at a rapid rate. Soon, the $30 million short-term loss looked trivial. He gained $750 million in the next 15 years.

So far, we've identified the Davis era, when Davis applied his principles alone, and the Shelby era, when the son and his father invested simultaneously but not in concert. Next came the Chris and Andrew era. Their grandfather was in decline, Shelby was continuing his Venture tenure, and his two sons ran their own mutual funds on the Davis strategy.

Raised in the 1960s and 1970s, Chris and Andrew learned about the magic of compounding and the Rule of 72, the family's complement to the Golden Rule. As a teenager, Chris worked part-time in his grandfather's office on weekends. Summers, he signed on as cook and chauffeur at the Davis house in Maine. He got along well with both sides of the Davis/Shelby divide.

Before he got to Wall Street, Chris passed through a "Viva Fidel" phase, when he denounced the "running dogs of capitalism"; a Dr. Doolittle phase, when he thought about becoming a veterinarian; and a Father Flanagan phase, when he flirted with the priesthood. From there, he veered into a Davis orbit, enrolling in a training program at a Boston bank, then taking a job at a small New York investment house. In 1989, his grandfather hired him as his apprentice. The job Shelby had rejected 30 years earlier ("He was too cheap to pay me anything"), Chris eagerly accepted.

Andrew, meanwhile, took a less eccentric route into the Davis domain. He majored in economics and business at Colby College in Maine, then worked for Shawmut Bank in Boston and PaineWebber in New York, before taking control of two funds (real estate and convertible bonds) that Shelby had launched with Andrew in mind.

The patriarch was ailing. In 1990, at age 81, Davis suffered a stroke. Convinced that Chris had made the most of his apprenticeship, Shelby hired Chris away from his grandfather to manage Davis Financial, another new fund intended to give the third generation a chance to prove itself. Chris moved his and his father's office from Wall Street to Fifth Avenue, but he kept a base in Wall Street by keeping in constant contact with Shelby at his downtown office in the World Trade Center. Chris inspired the rapprochement that brought Shelby to his father's bedside, where Shelby held his father's hand as Davis died in 1994.

Davis's ashes were buried in Maine and his assets were scattered among the Davis funds, so the spoils from two great investors were united at last. The third generation was now in charge of them.

This book is about investing in the long term, where the long term isn't 15 minutes, or until the next quarterly report, or even until the next economic cycle. Buying and holding is all the rage these days, and the Davises provide a 50-year case study not only in how to tend a portfolio but how to raise privileged children who break the trustafarian mold, work hard, earn their own keep, and allow the family fortune to continue to compound. Theirs is true long-term investing: not five years, or ten years, but perpetual. Their financial escapades cover the period from the late 1940s, when most Americans were afraid to own stocks, through the 1990s, when most Americans were afraid *not* to own stocks. Along the way, they invested through two lengthy bull markets, 25 corrections, two savage bear markets, one crash, seven mild bear markets, and nine recessions; three major wars; one presidential assassination, one resignation, and one impeachment; 34 years of rising interest rates and 18 years of falling interest rates; a lengthy struggle with inflation; stretches when bonds gained while stocks lost, or stocks gained while bonds lost, or gold gained while both bonds and stocks lost; and even a stretch when a savings account was more rewarding than the Dow in all its glory. As we see how the Davises negotiated these twists and turns, we learn about how stocks behave through good times and bad.

Looking through the Davis family tree, Mr. Market's twentieth-century history can be reduced to three periods of great gain and two periods of great loss, with interludes of drift and gradual recovery in between. The gains were made between 1910 and 1929, 1949 and 1969, and 1982 to the present. In each of these roughly 20-year uplifts, stocks were helped along by a fat economy, gee-whiz technology, rising corporate profits, and soaring valuations. Consumers had disposable cash and an inclination to spend it.

The two periods of great loss occurred from 1929 to 1932 and from 1970 to 1974. Most of the stock market wealth created between 1921 and 1929, and again between 1949 and 1969, disappeared in these pecuniary debacles. If you owned the hottest stocks in the hottest industries, your losses were maximized. Moreover, because the public was slow to buy on the way up, the mass of small investors came out of the round trip poorer for the experience. Investing via mutual funds was regarded as safer than buying naked stocks, but the average fund declined as much as, or more than, the average stock.

During the rebuilding phases, stocks drifted, rallied, and suffered demoralizing swoons. From the 1932 bottom, the rebuilding took more than 20 years; from the 1974 bottom, nearly eight years. In each restorative yin-yang, the public fell out of love with equities.

Throughout the market saga and the family saga, Davis stock-picking techniques have produced many happy returns, and readers may profit from applying them.

CHAPTER 1

DAVIS MEETS
HIS BANKROLL

S HELBY CULLOM DAVIS WAS BORN IN 1909, IN A nice neighborhood in the town that inspired the famous question: Will it play in Peoria? On the family tree, a passenger on the *Mayflower* dangled from his mother's branch and an original inhabitant of Jamestown looked down from his father's. His namesake and great-uncle, Shelby Cullom, was a one-term governor of Illinois, a four-term fixture in the U.S. House of Representatives, and a six-term fixture in the U.S. Senate.

For all the kickbacks, sweetheart deals, and other get-rich-quick schemes foisted on the electorate by the elected, it's a surprise that U.S. politics didn't create notable or lasting fortunes the way Third World politics did in the twentieth century. Journalists in every U.S. town, city, and county found plenty of corruption to write about, but corruption was somewhat democratic—otherwise, for all the money floating around, why didn't America develop a ruling class of millionaire mugwumps? Powerful senators with *Mayflower* pedigrees might have dined out on their lineage, but the lineage per se didn't pay the bills.

14

Davis's great-uncle Shelby Cullom wasn't in politics for the money. In fact, he devoted his political career to fighting the "moneyed magnates" who ran the railroads. He opposed Harriman, Vanderbilt, and other railroad tycoons as surely as he opposed polygamy. One man, one wife was a campaign issue in the nineteenth-century American farm belt, along with fair prices for farm freight.

Once the magnates had bought or driven off their competitors on key rail routes, they charged gougers' rates to ship cattle, wheat, corn, and other comestibles. Envisioning the same hordes of dollar signs, tycoons in other industries, from baking to matchbook making, conspired to monopolize. Faced with an epidemic of monopolizing, consumers cried "Foul!" and Washington responded. Congress passed and the courts upheld new laws to restore free enterprise through stricter regulation. Davis's great-uncle was part of this welcome, albeit ironic, solution. He pushed for the Interstate Commerce Commission, which was created in 1887 to thwart the railroad cabal. In 1912, at age 82, Senator Cullom was elected to a sixth and final term. He died in office. Davis, then age five, marched in the funeral procession.

In Cullom's lifetime, America's fastest-growing industry was railroads. Its managers, Davis later wrote, were "like generals of a vast Army." The iron-and-cinder superhighway—an ancient precursor to the Internet superhighway—excited imaginations and attracted more investors than any construction job in history. From the mid-1800s and beyond, the public paid for the laying of track coast-to-coast and exchanged cash for a never-ending supply of stocks and bonds. With the stock market in disfavor, railroad companies preferred to finance their expansion with bonds. In theory, these corporate IOUs were safer than stocks because issuers were obligated to refund bondholders' money, plus interest, while the issuers of stock had no obligation to stockholders. In fact, however, the "safer" alternative proved hazardous to at least two generations of railroad investors. Having gone the bond route, railroads were saddled with huge interest payments they often failed to make. During recessions and other crises, they solved their cash flow problems by defaulting on their paper and by drifting in and out of bankruptcy.

Investors in the "vast Army" learned an expensive lesson: There is no guarantee that a fast-growing industry with great future promise will reward its financial backers along the way. Railroads had been lauded as the nation's most reliable blue-chip companies, yet the payoff was unreliable at best. Stockholders saw their "conservative" rail holdings marked down in frequent panics and bear markets; bondholders were lucky to escape with their money back.

Foreign investors were the biggest losers in U.S. rail projects. The British, in particular, couldn't resist bankrolling the emerging U.S. market in the mid-1800s, just as Americans couldn't resist bankrolling emerging Asian markets in the late 1900s. Much British capital was lost in what turned out to be a gigantic, albeit unintended, charitable contribution to U.S. track laying and road building. Heed it well, ye global capitalists! Fast growth in the latest emerging phenom doesn't necessarily mean fat profits for foreign enthusiasts. The U.S. railroads proved that.

Davis was too young to grasp railroad finance, and his immediate family (father George, mother Julia Cullom) had nothing to do with stocks or bonds. They lived comfortably in Peoria, thanks to the income stream that came from a corner storefront owned by the family. This income stream subdued George Davis's pecuniary ambitions.

After he studied architecture at Princeton, George Davis had a brief and successful entrepreneurial debut. During the Alaskan Gold Rush, in 1898, he hustled out to the Pacific Northwest but arrived too late in the season to find and stake out a promising claim. Hearing that many earlier arrivals had neglected to bring winter feed for their horses, he chartered a barge in Seattle, filled it with hay, and shipped the load to Alaska. The hay was quickly sold out, at sellers' market prices. Prospecting in a mundane substance, George Davis outperformed all but a tiny percentage of the gold diggers. On a larger scale, Levi Strauss did the same thing with pants.

Once he'd returned to Peoria to marry into the Cullom clan, George Davis practiced architecture intermittently, if at all. He dressed like a Wall Street banker, insisted people call him "judge" (a nickname from college) and passed the time writing letters to the editor and picking up the monthly stipend from the storefront. He referred to this errand as "attending to my affairs."

Throughout Davis's childhood, the proceeds from the storefront rental provided a comfortable living: a local country club membership plus a prep-school-and-Princeton education for him and his brother, and enough cash left over to reward the two boys annually with $1,000 for not smoking. Their father, who suffered from lung disease and smoked, didn't want the mistake repeated.

Growing up with a ne'er-do-well father prepared the world's second greatest stock picker for successful investing, in a backhanded sort of way. From an early age, Davis was determined to work hard and avoid family welfare and all its degrading side effects. He held a variety of summer and afternoon jobs in Peoria. Family lore has him standing on a street corner, hawking a stack of newspapers that announced the end of World War I. This was standard schoolboy stuff, not nearly as imaginative as the enrichment scheme hatched by the world's greatest stock picker, Warren Buffett. According to his biographer, young Buffett paid his pals to dive for golf balls in the water hazards at the local links in Omaha, then sold the balls back to the pro shop.

17

Davis was long gone from Peoria by the time the Great Depression retarded the income stream and forced his family to economize. His father, the "judge," discovered frugality. "Use it up, wear it out, make do or do without," was George Davis's motto and mission. He took the mission so seriously that once—on a trip East to visit his son—he stopped at a train station, found the telegraph office, and wired a reminder back to his wife: "When you leave the house, don't forget to unplug the electric clock!"

Scholastically, Davis excelled at Lawrenceville and at Princeton. He was the managing editor of the campus newspaper at each school. At Lawrenceville, he was voted most likely to succeed. At Princeton, he joined a second-tier social club—Charter—then threatened to quit when Charter blackballed his Jewish roommate, Trivers. He stuck with Charter (at Trivers's behest) but preferred to socialize with a less starchy crowd. He shared the Bohemian disdain for conspicuous consumption: raccoon coats, silver flasks, gold watches, and so on. His father's frugality had rubbed off and later would pay off. His habit of living beneath his means freed his capital to make the most of itself.

Davis the student showed no interest in economics or finance. He majored in history and read widely on the Russian revolution. The first U.S. financial best-seller, *Common Stocks As Long-Term Investments,* appeared in the bookstores in 1924, when Davis was in prep school. The author, Edgar Lawrence Smith, argued that stocks were reliable and worth owning, even by widows and orphans. This contradicted conventional wisdom that pegged stocks as Wall Street's answer to a wager on a horse. Using words that will sound familiar today, Smith observed that Americans lived in a "New Era" of fantastic pecuniary promise.

In these "modern, enlightened times," Smith wrote of the mid-1920s, investors and consumers stood to benefit from the "emerging science of corporation management" that gave U.S. firms a lucrative advantage in the global marketplace.

At its 1921 low, the Dow traded at 63, a price it had fetched back in 1888. As prices rose toward the 1929 top of 381, so did the public's acceptance of Smith's enthusiasm. People who'd shunned the market a decade earlier eagerly embraced it late in the rise. Pioneer U.S. mutual funds—Massachusetts Investors' Trust, and State Street Investing Company—opened for business in Boston. The typical investor sought dividends, not earnings, and blue-chip railroad issues continued to attract a conservative faction looking for a safe return. At this point, the rails were called "America's 20 percent industry," because they bought 20 percent of all the iron, steel, coal, timber, and fuel oil produced and sold inside the country. The bullish line was that railroads had outgrown their untrustworthy adolescence and were now too well-established to fail. The railroad index had more than doubled over the decade.

Whether Davis read Smith's book is anybody's guess, but it made such a splash, he couldn't have avoided hearing about it, nor could he have avoided the gleeful newspaper accounts of quick fortunes made by the "margin millionaires" who borrowed their way onto Easy Street.

Though he was a quarter-century away from investing in earnest, Davis met his future bankroll on a French train. Textiles, not the storefront in Peoria, produced his seed capital, siloed in the trust funds of the woman sitting across the aisle. Kathryn Wasserman sized up her husband-to-be: ski-slope tan, tweedy British jacket, leather arm patches for sophistication—the uniform of the Ivy Leaguer. She noticed that his body language (shy eyes, slumped shoulders) didn't fit his preppy clothes. She sensed his discomfort with women. Figuring he'd never speak first, she broke the ice: "Is Geneva the next stop?"

They discovered they were both getting off at Geneva. They'd enrolled at the same Swiss summer school, sponsored by the Rockefellers, where bright students from around the world coagulated. The Rockefellers hoped a few of these high IQs would run their countries' governments someday, remember the fun they had together, and refuse to fight wars with one another. The goal was optimistic, and already the school had produced one promising alliance in transit: Davis and Wasserman.

Davis had a *Mayflower* pedigree; Wasserman, an Ellis Island pedigree. But they found they had a lot in common. Both attended status colleges (Princeton, Wellesley). Both studied Russian history. Both traveled in and around Russia before heading for Switzerland. Davis visited Leningrad and Moscow on an academic junket; Wasserman rode a horse through the wilds of the Caucasus. She slept in tents, shared campsites with gypsies, bartered with tribal chieftains, and rebuffed numerous lechers.

Older by two years, Wasserman had more hands-on romantic experience than the former editor of the *Daily Princetonian*. She'd been dating older men—her sister's "leftovers." Compared to them, Davis reminded her of a "kid brother."

Starting with their first date—an economical walk through a Swiss park—their romance blossomed on a budget. They swapped Peoria stories and Philadelphia stories. Davis learned how the three Wasserman brothers, Joseph, Howard, and Isaac, opened the Philadelphia Carpet Mills in 1895 and the Philadelphia Pile Fabric Company shortly after. The two entities were merged into Art Loom, a carpet company, that occupied an entire city block on Lehigh Avenue. Art Loom went public in 1925.

Joseph Wasserman, the chief decision maker, had prior experience in retail sales in New Mexico. His older brother, Isaac, found a way to slice a rug in half without damaging the weave—a technique that gave the Wassermans an obvious competitive advantage: they could make two carpets from one loom. The youngest brother, Howard, died of syphilis after refusing to take a Wasserman test (contributed to science by a distant relative in Germany) that would have detected the disease in its early stages.

U.S. Textile stocks became a glamour industry as consumption and machines loomed carpet boomed.

Joseph married Edith Stix, a fiery suffragette who showed her independence by siding with the workers in a strike against her husband's rug plant. When her husband warned, "They get their way, and Art Loom is finished," Edith ignored him—but not in bed. They produced two sons (one of whom died in infancy) and three daughters, Kathryn being the youngest. The Wasserman children were raised in the sexist tradition: the boys learned business; the girls learned art, music, and how to nab a husband. In those days, capable women did "women's work" in museums, hospitals, schools, foundations, and quasi-academic institutions. They were shut out of "men's work"—anything that had to do with business.

They traveled widely and filled their house at 6600 Wissahickon Avenue, Philadelphia, with fine antiques and exotic souvenirs of their frequent and ambitious globe trots. Visitors ogled the early English and Italian furniture, the Dutch and German paintings, the Fra Filipino Lippi, the Bronzino, the Gainsborough, the Syrian glass, and the 1,000-year-old Chinese sculptures. They'd crisscrossed Europe, toured Greece and Palestine, and traveled overland to Russia and the Orient. In the 1930s, they bought a sixteenth-century temple in China, had it dismantled and crated, and shipped it home. It became the star attraction in the Oriental wing of the Philadelphia Museum.

On one of their European trips, Kathryn spilled ink on a carpet in a fancy Paris hotel. Checking the label on the carpet, her father discovered she'd stained an Art Loom product. He sent the hotel a free replacement.

The Davis family's net worth was in decline; the Wasserman fortune surged on immigrant energy. Like his future son-in-law, Joseph loved hard work and hated spending; his wife loved spending and delegated work. At home, she rode around in chauffeur-driven comfort and filled the house with maids and cooks while the source of her extravagance hopped the streetcar to work and lunched from a brown bag. Kathryn sided with her mother on politics (Edith was a Democrat; Joseph, a Republican) and her father on frugality and belief in the virtue of paid employment. One summer, Kathryn answered an ad for a "literary position" that turned out to be selling World Book encyclopedias door-to-door. "My mother advised against it," Kathryn recalls, "but I agreed to take the job, as long as they didn't make me sell World Books to anybody I knew. I didn't want family friends to feel obligated."

World Book sent her outside her neighborhood. She devised her own sales ploy, which today's less trusting consumers would never tolerate. She'd stop a stickball game on the street, and ask one of the boys his name and where he lived. The boy would give her both bits of information—in those days, children weren't taught to stonewall a stranger. She'd find the house and ring the doorbell. The boy's mother would open the door (mothers stayed at home in those days) and Kathryn would introduce herself. "I've come to talk to you about your son, Tommy," she'd say, dropping the boy's name.

"What has Tommy done now?" The mother always suspected her Tommy was up to no good. "He's a nice fellow," Kathryn would volunteer, then segue into Tommy's education and how a World Book would help him. She returned to close the deal at night, when Tommy's father was home from work. In those days, fathers made all the decisions.

CHAPTER 2

FROM THE GREAT DEPRESSION TO THE HITLER CRISIS

I N THE FALL OF 1930, DAVIS AND HIS GIRLFRIEND returned from their summer in Switzerland to chase his and her Master's degrees at New York's Columbia University. They lived at the International House near the campus, attended classes, and worked on their theses. The future great investor glided through the Crash and its aftermath unscathed. Parental largesse paid his and Kathryn's school expenses, and the duo pinched pennies like typical college students. They were more absorbed in the news from Red Square than the news from Wall Street. As a nonstockholder, Davis was spared the financial trauma that turned many in his generation against stocks forever. Kathryn was spared as well. The Wassermans were part of a canny minority who kept their money in government bonds and lost nothing in the Crash that cost four or five million American shareholders a combined $30 billion. "The rug business is risky enough," Joseph Wasserman told his children. "I want to be conservative in savings." He maintained an all-bond portfolio until his death in 1937. Had he not, the seed capital Davis later plowed into insurance wouldn't have survived the 1929 to 1932 washout.

By 1931, the economy was moribund. Commodity prices hit lows that hadn't been seen since the 1870s. Falling prices begat falling profits in all types of businesses. Companies were forced to lay off workers and cut wages; as the rich got poorer, the poor got even poorer. Cash-strapped consumers spent less at the stores, store owners cut prices, profits took another dive, and the vicious cycle got more vicious. "The old car had to last another year," wrote Davis. "And the house went without new paint. And the frayed coat remained frayed."

It was a textbook case of deflation that baffled the pundits. Forecasters had predicted a Wall Street calamity, but there's no record of a well-known economist predicting economic calamity. Money seers were confident that the economy was "sound" and "too powerful to be stopped," and that the Federal Reserve System could engineer a happy outcome. By opening and shutting valves in the monetary pipeline, raising and lowering interest rates, and printing more cash when necessary, that magical agency had the power to liberate commerce from the extremes of boom and bust. Or so people thought.

Still, the Great Depression didn't destroy commerce, any more than the mislabeled Dark Ages destroyed culture. Zippo lighters, Frito corn chips, Skippy peanut butter, and Three Musketeers candy bars appeared on retail shelves in 1932. Revlon was created that same year. Life went on. People went shopping. Some bought rugs. Even in the worst of times, Art Loom stayed in business—thanks in large measure to the high tariffs that protected them from alien free-market competitors in Europe and Asia. Like other staunch Republicans, Joseph Wasserman applauded free markets and opposed government meddling—in theory. When it came to rugs, however, he opposed free markets and applauded the meddling. He urged federal trade authorities to impose higher tariffs on textiles.

Meanwhile, the studious couple graduated from Columbia with honors in the fall of 1931. Davis proposed marriage, using the old "two can live more cheaply than one" argument. Kathryn accepted. Davis demanded they keep the marriage secret until he landed a job and saw his name on a pay stub. On January 4, 1932, they wed on the sly at New York's City Hall. A journalist on the local gossip beat found out about the stealthy wedding, discovered that Kathryn came from a prominent Philadelphia family, and called her parents for comment. Though the ceremony proceeded without them, the Wassermans supported the marriage. Later, they threw a party in Philadelphia. Davis's father flew in for the festivities—his first airplane ride. He brought along the wedding ring worn by his wife, who had died while Davis was in college. In a reenactment of the City Hall ceremony, Davis slipped his mother's ring on Kathryn's hand. This family heirloom spared him an expensive purchase.

The same month Kathryn became Mrs. Shelby Davis, stocks hit bottom. The Dow Jones Industrials had slumped from an all-time high of 341 to an all-time low of 41—down 89 percent in two and a half years! This prolonged loss was far more devastating than the 1929 Great Oops, from which stocks made a snappy comeback, leaving the Dow down only 17 percent at year's end. But by 1932, investors were truly devastated. Losing 89 percent, who wouldn't be? Margin players, leveraged nine-to-one, owed for more than they had wagered. Their speculations often were backed by their houses and other assets, which the lenders acquired as partial payment. Gold stocks were about the only issues that hadn't betrayed their owners. The gold price was fixed by the federal government, and the metal was a popular hedge against doomsday. After it sold off in 1929, Homestake Mining stock recovered and then some; it hit an all-time high in 1932. This result compared favorably to the hundreds of stocks that continued to fall. Following the typical pattern, even the mighty General Motors dropped from $45 to $4. Meanwhile, a passel of corporate bonds, including allegedly "safe" railroad bonds, stopped paying interest. An abrupt decline in rail traffic in 1932, on top of costly strikes and labor disputes, drove railroads into default. Railroad companies had leveraged themselves almost as much as stock speculators; their debt equaled two-thirds of the industry's total capital.

Davis's future source of enrichment, the insurance industry, was in sorry shape as well. Stocks in reputable insurance companies, including several in business since the nineteenth century (USF&G, Continental, and Home), fell with the pack in 1929 to 1932. Home's $100 shares fetched $2 at the bottom. This was an extreme case, but not wildly extreme. Sour investments and shaky finances caused the demise of at least 39 life insurers from 1929 to 1934. Even the strongest companies faced an epidemic of defaults on the mortgages they held in their portfolios. After acquiring two million acres from farmers who stopped making payments, Metropolitan formed its own "department of agriculture" to babysit the property.

A related crisis erupted on the revenue side of the business when a large contingent of policyholders reneged on their monthly installments. The powerful Equitable lost nearly half its customers to cancellations. Many who canceled demanded a refund for the "surrender value." To any insurance company, no matter how well capitalized, the threat of mass redemption was as terrifying as a threat of mass withdrawals was to a bank. [The Insurance Company of North America (INA) was eccentrically rewarding. Thanks to its ultraconservative portfolio and strict underwriting, INA turned a profit every year from 1929 to 1935. Only once did it tap its "surplus" to fund the annual dividend to shareholders.]

Early in 1933, state insurance commissioners declared a moratorium on redemption—a way to avert a run on the industry's dwindling assets. A brochure titled "You Can't Turn the United States into Cash" and distributed by an industry-sponsored public relations firm explained that the moratorium was necessary to save insurers from total ruin and keep policyholders from losing all the protection they'd bought on their houses, their businesses, and their lives. "Companies became the victims of a financial situation for which they weren't to blame," the brochure said.[1] Only the kindness of regulators kept insurance alive. By allowing companies to value their portfolios higher than the depressed prices of the moment, the watchdog agencies permitted fictional solvency.

Banks faced a similar predicament when panicky depositors mobbed local branches, demanding their money back. No depository, large or small, kept enough cash on hand to cover such an exodus, so the panic was self-fulfilling. Hundreds of banks were forced out of business by desperate customers who lost their life savings because they had lost faith in the banking system. Deposit insurance hadn't yet been invented.

Insurance specialist Frank Brokaw began beating the drums for insurance stocks near the market's nadir of negativism. In 1932, his tiny brokerage house took out an ad in the *American Agency Bulletin* to proclaim: "Insurance stock prices have been forced down so far below anything justified by the condition of the companies that it appears certain the upward movement in sound issues will be correspondingly swift when it comes." Two weeks after the ad appeared, a Brokaw employee, E.C. Wilkinson, elaborated. Insurance stocks, Wilkinson said, were "selling for about fifty cents on the dollar of liquidating portfolio."

As so often happens on Wall Street, Brokaw was right on the analysis, but wrong on the timing. The insurance comeback didn't begin in earnest until Davis joined forces with Brokaw 15 years later.

Insurance didn't interest the newlyweds any more than stock quotes did. They were headed to Europe on an ocean liner, to return to the scene of their courtship, attend a world disarmament conference, and then pursue doctorates at the University of Geneva. Davis despaired of finding a new job with hordes of downsized workers desperate to regain employment. He preferred classrooms and conferences to a futile search for a paid position. On the ship, he and Kathryn were surrounded by fellow delegates to the conference. As a wedding present, the Wassermans gave them an upgrade to first class.

The job Davis doubted he'd land on shore came to him at sea. In the main dining room, he and Kathryn met Frederick William Wile, a CBS radio correspondent who was on his way to cover the conference. On the spot, Wile hired Davis as his assistant in Geneva, for $25 a week. While Kathryn attended the sessions, Davis worked in Wile's makeshift studio, scheduling interviews and baby-sitting the guests until they went on the air. During the live broadcasts, he stood next to Wile at the mike. To uphold the dignity of broadcasting, both wore tuxedos, even though this was radio and the listeners couldn't see them.

Radio stocks in the 1920s were as alluring as Internet stocks in the late 1990s, and in both cases the dazzle of the medium blinded investors to the realities of the business.

With Hitler coming to power and Japan threatening the Manchurians, the disarmament conference was a flop. An armament conference would have attracted more interest. A confirmed isolationist, Davis pegged Hitler as a serious warmonger, but he opposed a U.S. counterforce. He figured the Hitler problem would solve itself once the Germans and the Russians squared off and wiped each other out.

After the conference disbanded and Wile returned to the United States, Davis stayed on the CBS payroll as a roving radio reporter. He hustled off to Paris to interview Amelia Earhart—his first assignment. In a two-and-a-half-year stint, he crisscrossed Europe on his radio gig, and got two books published (one was his Master's thesis). Meanwhile, he and Kathryn each earned a PhD in political science from the University of Geneva.

When he was on the road, Kathryn was holed up in a rented room, doing her homework and writing her dissertation. (She got a better grade than Davis did.) Whenever they traveled together, even for a few days, they checked out of their current rental to avoid wasting money on unoccupied space. Finding new rentals took up a lot of Kathryn's time.

Late in 1932, Kathryn's parents invited the parsimonious duo on a trip to the Mediterranean and the Middle East—all expenses paid. Davis chafed at the luxury. In Egypt, he refused to stay at the high-gloss Shepheard Hotel chosen by his in-laws, even though the Wassermans were picking up the tab. He and Kathryn abandoned the Shepheard for more modest digs. On a jaunt through an Arab *souk,* Davis bargained a street vendor so mercilessly the vendor remarked to Kathryn: "He stingy man." "He stingy man" became a long-standing family joke.

In 1934, with twin doctorates in hand, the Davises returned to New York. Now a professional journalist, Davis looked for a writing job. After several months and no luck, Kathryn asked her brother Bill (his cronies called him "Wild Bill") for help. A well-traveled speculator who owned his own investment firm, Wild Bill connected Davis with the editor of an English-language paper, the *Advertiser,* in Tokyo. the *Advertiser* had an opening, and Davis was hired long distance. He and Kathryn were packing their bags when they got word that an earthquake had hit Japan and the paper's editorial offices were destroyed in a quake-related fire. The couple canceled their trip and stayed in New York. A clatter of dueling typewriters could be heard late into the night in their rental apartment on the Upper West Side. Kathryn did research for the Council on Foreign Relations; Davis produced freelance articles and a book about the French military. His byline appeared in highbrow journals such as *Current Affairs* and, later, the *Atlantic Monthly.* "Luckily," said Kathryn, "we didn't have to eat off our prose."

The 1930s—a low point in modern U.S. economic history—was the only decade in which workers produced less, businesses sold less, and the standard of living dropped in comparison to the prior decade. The decline in goods and services couldn't be blamed on a shortage of customers. The U.S. population grew by 15 million in the 1930s—mostly via immigration, not the maternity ward. During the decade-long commercial slump, pregnancy fell into sympathetic recession. Only 1 million U.S. births were recorded. The diminished number of pregnancies got the attention of the First Lady, Eleanor Roosevelt, who urged the nation to make "Babies, babies, babies."

The old buy-and-hold mentality was replaced by a quick-exit mentality. Edgar Lawrence Smith's best-seller, which touted the former, was superseded by Gerald Loeb's best-seller, *The Battle for Investment Survival,* which touted the latter and was a hot read in 1935. Loeb, a stockbroker and syndicated columnist, had ditched his equities before the 1929 Crash. This timely bailout made him famous and convinced him that stocks should be nimbly traded, not dumbly embraced. As his book title suggested, Loeb saw investing as warfare. To win the war, you had to keep fresh assets (cash) in reserve and move in and out of stocks "like a rabbit darting here and there for cover."

Loeb's strategy involved selling on 10 percent drops and buying on the rise—always with a finger on the panic button and a phone line open to the trading desk. He claimed it was "safer to buy and sell a dozen times starting at $40 and ending at $100 than just to buy and pay $40." When he sniffed a bear market, he escaped into cash, avoiding bonds altogether. Bonds, he realized, wouldn't always be a winning asset.

Loeb gave few clues about bear sniffing or nimble trading but advised avoiding stocks when the ticker tape acts "badly" and prices look "suspicious." There's no evidence he profited from his strategy, but he found a receptive audience in a generation known for its frayed nerves. Yet, just as the stock market had crashed when the economy was bountiful, the stock market soared when the economy was woeful. In the fiscal funk of 1932 to 1935, the papers were full of demoralizing tidbits: one out of four employable workers lacked a job; the song "Brother, Can You Spare a Dime?" was a radio favorite; corporate profits were in remission (Dow companies posted a group loss of 51 cents per share in 1932, the only year of negative earnings in the twentieth century); and President Franklin D. Roosevelt declared a bank holiday so bankers could close their doors on depositors who lined up to withdraw their life savings.

Wall Street then launched one of the most profitable rallies in its history.

Stocks were trading at giveaway prices. Solid Dow names were selling for half the market value of their factories, equipment, and bank accounts. Around the time of the Davis marriage, courageous investors who had a tin ear for public opinion and spare cash to put into disparaged equities quadrupled their money in four years. The Dow rose from 41 to 160, and the S&P 500 did even better. This unexpected bonanza was a good lesson for Davis. It reminded him that stocks don't read the papers or swoon in response to scary headlines. When they're priced for desperation, they can rally in the face of desperation, escaping the dumps while the companies to which they're attached are still wallowing in the dumps. For his part, Davis was about to enter the investment business unexpectedly. The Tokyo job fell through, and Kathryn's brother hired him.

It took a sick economy to involve Davis in Wall Street. Otherwise, he had the credentials and the smarts to land a career in journalism. But with no leads and no firm prospects in the media, he accepted his brother-in-law's offer to become a "statistician." (The term "stock analyst" hadn't yet been invented.)

The Davises rented an apartment in downtown Philadelphia, just off the landmark Rittenhouse Square. Davis got acquainted with the family at the elegant brunches, complete with finger bowls, held every Sunday at Kathryn's parents' house in suburban Germantown.

Wild Bill was the fastest talker and the biggest eater at these gatherings. Where Davis was socially reserved, his brother-in-law was boisterous. Where Davis was cautious, Bill was cavalier. Where Davis was economical; Bill was grandiose. "Bill made money to spend money," recalls nephew Louis Levy. "Davis made money to make more money. Bill ran up endless debts and flirted with financial meltdown. Just as he reached the brink of insolvency, he'd score big with his latest speculation."

In mid-Great Depression, Wild Bill engaged a high-priced architect, George Howe, to design and build a trophy mansion, which Bill named Square Shadows. In 1936, Square Shadows won the "House of the Year Award" from a popular architectural magazine. It came with a jumbo swimming pool for the children and detached guest quarters where Wild Bill harbored his mistress. Square Shadows was so lofty and inspirational, it was converted into a church after Wild Bill sold it.

Wild Bill's marriage never interrupted his amorous hyperactivity. His wife understood his "problem"—husbands were thought to be helpless victims of the Casanova disease, and philandering was widely tolerated. Wives of that era chose duty over divorce.

Bill had a roving eye for investments as well. He sent his money on numerous speculative flings. He got a hot tip from a banker in 1932: The German mark was falling. He bet against the mark and collared a huge profit, which helped to bankroll his investment firm and to put his name on Wall Street's map. In an article that appeared in the *Atlantic Monthly,* he correctly predicted that England would abandon the gold standard.

Ignoring the pessimism of the day, he started the Delaware Fund in 1934 and persuaded the du Ponts to become pioneer shareholders. Half the mutual funds from the 1920s had folded when Wild Bill launched his.

In his role as statistician and "field man" for the new fund, Davis visited companies around the country, looking for stocks with promise. He kept tabs on several key industries: airlines, autos, railroads, steel, and rubber. A decade later, in a speech to the State of New York Insurance Department, Davis recalled his "financial prospecting expeditions": "I used to swing regularly around a circuit that included Pittsburgh for the steel outlook, Chicago for general farm prospects, Detroit for the motor outlook, and Cleveland for machine tools and machinery. On occasion there were visits in between. On the whole we felt the broad business outlook was determined by the tale of these four cities. Gradually another city began to be included in the itinerary: Washington. Washington had become the fulcrum around which our entire economy revolved."

Davis also covered what he called the "second American revolution": labor strikes. He was on the scene when the United Rubber Workers shut down the tire factories in Akron, Ohio. A well-worn press card from his radio days got him into union halls, where strikers hatched strategy. Instead of the bomb-throwing "commies" that capitalists seemed to see in their nightmares, he found "plainly-dressed Americans stumbling through *Roberts' Rules of Order*."

"Could these workers," he asked rhetorically, "be the wild men we are all so afraid of?"

He witnessed the Great General Motors Strike of 1937. (From the Great Depression on down, every calamity in those days was "great.") The strikers, parading in GM cars, drove past the Fisher Body plants they'd temporarily put out of business. Davis rode along and listened to strikers' complaints. Low wages they could tolerate, but not the layoffs that came with every slump in auto sales. Their biggest gripe was the speedy assembly lines that exhausted the workers. Unions across America, said Davis, "cursed the modern pace."

While Davis roamed the country analyzing companies, Kathryn got a research job analyzing the Social Security system in Pennsylvania. She wrote a paper on the subject that impressed her employers. Meanwhile, Davis impressed his brother-in-law with his financial savvy. "Someday," Wild Bill told Kathryn, "your husband will be richer than I am."

By 1936, America showed signs it had shaken its malaise. Industrial output, auto sales, and retail sales were on the upswing.[2] Stocks were riding the bull for a fourth straight year. Taking advantage of the bullish momentum, a slew of private companies went public. Art Loom was public already, but its overseers decided to sell more shares while the selling was good. Joseph Wasserman hired a Wall Street underwriter to lead this latest offering. His son, Wild Bill, who considered himself the family guru on such matters, found a rival underwriter who agreed to sell the shares at a higher price than the one Joseph's underwriter had proposed. Faithful to his handshake, Joseph stuck with the original deal, even though it cost him money. The sale took place in 1937—an eventful year for the Wassermans, the Davises, and the world at large. Davis was promoted to treasurer of Wild Bill's mutual fund. Kathryn gave birth to the second Shelby Davis. The Nazis were building a war machine. Cancer killed Joseph Wasserman. The bull market ended. Davis and Wild Bill were headed for professional breakup: Davis bristled at Bill's shoot-from-the-hip attitude; Bill bristled at Davis's attempts to shun the family. The more powerful Hitler became, the less Davis wanted anything to do with his Jewish relations. He and Kathryn attended fewer Sunday brunches. In the biography Davis sent to *Who's Who in America,* Kathryn Wasserman became Kathryn "Waterman."

The Wassermans referred to Davis's new isolation policy as the Hitler crisis. In his own mind, Davis was no anti-Semite (he married Kathryn, after all). He behaved like an anti-Semite to spare himself and Kathryn from becoming victims of anti-Semitism, should Hitler invade the United States. In 1937, a German world conquest was a very thinkable prospect, and Davis was playing the odds. Many Americans shared his apprehension; the future of democracy was far from assured.

In apparent retaliation for disowning the Wassermans, Davis was passed over for partner at Wild Bill's investment firm; two newer and less talented employees were elevated instead. Wild Bill's excuse that his office mates disapproved of nepotism sounded phony to Davis. Convinced that Wild Bill had engineered the rejection, Davis submitted his "letter of retirement." He offered to stay on the job for six months until a replacement could be found. "Why don't you just leave now?" Bill said. Davis did. Joseph Wasserman wasn't around to witness the feud. He died a few weeks before Davis walked off the job. He knew he was dying when he took his wife on a South American cruise. They danced their way from port to port, never discussing his terminal illness until he checked himself into a Boston hospital on their return. He chose Boston for its proximity to the Wasserman summer home on Cape Cod. He spent his final days in the hospital's cancer ward.

Davis and Kathryn joined the bedside vigil, then returned with the rest of the family to Philadelphia for the funeral—held within 72 hours of Joseph's death, in keeping with Jewish custom. At the cemetery, Davis stood with his in-laws and tossed flowers into the grave. Wild Bill's clear-eyed appraisal—"The future of the world does not lie on carpets,"—proved prophetic. Soon, imports brought U.S. mills to a standstill. Already, Art Loom's stock price was falling fast, along with prices of most publicly traded issues. After a glorious five-year gambol, the bull was felled. Its primary assailant was the Federal Reserve, which raised interest rates early in 1938.

By March of that year, the Dow was chopped in half and the magic of compounding went into reverse. To return to the break-even point after this 50 percent decline, stocks had to rise 100 percent, a result that was 15 years away. Even with a 100 percent recovery, the typical stock would be priced far below its 1929 high. As the market gave up its gains, the economy suffered a recessionary relapse. An additional two million Americans joined the unemployment lines, and industrial output dropped faster than it had in mid-Depression. As Davis noted, "The bottom fell out and business declined more precipitously than during the 1929 to 1932 panic." The onset of war in Europe, in September 1939, destroyed any chance for a significant rally. Bullish scholarship, the kind found in Edgar Lawrence Smith's best-seller, was supplanted by bearish scholarship, such as Robert Lovett's article that appeared in a 1937 *Saturday Evening Post*.[3] "No investment is safe or unchanging enough to 'put away and forget,'" Lovett wrote, in direct contradiction to the now disparaged buy-and-hold theory. For proof, he cited the startling rate at which leading companies of the era had declared bankruptcy or had stopped paying dividends. Moreover, because corporate failures were removed from the Dow, the S&P 500, and other popular stock "averages," Lovett said, the return from investing in stocks was far less than it was made out to be. Official calculations didn't reflect the total losses suffered by investors who bought stock in companies that went bankrupt and had nothing to show for their investment.

Bored with the stock slump, Bill Wasserman sold the company that ran the Delaware Fund soon after his father died and his brother-in-law took a hike. Dumping this promising endeavor was typical of Wild Bill's impetuosity–"an elephant charging down the road," nephew Louis Levy describes Bill's investment style. He opened his wallet to an unending procession of imaginative products: from sanitary toilet seats to "mobile dwelling units,"—a precursor to modern RVs and house trailers. He was enthralled by the latest gee-whiz, but bored with details such as: Can these inventors run a business? Often, they couldn't, and his gee-whiz portfolio suffered accordingly. Once in a while, he'd snag a winner, but his prospecting in fantastic realms was far less lucrative than Davis's loyalty to dull insurers. Bill lived to regret the Delaware Fund sale. The fund and its management company prospered for the next 50 years.

Davis, meanwhile, stopped analyzing stocks and returned to his typewriter. Kathryn was absorbed in motherhood; the second Shelby Davis had been born at the onset of the 1937 bear market. An Irish nurse helped with Shelby and freed Kathryn to pursue civic affairs part-time. She volunteered at the local Planned Parenthood unit and was elected head of the League of Women Voters in her area. She worked on a state-funded project that trained domestics and advised them of their rights. Davis got a contract to ponder the causes of the Great Depression, what prolonged it, and how a recovery might play out. Now, the history buff was writing about economics. He sent the manuscript for *America Faces the Forties* to his publisher at the end of 1938.

The book was a modest hit, got good reviews, and attracted a sizable readership that included Thomas E. Dewey, Governor of New York and Republican Presidential hopeful. Dewey enlisted Davis as a speechwriter and economic adviser.

CHAPTER 3

BEYOND THE
REAR-VIEW MIRROR

HEN DAVIS WROTE *AMERICA FACES THE FORTIES*, he was still several years away from becoming a full-time investor, but the topic laid the groundwork. It forced him to face the trauma that caused most of his generation to reject stocks forever. In the standard postmortem of the Great Depression, greed and capitalist excess were popular culprits, and in the hearings that established the Securities and Exchange Commission, Wall Street bankers were pilloried for self-dealing and for enriching themselves at public expense. The lesson that many took from the finger-pointing was that stocks were a rigged game and a sucker's undoing. Investors had a new love interest: bonds. The 1930s turned out to be the only decade in the century in which bonds succeeded while stocks failed. Actually, only one type of bond put investors on a secure, winning track: U.S. Treasuries. Corporate bonds were fickle companions; many corporate borrowers were too strapped to make interest payments. Latin American bonds, sold in large quantities to the American public by zealous brokerage firms (the first time public enthusiasm was aroused by offshore investment), defaulted en masse, again leaving the gullible buyers holding an empty bag. But Treasuries, the Wassermans' favorite asset, were reliable income producers and surprisingly rewarding performers.

It wasn't that Treasuries performed well per se, but that everything else performed badly. With stable to receding interest rates, government bonds held their value while prices of consumer goods, houses, and whatever else money could buy—including stocks—declined across the board. Unless they played the 1932 to 1935 rally, stockholders wished they were bondholders and bondholders like the Wassermans were elated they weren't stockholders.

In rethinking the 1930s, Davis found the actual causes of mass impoverishment to be quite different than prevailing opinion had supposed. At his brother-in-law's firm, he'd studied the ups and downs of companies and their industries. Now, he studied the big picture and found that government policy, not corporate venality, was the principal cause of the years of economic inertia that followed the 1929 Crash. In his view, Washington was more responsible than Wall Street for factories being "strangely inactive" while consumers lacked for shoes, clothing, and other necessities. There was no denying that fantastic and unsupportable stock prices led to the Great Oops, and that by raising interest rates in 1929, the Fed had knocked the bull off stride. But if greedy capitalists caused the Great Depression, as Wall Street's critics had never tired of contending, what accounted for the different economic outcome in England?

As Davis observed, stocks collapsed in both countries, but while the U.S. economy sputtered in the 1930s, British output actually rose. Conversely, the British economy had sputtered in the 1920s, while the U.S. version purred along. The most plausible explanation for this trans-Atlantic flip-flop, Davis argued, was the ballot box. Probusiness Republicans ran the U.S.

Government in the 1920s and were toppled by antibusiness Democrats in the 1930s. Antibusiness Liberals ran the British Government in the 1920s and were toppled by probusiness Conservatives in the 1930s. Though his conclusion was admittedly simplistic, Davis saw how political and regulatory blundering turned a stock market mishap into a global catastrophe.

On the U.S. side, Davis explored the factors that prolonged the slump. Practicing what economist John Maynard Keynes was about to preach, President Roosevelt had pushed for huge increases in government spending to stimulate a commercial revival. To wield this Keynesian prod, the White House launched costly campaigns to pave roads, build dams, upgrade the national parks, and so on. By the late 1930s, it was obvious these measures hadn't succeeded.

Where had the Roosevelt plan gone awry? The government that spent more also taxed more, and "the more the tax burden rose, the more private investment was inhibited," Davis noted. Between the regular tax and a Roosevelt-inspired surtax, the top rate on personal income reached 56 percent in 1932–double the levy of 1925. Four years later, in 1936, the top rate was kicked up to 62 percent. In 1937, an undistributed corporate profits tax was imposed. In Davis's opinion, that tax broke Wall Street's back. "Companies were in retreat," Davis recalls of the aftermath. "Capital went on strike." The 1932 to 1937 stock market rally quickly turned to row.

To Davis's way of thinking, the entire U.S. Tax Code was ill-conceived. It rewarded holders of municipal bonds with zero tax, and, thanks to this generous feature, money poured into state and local government projects financed with municipal bonds. Worthy or not, government projects added nothing to the nation's economic output. Private enterprise made a country wealthier and more productive, created new jobs, invented new merchandise. Yet, in spite of capitalism's relative merits, investors in private enterprise were punished with high taxes on stocks and corporate bonds, while investors in public works were spared all taxes. Thus, the Tax Code retarded prosperity.

While his administration stymied commerce with a hyperactive IRS, Roosevelt cowed businessmen and investors with anticapitalist harangues. The nation's CEOs, Davis wrote, never missed an opportunity to denounce the "malefactors of wealth" and the "selfishness of organized money" in the papers and on the radio. In the press and at the White House, profit was public enemy number one, fingered as the cause of suffering and poverty around the world, where later it would be celebrated as the solution. A Roosevelt adviser, Stuart Chase, in a confidential memorandum for New Deal ghost writers, pointed out certain "good" and "bad" words to use in speeches and articles. "Public interest" was good. "Savings" was good—it reminded people of Ben Franklin and *Poor Richard's Almanac*. "Profit" was taboo.

Tycoon bashing played well in the union halls and on the unemployment lines, but it spooked entrepreneurs and their bankers into keeping their cash on the sidelines. Money that could have built new companies or revived old ones was parked in government bonds or Treasury bills. With financiers afraid to finance, the economy continued to stagnate, in spite of the Keynesian prod.

Besides vicious taxation and Roosevelt's harangues, Davis identified three other Depression enhancers: (1) Congress's slapping stiff tariffs on foreign products to shelter U.S. manufacturers, (2) collapsing currencies abroad, and (3) corporate mergers. (Given the merger mania and the multiple currency crises in the late 1990s, plus the vigorous debate over free trade, all three have contemporary relevance.)

How could mergers depress an economy? Davis explained as follows. Big companies combined to make bigger companies, until a few names (General Electric, DuPont, General

Motors, and U.S. Steel) dominated their respective industries. With these giants throwing their weight around, smaller, more innovative enterprises scrambled to survive. In the auto industry alone, a procession of car makers (Stutz, Reo, Auburn, Hupmobile, Willys-Overland, Hudson, Packard, Studebaker, and others) went bankrupt or were consumed by more powerful rivals.

The currency collapse began with the fall on the German mark in the early 1930s, a move on which Davis's brother-in-law had made his most profitable bet. Germany was still deep in hock to the victorious Allies for World War I reparations. The Allies proposed a moratorium on German war debts to give the losers more time to pay, but France took a hard line and rejected any debt relief. The Germans promptly defaulted on their payments, which inspired other debtors to do the same. The currency markets were in turmoil. "Within weeks," Davis wrote, "England and 30 other nations watched the value of their currencies drop 40 percent." In the United States, the dollar held its value, but prices of grain, timber, and other commodities took a dive. A strong greenback put U.S. businesses at a crippling disadvantage. Foreign competitors could afford to cut prices on goods they sold in the United States because they were paid in almighty dollars, whereas foreign consumers couldn't afford to buy U.S. products because their local money had lost its buying power. Several countries closed their borders to imports.

The U.S. Secretary of State, Cordell Hull, fought for open borders, even though free trade was wrecking the home economy. Alien merchandise flooded the country while unsold U.S.-made goods piled up in warehouses, grain silos, and cargo bins. "The foreigner," wrote Davis, "turned a slump in American business, as had been experienced before, into panic and utter collapse."

Companies fired workers to cut costs. The U.S. unemployment rate jumped from 7.8 million to 13.7 million, rousing politicians to action. Seeking a foreign-trade repellant, soon after the Crash, Congress had enacted the Smoot-Hawley law, which slapped hefty tariffs on imported merchandise. Smoot-Hawley was no match for global deflation. Prices for almost everything continued to fall. Businesses struggled to eke out a profit. Consumers already had shrugged off President Herbert Hoover's "buy more" campaign. Under President Roosevelt, they bought even less. The U.S. Farm Board exhorted farmers to plant fewer crops. (With a reduced food supply, prices would surely rise.) Desperate for cash, farmers planted more.

Unlike most of his contemporaries, Davis refused to let the sad story he'd just retold dampen his enthusiasm for the coming recovery. About business and finance, Davis was congenitally optimistic, an indispensable trait for any shareholder. As brokerage houses would later say during prosperous times, "Past performance is no guarantee of future success," but at the end of the worst decade in modern history, Davis realized that past performance was no guarantee of future failure. He was a student of history and a believer in cycles. He never lost faith in Edgar Lawrence Smith's credo that stocks pay off in the long run. He looked beyond the breadlines, the gloomy headlines, the ravages of deflation, and the national disgust with Wall Street brokers and bankers. He focused on America's lucrative knack for innovation.

To the popular lament, "There's nothing left to invent," Davis found a refutation in the typical U.S. dwelling. Hadn't General Motors just installed a battery in every new vehicle, making a relic of the hand crank and bringing "the ladies into the car market"? Hadn't an array of new labor-saving gadgets gentrified chores and boosted demand for electricity? Electricity consumption per household nearly doubled in the 1930s, so there was no Depression in kilowatt-hours. If invention was passé, Davis asked himself, what explained the deluge of applications in the U.S. Patent Office? He gave a quick rundown on the latest advancements: air-conditioners; nylon (invented by DuPont in 1938); television ("a major industry in the making"); radio facsimile broadcasting; no-knock gasoline; the "continuous spinning machine"; new plastics and fiber products; corrugated board made from chestnut husks (Mead Corporation); latex foam sponges (U.S. Rubber); and germ-killing lamps (Westinghouse).

In spite of the exciting developments that surrounded them, many Americans expected more economic hardship ahead. Howard Scott, leader of the "Technocrats" (actually, they were antitechnocrats), was a big draw on the lecture circuit. Large crowds heard him blame the Depression on mechanical and electronic advances that caused workers to lose their jobs to gadgetry. At a well-attended banquet at a posh New York hotel, business notables listened to Scott's Luddite solution to the nation's woes: Destroy machinery and revert to handicraft, hoe, and horse-drawn plow.

Davis didn't buy the Technocrat lament. He predicted the three "sleeping giants" of industry (railroads, utilities, construction companies) would awaken in the 1940s. He saw new jobs opening up as 130 million consumers returned to the stores and filled the checkout lanes in a nationwide rush to satisfy their pent-up demand for goods and services. In the Davis crystal ball, the biggest threat to U.S. prosperity was legislation proposed by various states to protect home industries with tariffs, just as nations-at-large had protected their manufacturers. He doubted such tariffs actually would be imposed, and he was right.

He was convinced that a world war was imminent, and that it would hasten economic revival. He sensed that the public was "far better informed about our capitalistic system" than it had been in prior decades. Though he was no fan of Roosevelt, he was open-minded enough to realize that Wall Street's nemesis had changed business forever, and not entirely for the worse. For starters, Roosevelt's jumbo government had created a "semi-managed economy." Social Security, unemployment, and government salaries would provide a steady flow of money into consumers' bank accounts, keeping cash in circulation and making future recessions less severe. Deposit insurance would take the risk out of banking, and protect the nation's savings. All that was needed to revive a half-dead economy, Davis concluded, was to have the "breath of business confidence blown into it. When this occurs, the response of the American people will be great. . . .

"A major movement in population, made possible by the motor car, is ready to take place, aided by streamlined financing. . . . A higher standard of living seems almost certain to come. And it will come sooner if public policies that are at the same time pro-social and pro-business are adopted."

On the inflation front, Davis saw no cause for alarm. "Prophecy is always dangerous," he wrote. "But with industrialists intent upon keeping plant capacity sufficiently large, with enormous potential agricultural production, and with the government resolute in taking firm measures to prevent the rising prices from getting out of hand, as I expect it will be, the dangers of unbridled inflation ought to be postponed until after the Forties." As for the shortcomings of Roosevelt's New Deal: "We now have the knowledge of what has been wrong with it. One has only to compare the most recent diagnoses with those of the early New Deal." By 1937, Davis was happy to report, Roosevelt's sermons that decried the "forces of evil and the malefactors of wealth" were no longer taken as gospel.

CHAPTER 4

A LAST HURRAH
FOR BONDS

> After the great market decline of 1929 to 1932, all common stocks were widely regarded as speculative by nature. A leading authority stated flatly that only bonds could be bought for investment.
> Benjamin Graham, *The Intelligent Investor*

SHELBY WAS BORN IN 1937; HIS SISTER, DIANA, IN 1938. Soon after Diana's birth, Davis was hired by Governor Dewey, and the family exited Philadelphia and moved to Scarborough-on-Hudson, New York, where they rented the guest quarters on a local estate. Kathryn hired a baby nurse and a cook—household help was cheap in the area. She volunteered part-time for the League of Women Voters. Davis worked in Albany, in the governor's office, and came home on weekends. After Dewey lost the presidential nomination at the 1940 GOP convention, Davis returned to freelancing. He was named financial editor of *Events* magazine, an offshoot of the widely read *Current History.* He wrote a series of lengthy articles on key U.S. industries (shipping, steel, and so on) for the *Atlantic Monthly,* and knocked off another book: *Your Job in Defense.*

In 1941, Davis invested in Wall Street in a curious, back-handed way. Kathryn had saved $30,000—her father had provided all his children the same amount so each of them could buy a house. Davis and Kathryn had continued to rent because Davis thought houses were too expensive to maintain. He'd watched Wild Bill throw money at his mansion, Square Shadows, and was determined not to repeat the extravagance. Then, in 1941, the man who had refused to spend family money on a house bought a seat on the New York Stock Exchange. He had no use for the seat, purchased from one Nathaniel S. Seeley. At this point, reviving his short-lived career in the investment business hadn't occurred to him. He bought it because he couldn't resist the $33,000 price tag. An identical seat had fetched $625,000 in 1929. To Davis, it was like finding a valuable antique at a garage sale.

A year after his purchase, identical seats were selling for $17,000, so Davis didn't catch the absolute bottom of the stock exchange membership trade. Still, he'd bought very low. The seat market rallied to $97,000 in 1946, then stalled in the early 1950s but never fell below $38,000. By the time Davis died in 1994, his seat was worth $830,000 (May 1994). Buying stingy became a Davis hallmark.

Wild Bill's roving eye roved across continents. He did a hitch in the Air Corps, then shipped out to Australia as part of an economic advisory team. In Melbourne, he met an attractive young woman and coaxed her into a hotel room, after checking them in as "Mr. and Mrs. Smith." The next morning, the local paper ran a front-page article (with a large photo) welcoming Wasserman to the city. As he passed the check-in desk with his girlfriend in tow, the desk clerk held up the front page and said: "Glad to have you with us, Mr. Smith."

Bad eyesight kept Davis out of the military. He continued to oppose sending U.S. troops to fight Hitler, and became a prominent campaigner for the "America Firsters," a group that urged the United States to mind its own business. America First didn't win popularity contests, and Kathryn's affiliation (she joined the Firsters in support of her husband) led to her ouster from a committee post at the Westchester County League of Women Voters in 1941. The flap over her dismissal made the *New York Times*.

Despite his isolationism, Davis wasn't against contributing money and materiel to the anti-Hitler cause. In 1942, he landed a job at the War Production Board in Washington. The Board helped convert U.S. manufacturers into wartime suppliers. He took a room at the Princeton Club, and often drove by the German embassy late at night and saw lights—proof that the Nazis were working overtime. Once again, he was a weekend husband and father.

A third child, Priscilla Alden, died of respiratory failure in the maternity ward in 1942, after a nurse removed her too quickly from an oxygen tent. Kathryn couldn't bear to look at the tiny corpse, but Davis forced himself to peek. He reported that the baby had lovely feet, like his feet. Kathryn counted Priscilla as a war casualty because the best nurses and doctors had joined the military, leaving behind a ragtag staff. The grieving mother spent a few weeks with her family in Philadelphia. Priscilla was buried in the Davis family plot in Peoria.

Families nationwide subsisted on war rations—everything from gasoline and coal to shoes and meat was allotted by coupon. Heeding the call to grow food at home, so farm produce could be delivered to the troops, the Davises planted vegetables in a backyard "victory garden" and potatoes on the front lawn. On their father's orders, Shelby and Diana got up early to pull weeds and to gather eggs from the chicken coop. Davis assumed the children enjoyed these rural chores; Kathryn informed him that they hated them. "Maybe," she said hopefully, "they'll like them better in 20 years when they have their own garden." Every Saturday, the family walked two miles along Route 9 to the neighboring town of Ossining, New York, to see a movie and eat ice cream cones. Kathryn left the car in the driveway. It was unpatriotic to waste gas when the military needed every gallon it could pump. It was also unpatriotic to leave drapes open if a room was lit at night. Americans shuttered their windows and darkened their yards so that enemy planes couldn't target populated areas. A beam of light shining through a window was a breach of "blackout" security, and neighbors were asked to report it to the local air raid warden.

For at-home entertainment, families gathered around a radio or a record player operated with a hand crank. The Davis's record player was installed in the upstairs bedroom, dubbed "the Davis Nightclub," where the children saw their parents dance and heard their first jazz albums. Downstairs, at the breakfast table, they formed a "barnyard orchestra," and brayed, oinked, clucked, mooed, bow-wowed, and baaed on cue. Shelby was the designated clucker. He liked chickens because he made a nice profit selling the eggs he gathered from the family chicken coop and sold with Diana. "We encouraged his door-to-door salesmanship," Kathryn recalls, "but we didn't realize he'd deplete our entire egg supply."

War in Europe tranquilized the New York Stock Exchange. Giddy buying in early 1939 ended in the fall, and a protracted decline followed. The popular theory that wars are bullish, based on the Dow's 1915 record advance, was disproved at the NYSE, which reached its 150th anniversary in a catatonic funk in 1942. On February 14 of that year, only 320,000 shares were bought and sold. It was a typically boring session; the trading floor resembled a lazy tropical resort. On August 19, 1940, the exchange had set a record for inactivity with only 129,650 shares traded—the lowest volume since 1916.*

World War II produced an industrial renaissance, just as Davis had predicted in his book. Once the United States entered the fray, stocks rallied. The Dow more than doubled from 1942 to 1946. The government became the nation's biggest consumer. From steel to rubber to dry goods to munitions, companies retooled their factories to satisfy the only buyer that mattered: Uncle Sam. Among thousands of businesses given new life in the military retrofit was Art Loom. The looms were rebuilt to make uniforms instead of carpets, and the company's profits rose accordingly. Joe Wasserman had advised against "going overboard" on government contracts, but going overboard paid off, at least momentarily. Eventually, Art Loom was acquired by Mohawk, the largest carpet maker in the country.

To quell the inflation it had created, the Roosevelt administration tried to control prices by rationing everything from wheat and sugar to nylon stockings. Consumers chafed at the restrictions and the government-induced austerity. Telephone workers struck for higher wages; coal miners, for meat. The wheat shortage begat a bread shortage, and the Roosevelt White House published the first official federal cookbook: *How to Make Bread-Free Lunches and Dinners.*

Back in Scarborough, Kathryn was having her own domestic problems. Her paid help resigned. "The kids will starve," she told her husband. "I'm a terrible cook." Davis suggested she become a "speed chef" and make a game of it.

---

*Several facts and figures cited in this chapter (the trading volume on the New York Stock Exchange, Joseph Schumpeter's bearish outlook, deflationary expectations for the late 1940s, the rise in federal spending during World War II, the Thomas Parkinson quote about "fictitious money," and the 34-year decline in bond prices) first appeared in James Grant's *The Trouble with Prosperity,* Times Business/Random House, 1996.

Keeping a close watch on the clock, she learned to put a dinner of Campbell's soup, Birdseye peas, and broiled steak (when she could find steak) on the table in 15 minutes or less.

Once she got the hang of solo homemaking, Kathryn wrote an article for the *Ladies' Home Journal,* "Household Servants Are Gone Forever," lamenting the wartime shortage of capable help and the plight of domestics who were underpaid, overworked, and often abused. Her piece was reprinted in *Reader's Digest* and debated in Congress and elsewhere. In 1944, Dewey returned to the New York governor's mansion, and he repaid Davis for his campaign work by naming him deputy superintendent in the state's insurance department. Davis could just as easily have been named deputy superintendent in the traffic department or the public relations office, but this chance appointment introduced him to the industry that would make his fortune.

He was assigned to the state's Manhattan outpost—a cluster of offices at 61 Broadway, on the outskirts of Wall Street. His ongoing mission was antibureaucratic: simplifying forms, streamlining procedures, revamping the accounting rules to make insurance reports easier to understand. He commuted between Manhattan and the rented cottage in Scarborough, but halfway through the first year, after Davis noticed irresistible bargains within commuting distance of Manhattan, Kathryn went house hunting.

A real estate agent showed her a three-story Colonial perched on three acres in Tarrytown. It had an unobstructed view of the Hudson River. The seller was a Mrs. Newberry, widow of the founder of a chain of five-and-ten-cent stores. Kathryn liked the river view but not the suburban neighborhood, and she knew Davis, given his druthers, would rather live on a farm. After Kathryn insisted she wasn't interested, the agent coaxed her into making a $5,000 offer. She was so sure of Mrs. Newberry's immediate rejection of this low-ball insult, she didn't bother to consult Davis before drawing up the contract.

Less than an hour later, the agent called with congratulations. Mrs. Newberry had accepted. "She decided to take a tax loss," Kathryn said. "When my husband came home that night, I told him we'd bought a house in Tarrytown. He cheered up when he heard the price. From then on, I was the designated house hunter for the family."

[Davis, who paid cash for his house, would soon be buying stocks with borrowed money (margin). After its losses in 1929 to 1932, the public disparaged margin investing, yet people routinely bought houses with margin loans, aka mortgages. Though they didn't think of mortgages this way, leverage in residential real estate was a main reason their houses gave them their biggest investment gains over the long term. Davis was confident that leverage applied to stocks was a far more potent profit booster than a mortgage, so he pursued the former and ignored the latter.]

Thus, the Davises became seat owners in 1941 and homeowners in 1945—the year when the surviving combatants came home from World War II, and the war rally in stocks was nearing its end. Even with the rally, the Dow and other major indexes sold below their 1929 prices. Potential investors were traumatized by fear of a depression encore, discouraged by the high taxes on dividend income (capital gains were taxed relatively modestly, but who had any?), and convinced that peace was bad for business. Some expected the falling birthrate would subvert future prosperity (an idea advanced by economist Joseph Schumpeter). Most continued to favor the winning asset of the 1930s: bonds.

Davis didn't share the public's enthusiasm. Though bonds had won the decade, he realized that stocks were superior wealth producers. A stock was a slice of corporate ownership, and, if the company thrived, its upside was unlimited. A bondholder's reward was getting money back, plus interest, no matter how well a company fared. Moreover, though governments depended on bond sales to finance their activities, history showed that regimes of all types had subjected their loyal bondholders to inflationary practices, particularly during and after major wars. World War II was no exception. The war effort that had revitalized industry had been stunningly expensive. Costs ran far beyond the wildest estimates. In 1943, the government spent an abacus-warping $72 billion, which, thanks to the war tab, was $16 billion over budget. To put this in perspective, all the shares in all the companies listed on the New York Stock Exchange were worth only $36 billion. One year's federal outlay exceeded the market value of an all-star lineup of America's leading corporations by half.

There was a predictable hitch: The government lacked the funds to support the wartime spending spree. It solved the problem the old-fashioned way—by raising taxes, selling bonds, and printing fresh cash on federal presses. The strategy was classic: War debts were paid with cheap money, even though cheap money was inflationary. In a clumsy attempt to mollify investors, the Treasury Department put a "cap" on the interest it paid on its own bonds. Bond prices don't fall if interest rates don't rise, so bondholders were temporarily spared the losses that might have cooled their enthusiasm.

The reprieve was short-lived. Investors who bought Uncle Sam's debt were victims of a triple swindle: (1) the cap on interest rates denied them a fair market return; (2) the inflation aroused by government printing ate away at the value of their principal; and (3) in the top brackets, their bond income was taxed at 94 percent. Meanwhile, ad campaigns insisted it was patriotic to buy bonds, and the sheepish patriots dutifully bought all the inventory the government dared print.

Average investors couldn't afford bonds, which customarily sold in $100,000 lots. Millions of Americans parked their money in savings accounts at the local bank or savings and loan, protected by the newly authorized Federal Deposit

Insurance Corporation (FDIC). Depositories paid them a paltry noncompetitive rate of interest, but savers didn't seem to mind. They were more interested in preserving their capital than in augmenting it.

The biggest dupes in the triple swindle were fat cats and institutions (pension funds, insurance companies, and their ilk). These sophisticated types who could afford bonds might have seen the folly in owning government paper in the late 1940s, but most didn't. Fanciful arguments tranquilized the bond bulls. They believed that because bonds were profitable in the past decade, they'd be profitable in the next. They convinced themselves that the Fed could keep interest rates from rising, indefinitely. A government that controlled the price of pork chops, it was widely assumed, could also control the price of money.

Besides, hadn't the inflation aroused in World War I been subdued after peace was restored? That being the case, the "history repeats itself" school of finance predicted that the inflation born in World War II would vanish just as readily. Moreover, the deflation of the 1930s raised expectations of more deflation to come.

Davis rejected these arguments. He became an antibond maverick. The recent past had told people bonds were attractive and safe, but the present was telling Davis they were ugly and dangerous. Interest rates were fast approaching what economist John Maynard Keynes called the "balm and sweet simplicity of no percent." Keynes was exaggerating, but not by much—the yield on long-term Treasuries hit bottom—2.03 percent—in April 1946. Buyers would have to wait 25 years to double their money, and, to Davis, this was pathetic compounding. He saw the threat in the "sea of money on which the U.S. Treasury has floated this costliest of wars."[1] With the government deep in hock and forced to borrow another $70 billion to cover its latest shortfall, he was certain lenders soon would demand higher rates, not lower. The most reliable inflation gauge, the Consumer Price Index (CPI), rose sharply in 1946. Bond bulls turned a blind eye to the inflationary outbreak and ignored a basic lesson from Investment 101: Avoid bonds when the Consumer Price Index is rising. A second lesson—avoid bonds after a costly war—convinced Davis that the bonanza in government paper was over.

He turned his job at the state insurance commission into a soapbox. In the prior decade, insurance companies and pension funds had routinely filled their portfolios with safe-haven Treasuries. Now, given the high risk and low yields in the bond arena, he advised industry leaders to reduce their Treasury holdings and buy more real estate, mortgages, or stocks. In person and in print, he fought the prevailing antistock bias and the irrational exuberance of bond buyers. In the lead article in the *Analyst's Journal,* in July 1945, he wrote:

> Instead of breaking their bondage to bonds, life insurance companies over the past four years have patriotically engaged in the greatest bond buying spree in history. . . . A healthier development would be for them to maintain diversified interests in the American economy, as they did formerly.

Part of the problem was regulatory, and Davis pushed for changes in the rules. In some states, including New York, it was illegal for insurance companies to own any stocks at all. More lenient states allowed insurers to own small quantities. Chastened by the Crash of '29 and its aftermath, insurance executives feared and loathed stocks as much as the regulators did. At a famous hearing in 1941, Frederick Ecker, president of Metropolitan Life, blamed stocks for the Depression-era failure of 60 life insurance companies outside New York. The fact that no insurer failed inside New York, Ecker said, proved the wisdom of New York's just-say-no policy toward equities.

On his contrarian crusade (pro-stock, antibond), Davis had few supporters. Inside the family, his brother-in-law lobbied for stocks in the Wasserman trust, and agreed with Davis that Treasuries and other government issues were nothing more than "certificates of confiscation." In political and business circles, a prominent Roosevelt adviser, Sumner Pike, shared his viewpoint, as did Thomas Parkinson, the president of Equitable Life. The straight-talking Parkinson, who had run Equitable for 25 years, lambasted his colleagues for not speaking out against the government's overactive printing press. "The country," Parkinson said, was "being used by an uncontrolled Treasury to create more and more fictitious money under the cloak of respectability of the Federal Reserve System."

Parkinson and other desperate insurance moguls sought higher yields in the junk bonds of the day, issued by "disgraced public utilities and troubled railroads." The sweeter return came at a price—the extra risk that these shaky companies might default on the payments. In time, many did. Defaulted junk bonds caused big losses in insurance company portfolios.

"For at least a decade, the life insurance industry earned a lower yield on its investment than it had promised to pay its policyholders," Davis remarked. If something didn't give, the insurance industry would go bankrupt.

Parkinson, like Davis, believed bond yields wouldn't stay low forever. "You know," he told the Bond Club of Chicago in November 1945, "unanimity of opinion is a danger sign. When everybody thinks that interest rates are going to remain low or go lower, look out." Meanwhile, Davis "almost pleaded" with insurance companies to add stocks to their portfolios, and with regulators to repeal the no-stock rule. The pleas were widely ignored.

Is it a cruel joke that the most popular asset of each era will impoverish its owners? Every 20 years or so in the twentieth century, the most rewarding investment of the day reached the top of its rise and started a long decline, and the least rewarding investment hit bottom and began a long ascent. These turning points enriched a small group of nonconformists who caught the turn, but the majority continued to put their money on yesterday's proven winner. The majority's loyalty cost them plenty.

In the late 1920s, yesterday's proven winner was stocks, and the love-in for equities wrecked the net worth of a generation. A skeptical minority escaped into government bonds, a move that gave them an excellent and steady income for the next 17 years. Stocks never fully recovered. The late 1940s brought another turning point. By that time, bonds were yesterday's proven winners and were hailed as the safest and smartest investment. What followed was a 34-year bear market in bonds that lasted from the Truman era to the Reagan years. The 2 to 3 percent bond yields in the late 1940s expanded to 15 percent in the early 1980s, and, as yields rose, bond prices fell and bond investors lost money. The same government bond that sold for $101 in 1946 was worth only $17 in 1981! After three decades, loyal bondholders who had held their bonds lost 83 cents on every dollar they'd invested. Ignoring the scene in the rear-view mirror, Davis focused his attention on navigating the future.

CHAPTER 5

A CRIB COURSE
IN COVERAGE

I N THE AFTERMATH OF WORLD WAR II, DAVIS was a minor cog in the Dewey political machine and an outspoken functionary in the New York State insurance department. For four years, he'd pored over the latest reports each company was required to file with the state agency. What he couldn't finish during the workday, he took home in a shopworn briefcase. His evening reading spot was a padded chair near the fireplace.

He had lobbied with little success for more stocks and fewer bonds in the insurers' portfolios. His seat on the NYSE was an indirect investment in the future of equities, but, beyond that, Davis hadn't yet capitalized on the great recovery he'd foretold. Now, his regulatory duties immersed him in balance sheets, income statements, and other bean-counting activities. He became expert in grasping the inner workings of a supposedly dull industry, and the details engrossed him.

A perpetual student of history, Davis studied insurance from its ancient beginnings, as summarized in the following crib course on the subject. (Readers who find this material less fascinating than he did can proceed to Chapter 6.)

According to academic sources, insurance "dawned" as far back as 4000 B.C., which makes it a candidate for the world's *second* oldest profession. Over the centuries, various cultures have contributed new types of coverage, but the basics of insurance have otherwise stayed the same.

Frog, grasshopper, pestilence, firstborn, and flood insurance weren't available in biblical times. The first known policy, the "bottomry contract," covered sea freight. Bottomry was popular with seafaring Babylonians and Phoenicians. In the ancient Code of Hammurabi (circa 1750 B.C.), a terrestrial insurance angle appeared: "If a life [has been lost], the city or district governor shall pay one mina of silver to the deceased's relatives." In addition to pioneering group coverage, Hammurabi was tough on pilferers in the fire department. Any fireman caught stealing property while putting out a fire was thrown into the fire.

Widows of Greek shippers who went down with their cargo were awarded an income stream—the first life insurance on record. In describing these early policies, Demosthenes became the first literary heavyweight to tackle a subject that has bored writers for centuries.

Rome's contribution to insurance heritage was the Burial Society, which offered prepaid interment at favorable group rates. Burial policies begat health-care policies. Fraternal organizations paid retirement and disability benefits to Roman GIs. In A.D. 200, an ingenious bean counter, Domitius Upianus, devised an annuity value table, used by Italian insurers to set rates. In parts of Tuscany, Upianus's table was still in vogue 1,600 years later.

European fire insurance has been traced back to the village of Verambacht in A.D. 1240. According to local law, "the person whose house burned down is to be indemnified without delay by the whole village." In the 1500s, English "slush funds" reimbursed guild workers for losses due to everything from sickness to fraud. English burial societies covered expenses for people who "wished to be interred in a genteel manner." In London, a well-preserved life insurance policy from 1583 was unearthed four centuries later. It belonged to William Gybbons, who, with excellent timing, expired 17 days before his coverage did.

Neapolitan banker Lorenzo Tontine, launched the first "Tontine" in 1653. Here, various players put up "x" amount per month, in a macabre Italian version of *Survivor*. When the first player died, his relatives got a small payoff. Relatives of the next dead player got a bigger payoff, and so on, until the last living player took home a giant lump sum. Tontines were popular entertainment and caused a lot of joy and murders.

Before observing the comet in the late 1600s, astronomer Edmund Halley invented a mortality table to help insurance CEOs figure out how much to charge their customers. At that point, typical English clients could protect themselves at work, in the bedroom, the outdoors, and the hereafter with highway robbery insurance, chastity insurance, marriage insurance, baptism insurance, apprenticeship insurance, widowhood insurance, and unemployment insurance.[1]

The Great Fire of London, in 1666, destroyed a half-square-mile of real estate, including 87 parish churches, and put numerous insurers out of business—an option they preferred to admitting they had no money to pay claims. Several new companies rose from the ashes and took advantage of the belated boom in fire policy sales. Three of those enterprises still exist today, as divisions of modern conglomerates.

Forty years after the Great Fire, a great "South Sea Bubble" was formed on the London Exchange. Many dot-com-type enterprises of dubious merit went public at carbonated prices, along with at least 20 newcomers to the insurance field, one of which insured heavy drinkers against "excessive consumption of rum." When the bubble popped and stocks were marked down 70 to 90 percent, insurers and noninsurers went pfft.[2]

The famous Lloyd's of London survived the bubble by not being publicly traded. Lloyd's got its start as a coffeehouse with a liquor license, which explains its popularity with seafarers. Between drinks, they picked up their mail here, along with the latest shipping gossip read aloud by comely barmaids. After the owner, Edward Lloyd, died in 1713, the place was gentrified with booths, but a salty atmosphere lingered. Between drinks, patrons bought marine insurance from agents who'd infiltrated the premises. Realizing insurance was more profitable than coffee and whiskey, Lloyd started underwriting.

Thanks to brilliant odds making, Lloyd's continued to pay out less money in claims than it took in to insure those claims. Its private financial backers, called Names, pocketed large and generally reliable profits for more than two centuries.

On the U.S. side of the insurance market, the industry wrapped itself in flags and rode the coattails of Revolutionary celebrities. An American eagle perches above the headline in the lead article in the premiere issue of the *Journal of Insurance,* published in September 1923. Here we learn that as early as 1752, a civic-minded "party of forefathers" led by Ben Franklin met at a Philadelphia courthouse to organize local fire insurance. Although textbooks often neglect to mention this gathering, industry sources remind us of its lasting importance to future home owners. Early American fire insurers helped many more people over time than, say, the perpetrators of the so-called Boston Tea Party who get more credit.

Before Franklin got involved, the typical colonist in Philadelphia was forced to buy coverage from British sources, as local coverage was frowned upon. A policyholder with an insured loss waited months before London acknowledged the claim, let alone paid it.

Though Franklin gets all the credit, it is only fair to mention that fire insurance made its American debut in Charleston, South Carolina, 15 years before the kite-flying electrician wrote his first policy. Unfortunately for the Charleston policyholders, after four years of vigorous sales, the pioneer insurer went out of business just as a pile of claims was filed from a citywide blaze. It wasn't the last time an insurance company was long on promises and short on cash. Facing its own rash of claims in Philadelphia, Franklin's company refused to insure any house with trees in the yard. A competitor, Green Tree Mutual, sprung up to offer coverage to tree owners.

Meanwhile, other notable patriots realized that a new nation, especially a nation of wooden buildings, couldn't long survive without protecting its real estate. Alexander Hamilton took time out from political wrangling to found Mutual Assurance of New York, while John Marshall, original chief justice of the U.S. Supreme Court, launched the Mutual Assurance Society Against Fire on Buildings in Virginia. One of Marshall's best customers was Thomas Jefferson, who bought a policy for his Monticello mansion.

From the mid-1800s onward, start-up insurance companies named themselves after deceased patriots (Franklin, John Hancock, Paul Revere, etc.) to create the impression of longevity, tradition, and high character. A few canny underwriters launched when the patriots were still alive have survived two centuries of plagues, wars, piracy, fires, earthquakes, reckless drivers, fraudulent claims, and greedy lawyers, proving that clever and prudent insurers can outlast most types of businesses.

In 1792, the Insurance Company of North America (INA) was hatched by two speculators who imported the "Tontine" concept from Europe with minimal success.[3] They dropped the Tontine business in favor of selling standard fire, marine, and life insurance in Philadelphia. On the fire front, they competed directly with Ben Franklin. Their first year was profitable, and they sent investors a nice dividend. Then a yellow fever epidemic hit Philadelphia. Residents protected themselves by smoking cigars, lighting bonfires, firing muskets in the air, closing their windows, sprinkling vinegar around their beds, and attaching leeches to their skin. In spite of these efforts, funeral parlors worked overtime. To avoid contamination, George Washington and Thomas Jefferson both left town.

A flurry of claims convinced INA to drop life insurance and specialize in fire and marine protection. This was the heyday of American clipper ships, the oceanic sprinters that outraced beamier British cargo scows across the Atlantic. Clipper operators bought insurance, and for a brief period, the sellers thrived on hefty premiums and minimal claims. INA invested its windfall in mortgages and bonds that built roads, bridges, and canals nationwide.

In predictable fashion for this industry, a string of fat years was followed by a string of lean years. INA was thwarted on several fronts: skirmishes with the British disrupted trade and created losses; piracy and deliberate "wrecking" of U.S. ships added to the losses; British steamboats took business away from the clippers. But the insurers' worst enemies weren't wreckers, steamboats, or gunboats. They were rival companies that invaded INA's markets along the Eastern seaboard. High profits attracted a mob of competitors. Freelance salesmen, called "out-of-door underwriters" sold cut-rate policies al fresco. A vicious price war killed everybody's profits.

Still, INA could count its blessings. By refusing to do business in New York, it sidestepped claims from the Great Fire of 1835 that ruined all but three of that city's insurers. It survived the financial panic of 1837 that resulted in multiple bank failures and insurance collapses, and caused Pennsylvania, the richest state in the country, to default on its debts.

From the investment angle, there were two types of insurers: "stock companies" that sold shares on Wall Street, and "mutual" companies owned by the policyholders (the same way mutual savings banks were owned by depositors). Stock companies had caught on in the East, while mutuals proliferated in the Midwest. In the wake of the 1837 panic, mutuals gained further popularity.

In 1850, New York had passed its first general insurance law. Other states followed New York's lead, setting up agencies to police an industry that attracted a continuous cast of scoundrels. Soon, the federal government imposed its own regulations, but these were stymied by the U.S. Supreme Court, which ruled (*Paul v. Virginia,* 1869) that insurance didn't involve interstate commerce and therefore was immune from federal oversight and exempt from antitrust legislation.

State regulators didn't quell the surging popularity of selling policies. After the latest financial panic in 1857, hundreds of merchants left their bankrupt businesses and opened insurance offices. Disaster claims from the Civil War undid most of these poorly capitalized providers, but at war's end, another spate of new companies of doubtful standing filled the void. Ex-soldiers from both sides of the war enlisted as roving agents, expanding the market for local moms-and-pops. Some went public, while others operated as mutuals. Some were reputable in theory, but lacked the wherewithal to bankroll a true catastrophe. Others were scammers who pocketed premiums and skipped town as soon as big claims were due. Either way, claimants were stuck with losses they'd supposedly paid to avert.

Factory insurance was on the rise as a post-Civil War manufacturing boom doubled the number of insurable plants. INA sent its sales force inland, writing policies for the settlers who heeded Horace Greeley's advice to travel West. Insurance covered homesteads, wagon trains, saloons, feedstores, railroads, and mines. Reputable insurers lobbied for reforms to foil their shady competitors. Like oil tycoons in the twentieth century, insurance tycoons in the nineteenth century formed cartels to boost rates and preempt price wars.

Thus, the National Board of Fire Underwriters was organized in 1866 to put an end to the ruinous free market free-for-all with "uniform rates and commissions." This goal was elusive and its supporters hypocritical, as member companies routinely cut prices sub rosa and subverted the uniform rates they pretended to favor. (In 1921, a similar attempt to cartelize, the Surety Association of America, met with similar futility.)

In 1871, Mrs. O'Leary's cow kicked over a lantern in Chicago, resulting in $90 million worth of insured losses and undoing nearly 200 companies that provided the coverage. INA paid $650,000 to 180 claimants from its well-fortified bank account and still had enough cash to pay its annual 10 percent dividend to shareholders. By making good on its promises, INA attracted new customers.

The Great Fire of Boston broke out 13 months later, leaving $100 million in losses and destroying 50 insurers. The 1906 San Francisco earthquake/fire did $400 million in property damage and wrecked 20 insurance companies. That city's water mains crumbled in the quake, leaving fire hoses dry and giving the flames free rein. Eight months before the blaze, the National Board of Underwriters had chided its San Francisco associates for reckless coverage, and warned that the fire department "cannot be relied upon to indefinitely stave off the inevitable."

Called a "harebrained fad" by skeptics, the motor car created a vast new territory for policy prospecting. According to dusty records, the first customer was Dr. Truman Martin of Buffalo, New York. Dr. Martin's policy came from Traveler's, the strongest casualty underwriter of the late 1800s. He was insured for damages his car did to others.

The founder of Traveler's, James Batterson, was the son of a Connecticut stonecutter who made a quick fortune in grave markers, studied Latin and Greek, and befriended Abraham Lincoln. In 1864, he began to insure wayfarers against accidents. As the first underwriter of this hazard, he picked rates "out of the air." In 1866, Traveler's added life insurance, followed by auto insurance.

At that point, INA already had made it through financial crises in 1819, 1837, and 1857, on its way to surviving similar crises in 1873, 1893, and 1907. Thanks to conservative investing, INA came through the 1929 Crash with relatively minor damage. At the market's nadir in 1932, the company's stock and bond portfolio had a market value of $52 million, down from a $77.7 million pre-Crash high. Its own shares, traded on the New York Curb Exchange (the precursor to the American Stock Exchange) took a comparatively mild fall: $87.50 at the top to $32 at the bottom. By the end of 1935, the price had rebounded to $76.50. Few issues could boast of such a revival.

In the mid- to late-1930s, the industry made a brisk recovery, and a few stocks rebounded with gusto. USF&G, the largest casualty underwriter in the country, saw its share price rise 1,145 percent into the mid-1940s. The S&P 500 rose a comparatively disappointing 77 percent over the same stretch, while a typical casualty company (judging by Best's Casualty Index) rose 248 percent.

Finally reversing its long-held prior opinion, in 1944, the Supreme Court ruled that insurance qualified as interstate commerce. The latest test case reached the court after a regional cartel, Southeastern Underwriters, was indicted for fixing rates in violation of the Sherman Anti-Trust Act. Appalled at the judicial flip-flop that threatened to end a century of kinder, gentler state oversight, the insurance lobby swarmed Capitol Hill to goad Congress into passing new legislation (the McCarran-Ferguson Act) giving the states sole power to regulate the industry.

Along with Traveler's, Aetna, and Cigna, INA had persevered through a long stretch of manmade and natural property damage (wars, floods, hurricanes, earthquakes, and fires that scorched three major U.S. cities). This handful of insurers had whistled past the graveyard of bankrupt railroads, textile mills, steel mills, retailers, and wholesalers. In spite of all the calamities whose victims they reimbursed, these big names had proven themselves. So had Lloyd's of London, which formally incorporated in 1871. By the twentieth century, Lloyd's was the most famous insurance powerhouse in the world, as solid and permanent an institution as the British Empire itself. Its unsinkable reputation caused one writer to dub Lloyd's the "Titanic of Insurers" in 1911, the year the ship was launched and before it hit the iceberg.

Did insurance investing always produce stable, reliable, and attractive returns? Hardly. For every long-term survivor, dozens of companies had succumbed to panics, depressions, optimistic underwriting, expensive settlements, inflated claims, inept management, and bad luck. In the 1960s and beyond, even Lloyd's lost its knack for making money, and at one point its survival was in doubt, almost making the Titanic tag belatedly apt. Lloyd's investors (the "Names") lost plenty, along with less celebrated investors, in a slew of hapless insurance companies that stayed in business although they were only marginally profitable. Davis was aware of this when he made his initial stock purchases.

CHAPTER 6

FROM BUREAUCRAT
TO INVESTOR

DAVIS LEFT HIS STATE JOB FOR THE STOCK MARKET in 1947. Kathryn recalls her family's reaction to Davis's sudden exit from secure government work: "They thought it was a little crazy."

Bell Labs came out with the transistor that same year. Sony was born. Ajax, "the foaming cleanser," appeared on the shelves. "Cold War," a phrase coined by financier Bernard Baruch, entered the vocabulary. In a speech at Harvard, General George C. Marshall introduced his Marshall Plan to help Europe dig itself out of the rubble. Congress passed Taft-Hartley, a law designed to weaken labor unions. The first assembly-line houses were ready for occupancy in Levittown. Jackie Robinson broke the color line in baseball. The electric guitar made its debut. Stocks were still widely disparaged. The Dow stood—or reeled—at the 180 level, half off its 1929 high. Chemicals and autos hit new lows in 1946; rails and aircraft fell in 1947; and drugs and utilities went down a year later.

Investors faced the following choices. They could go the bond route, clip a 2.5 percent annual coupon for 30 years, and pay brutal taxes. Tax-free compounding [in IRAs, Keoghs, and 401(k) plans] hadn't been invented. The vast majority of Americans who couldn't afford bonds continued to store their liquid assets in savings accounts. In another example of how financial institutions were spared the rigors of the competitive free enterprise system they financed, all banks paid the same low-ball interest rates to depositors. The fix was in, imposed by the feds to guarantee bankers a source of cheap capital they could lend out at much higher rates, producing a favorable "spread." The wider the "spread," the greater a bank's margin of profit and safety, and the less chance it would fail. Bankers could worry less, keep bankers' hours (10:00 A.M. to 3:00 P.M., Monday through Friday), and play more golf.

Meanwhile, the interest paid to depositors, minus the taxes paid on the interest, didn't come close to beating inflation. That being the case, the savings account was guaranteed to deplete wealth. Year after year, dutiful savers lost money and rarely complained about it.

What about the stock route? Davis hadn't worked as an analyst for 10 years, but he'd kept up with developments. He knew stocks hadn't escaped the bargain basement. The Dow sold at 9.6 times earnings, only slightly above its book value. The average Dow company paid a 5 percent dividend, double what investors could get from Uncle Sam's bonds. Beyond the Dow, in almost every sector of the market, dividend yields far exceeded bond yields. On top of the yield, stockholders got the chance for capital gains.

Still, the public wasn't buying. Over 90 percent of the respondents to a Federal Reserve Board survey said they were opposed to the purchase of common stocks. As Davis put it, the masses held a "collective grudge against the market." The nation that fought and won the war to rid the earth of its biggest devils avoided the devil's money pit on Wall Street. The mutual fund industry, prominent in the 1920s, had all but disappeared. Only 300,000 Americans owned shares in funds. Few people wanted to bet on American business, but Davis couldn't help noticing that business was on an upswing. American factories stood alone in the world—their foreign competitors had been obliterated in the war. Multinationals in the United States boosted their profits abroad by capturing European markets without resistance. Four former enemies—Italy, Austria, Germany, and Japan—became wards of the Allies. And America had the Bomb.

The release of postwar energy was more powerful than the Bomb. It cured the lingering Depression. Through the 1930s and into the 1940s, a mass market hardly existed in America. Restaurants, motels, and most stores were local. Nearly half of the nation's families earned less than $20 a week. They struggled to keep themselves fed, clothed, and sheltered. They emptied their wallets for necessities, with zilch left over for amenities. For these subsistence-level earners, "shop till you drop" was as alien a concept as surfing the Web.

Postwar prosperity brought what economists call "discretionary income" to millions of new retail customers who suddenly found themselves with cash for non-essential purchases. This extra cash had a fantastic multiplier effect. After a frustrating stretch of rationing and coupons, of regarding gasoline as an extravagance, butter and sugar as luxuries, meat as a treasure, and a new pair of nylons as an impossible dream, Americans exercised their freedom to shop. People bought everything and anything, and stretched the definition of "necessity" to include whatever caught their fancy.

Giddy with triumph and flush with separation pay, ex-GIs had more spending money in their pockets than any working-class population had ever amassed. They were acquiring houses, cars, and college degrees financed on the GI Bill. The housing boom led to a small appliances/home repairs/furnishings boom. The baby boom led to a diapers, laundry soap, pram, and crib boom. Nationwide, manufacturers thrived on the pent-up demand and switched quickly from a satisfy-Uncle-Sam mode to a satisfy-the-local-shopper mode. Cash registers from coast to coast merrily rang up sales, and gratified merchants added floor space and opened new stores. The economy kicked into high gear. Inflation was on the rise, but profits rose faster as improved machinery helped workers produce more goods per hour. Had Davis been assigned to the traffic department, the utility department, or the press office, he might have seen a great potential in auto stocks, electric companies, or newspaper stocks. But, as Peter Lynch would later advise, he specialized in what he understood—an industry that was overlooked by analysts and ignored by brokers.

Insurance was a trivial pursuit on Wall Street. Many insurance issues traded in the minor leagues of stock exchanges—the neighborhood stock parlors that comprised the "over-the-counter" market. As Davis had noticed, small stocks outran big stocks in the postwar era. He surmised the reason: Small companies could hike prices and control wages without "fear or threat of Congressional investigation or labor union pressure." In theory, the typical insurer enjoyed this advantage, but Davis was aware of a lingering absence of profit. Dow companies doubled their earnings from 1942 to 1947; fire insurers earned zilch. "The fire insurance industry is less profitable than at any time since the San Francisco fire [of 1906]," Davis said in one of his many speeches. "The rest of the business world has been feasting on the greatest bonanza America has ever seen. . . . My shirts cost more, my coal costs more, my bread costs more, my pork chops cost more. Practically everything I know of costs nearly twice as much as it did before the war—except fire insurance."

Davis blamed the earnings slump on low-yielding bonds held in insurers' portfolios. The industry got such a minimal payoff on its capital, it had trouble setting aside the necessary "reserves" to cover future claims from policyholders. "Typically, the biggest problem for a life insurance company is selling policies," Davis told a group of industry leaders in 1946: "Today, the bigger problem is [how to invest] the proceeds."

Though the lack of earnings was superficially disturbing, Davis was convinced not only that stocks in general had a prodigious upside, but insurance stocks offered extreme reward at minimal risk. Without formal CPA training, Davis had learned the quirks of insurance accounting—designed to satisfy state regulators, not inform potential investors. Like a gold miner who wore rags to the claims office to avoid calling attention to his lucky strike, the industry presented itself in as poor a light as possible. When an agent sold a new policy, the commission was 120 percent of the first month's payment. Thus, each new sale created a loss on paper.

Davis devised various rules of thumb to compensate for this and other anomalies. The typical insurer, he discovered, was selling for less than "book value." The bonds and mortgages held in its fixed-income portfolio were worth far more than the market price of the company's own shares. Any buyer of those shares got his or her money's worth—and then some—in a slice of the portfolio. As a bonus, the buyer got the ongoing insurance business thrown in for free, and as if that weren't enough, the buyer received the annual 4 to 5 percent dividend, or double the yield on the beloved long-term Treasury bond.

With a bit of pencil pushing, the tangibles and intangibles could be assessed. Underneath the drab earnings, the insurers' portfolios were merrily compounding, as bond interest and mortgage payments rolled in. In his earlier role as Wild Bill's analyst, Davis hadn't differentiated compounding machines from other types of companies, but the regulatory job had taught him this crucial distinction. Where manufacturers expended capital to devise a salable product, then spent more to upgrade their factories and improve the merchandise, insurers took in cash from every new customer and spent belatedly, when claims were filed or policies matured.

Bonds and mortgages in the insurers' possession were bought with customers' money. Assuming unexpected claims didn't deplete the portfolio, an insurer could amass a gigantic hidden asset that someday would belong to the shareholders. Patient investors could wait for the hidden asset to grow, expect other investors to discover it, and then bid up the price. Other people's installment payments, plus interest, then became their own life savings instead.

This shareholder alchemy required no boiling cauldrons, potions, amulets, or magic words. Any stock picker could benefit, and the how-to aspects of so-called "value investing" were fully described in Ben Graham's *Securities Analysis,* first published in 1934. Graham resolved the popular confusion between speculating and investing by arguing that stockholders could be investors or speculators, depending on what they bought and how much they paid for it. Graham advised buying shares in businesses that were selling for less than the liquidation value of the assets. That way, the chances of losing money were drastically reduced. People who looked for a payoff at minimal risk were investing. People who paid silly prices for the unrealized potential of celebrated upstarts in promising but unproven endeavors were speculating.

Although he was a nonentity to the general public, Graham had a cult following among the actuarial cognoscenti. His most ardent disciple was Warren Buffett, but Davis also had studied Graham's writings and admired his ideas. In 1947, Davis was elected president of Graham's stock analysts' organization.

On top of their allure as value players, insurance companies benefited from a surge in the demand for policies. Newlyweds with new houses and new cars in the driveway needed three kinds of coverage: life, home, and auto. The lead story in the July 1948 issue of Kiplinger's magazine, the *Changing Times,* caught Davis's attention. It was entitled: "What a Young Man Should Do with His Money." The first bit of advice: "Start by buying at least $20,000 of life insurance." A decade earlier, one-third of the nation's savings had been tied up in life insurance; in the 1940s, that percentage increased. War had been bullish for insurance agents. Record sales were reported after the attack on Pearl Harbor. Customers bought more policies and faithfully paid the premiums. "Lapses" (the industry's euphemism for nonpayment) and "surrenders" (some people simply gave up their policies) hit all-time lows in the 1940s. By 1944, 159 million policies were in force nationwide; nearly 16 million of them belonged to military personnel. GIs who took out insurance for five years were persuaded to convert to 20-year policies. Davis noted another boon for the industry: the "bull market in longevity." When it came to dying, policyholders were taking their time. They were alive and paying premiums—as opposed to dead, with their heirs collecting on their policies. Insurers, Davis said, were "growth companies in disguise"—growing like crazy but "people don't think of it that way." Electric utilities fit the same category in the 1950s. Much later, Davis's son found disguised growth opportunities in consumer companies in the 1980s and financial companies in the 1990s.

The more he learned about the industry he regulated, the more Davis was convinced he'd stumbled onto a mother lode. In case after case, he found companies selling for less than book value, paying hefty dividends, and offering superior long-term compounding. With his boss and mentor the odds-on favorite to win the presidency in 1948, Davis could have hung on Dewey's coattails, expecting to ride them to Washington. But a chance at a high-level Washington gig didn't interest him as much as the insurance business. If the companies he regulated couldn't be persuaded to put more common stocks in their portfolios, at least he could show the world at large why they should put insurance stocks in theirs. To that end, he submitted his resignation.

To gain a base of operations, Davis bought a controlling interest in Frank Brokaw & Co., which advertised itself as the "oldest specialist in insurance stocks." Brokaw had been pounding the table for his favorite insurers since the 1930s. Bad timing undid him, and his firm was on the ropes. Davis decided he could benefit from Brokaw's staying power by keeping the "oldest specialist" tag, erasing "Brokaw," and re-naming the enterprise Shelby Cullom Davis & Co. His seat on the New York Stock Exchange came in handy. It gave him access to the trading floor and a license to do business alongside the big-league Wall Street houses. His was now a "member firm" with all rights and privileges attached. Davis allowed Brokaw to stay on as his partner, at least temporarily, but several months into the new arrangement, Brokaw dissolved the partnership by drowning in the Atlantic Ocean. The coroners ruled his death a suicide.

Davis now had the office to himself. It was located at 110 William Street, just off Wall Street—the financial equivalent of off-Broadway. It contained twin desks and two black phones. The phone number (in May 1948) was Beekman 3-0626. Kathryn served as the in-house answering service. "It was easy work," she recalls, "but boring. Nobody called. I sat there reading a book."

In the country at large, wartime austerity had given way to peacetime spending, but in the Davis household, austerity was still in effect. The resident stock picker emerged from his bedroom at 6:00 A.M., cooked his own breakfast on a hot plate in the bathroom, ate while he dressed, dressed without noticing what he was wearing, grabbed his briefcase, and called for Kathryn to drive him to the train station. He caught the 7:00 A.M. commuter from Tarrytown to New York. His neighbors opted for the 8:00 A.M. club car, which gave them more time to sleep and a cushier ride. Davis preferred an earlier start and nobody to bother him while he read the *Wall Street Journal*. He also liked getting a jump on the Wall Street crowd. The lower fare at 7:00 A.M. was a bonus.

As a member of the private sector, Davis addressed the Insurance Accountants Association at the Hotel New Yorker on May 12, 1948. "My topic today is close not only to the hearts but indeed to the very lives of those who look to fire insurance for sustenance," he said, as if he were facing a roomful of heroic fighters instead of pencil-pushing Dilberts. His speeches were heavily salted with "very," "indeed," and "I need not remind you," as in: "This is a great industry, I need not remind you, one of the oldest and most honorable in America. . . ."

He described how policyholders weren't the only people who benefited from a robust insurance industry. A "large and silent body" of shareholders—including universities, hospitals, missionaries, and others—had invested part of their savings in insurance stocks. "They all suffered when regulators rejected rate increases and squashed industry profits." More profit, he thundered, meant more jobs and more prosperity at large.

During 1947 and 1948, he'd crisscrossed the country several times, pounding the table for insurance stocks. He delivered the pitch to foundations, pension funds, and wealthy individuals, just as his drowned partner had done, with minimal success, a decade earlier. He expected that whoever bought shares on his recommendation would let him handle the trades, and he could pocket the commissions. "Would you buy Standard Oil at half today's price?" he asked his audiences. The crowd always hollered "Yes!" Insurance stocks, he enthused, offered them the same discount. The typical insurer was selling for half the value of its captured assets. This, he said, was "the greatest fire sale in history."

"I myself have been battering against the doors," Davis admitted, describing the effort to raise capital for seven insurers about to go public. His firm was the smallest of several syndicates involved in this underwriting. He expected his coast-to-coast road show to rouse buyers, but it didn't. "Apparently," Davis snorted, "the horny-handed savers of this country will not pay one plugged nickel for those assets. . . ."

One of the new public offerings was Aetna. Existing shareholders had first dibs on the shares, but took only half their allotment. Davis and his cohorts in the other syndicates struggled to unload the remainder.

"Why, under such circumstances . . . did I not have to beat off would-be purchasers with a club?" Davis asked—and then answered his own question. First, stocks were still anathema to most people. President Harry S. Truman had lampooned Wall Street so gleefully during the 1948 campaign that his victory caused Charles Merrill, founder of Merrill Lynch, to take out newspaper ads to rebut the President's attack:

"Mr. Truman knows as well as anybody: There isn't any Wall Street," scoffed Merrill. "That's just legend. Wall Street is Montgomery Street in San Francisco. Seventeenth Street in Denver. Marietta Street in Atlanta. Federal Street in Boston. Main Street in Waco, Texas. And it's any spot in Independence, Missouri, where thrifty people go to invest their money, to buy and sell securities."[1]

Would-be purchasers had given Davis the following reasons not to buy his favorite insurers: (1) Wars cause a "general loosening of morals." Returning GIs will set fires and burglarize their neighbors. Insurance companies will be stuck with the bill. (2) Insurers had recently paid a whopping claim from an explosion at a nitrate plant that killed 576 people in Texas City, Texas, in 1947. Another mega-disaster might put them out of business. (3) The oft-predicted atomic warfare was an

insurance nightmare. Imagine the claims from World War III!
(4) Nuclear power plants would leave a radioactive mess, causing another huge insurance tab.

The frustrating road-show flop was a blessing in disguise. In the *Intelligent Investor,* a sequel to his famous *Securities Analysis,* Benjamin Graham had written: "[To] enjoy a reasonable chance of continued better-than-average results, the investor must follow policies which are (1) inherently sound and promising, and (2) are not popular on Wall Street." Davis devoted his new career to this two-part maxim. If shortsighted audiences ignored his recommendations, he'd take his own advice. His underwriting and brokerage operations quickly became secondary to his own portfolio. He turned his attention to buying sound and promising companies in this unpopular industry.

Investing through his licensed firm gave him two key advantages over the typical neighborhood stock picker: (1) he could buy more shares on margin because the SEC gave firms more leeway to borrow money than it gave individuals, and (2) a firm paid a lower rate of interest. A large crowd of unwary enthusiasts had bought stocks on margin and lost their life savings in 1929, but Davis was comfortable borrowing the maximum the SEC allowed—slightly more than 50 percent. Unlike his hapless predecessors, who bought stocks at sucker prices on margin, he figured the cut-rate prices for insurance companies gave him a safety net.

"My father hated taxes," says Shelby, "so margin became his favorite weapon against the IRS. The interest he paid on his loans was tax-deductible, and his deductions wiped out the taxes he'd otherwise have owed on the dividends he got. Also, by raising the stakes on his investing, margin kept him focused."

Davis continued to travel widely—not so much to tout companies to others, but to analyze them for himself. He visited CEOs in Hartford and elsewhere, quizzing them on recent results and plans for the future. Face-to-face meetings helped him separate the "bluffers from the doers." Today's Wall Street analysts make corporate house calls as a matter of course; Davis pioneered the practice. CEOs routinely announced goals for the future. Davis challenged them to provide details. It turned him off when a company made definitive predictions about its long-term profit growth but was vague on how it planned to achieve it. One of Davis's favorite questions was: "If you had one silver bullet to shoot a competitor, which competitor would you shoot?" He'd get the answer, and make a note to research the competitor's stock. A company that was feared by its rivals must be doing something right. "Meeting with my partners," he called these fact-finding forays; since history taught him great civilizations are built by great leaders, he looked for great leadership in executive suites.

Once he had opened his firm, Davis sought out Graham, Warren Buffett's professor at Columbia University. Graham was on a mission to transform stock analysis from a rustic craft to a serious profession. To that end, Graham lobbied for better training and certification for Wall Street's bean counters, and more reliable accounting from public companies. His efforts led to the creation of the New York Society of Security Analysts (NYSSA), which, by the mid-1940s, had attracted 1,000 members.

Davis joined the NYSSA to drum up business and to support Graham's campaign. At this point, analysts were low-pay, low-profile, and low-priority people on Wall Street. They did research for institutional clients (pension funds, among others) but had minimal contact with the public. Their budgets were tight. Some grumbled about having to pay the $5 annual NYSSA dues that covered general expenses, plus a small surcharge for the weekly lunches at which corporate emissaries gave generally flattering reports on their companies' recent activities. Members who balked at paying the lunch tab got "noneating listener" passes for free.

Judging by the minutes, the main topic of discussion at NYSSA executive meetings was the quality of the food and table service at Schwartz's, the restaurant where the lunches were held. The food topic took up hours of debate and staff time. For instance, on July 8, 1946, the executive committee reported that Schwartz's manager, Harry Beck, requested the lunch charge be raised from $1 to $1.15. The request was granted, as long as Beck kept his promise to expand the menu. At a subsequent meeting, the question of how to pay the extra 15 cents came up. Somebody proposed dunning nonmembers with a guest fee. Davis, then chairman of the program committee, was asked to study the matter.

Davis quickly advanced from program manager to NYSSA president. He won the 1947 election by 67 votes. From the start, he was absorbed in the ongoing restaurant controversy. A committee was formed to recommend a nicer place, but the search was called off while the analysts' lawyers hashed out a new deal with Schwartz's lawyers. A clause in the latest contract had stipulated that Schwartz's lunches should be "at least as good" as lunches served in competing establishments.

At a September 1947 meeting, it was reported that Schwartz had installed a new stairway at his own expense. The following February, the membership agreed to allow Schwartz to rent out the analysts' dining room to other parties during the Christmas season. In return, Schwartz agreed to cancel a claim against the analysts for unpaid lunch tabs. The question of whether to install filing cabinets in the office was also raised, along with the cost of air conditioning and a $150 bar bill to be paid in advance of an upcoming NYSSA party.

In January 1948, a motion was entertained to bump the lunch fee to $1.25, and once again to lobby Schwartz for better food. In March, a disgruntled analyst suggested posting the names of delinquent dues payers on the NYSSA bulletin board. In May, as the Davis presidency ended, proposals to find more exciting speakers, improve the décor in the dining room, install new ceiling lights and cork-board panel, and eliminate "electrical fixtures underfoot" were entertained.

Throughout this period, Benjamin Graham was always trying to "get things back on track." As the minutes show, analysts weren't taken very seriously and seemed to have a lot of spare time on their hands. Otherwise, they would have had better things to do than analyze Schwartz's.

Meanwhile, Davis's early stock picks were merrily compounding. He'd started his fledgling company with $100,000 in assets ($50,000 cash plus the seat on the NYSE, valued at $50,000). By the end of year one, his net worth was pegged at $234,790. Seven insurance stocks gave him the kind of liftoff that today's investors might associate with high-tech names. His biggest holding was a relatively large insurer, Crum & Forster (later absorbed by Xerox). The others were smaller and obscure. They traded in the financial boondocks known as the over-the-counter market, and increased sales and profits at a Microsoftian clip.

While the Dow went south (down 24 percent from 1947 to 1949), Davis's portfolio went north. He was in the right stocks and the right industry, and his rapid moneymaking got a considerable boost from leverage. He borrowed $29,000 the first year and continued to borrow to the maximum throughout his career. For unknown reasons, trace amounts of U.S. Steel and United Air Lines "preferred" shares appeared in his holdings. Plenty of money managers would have advised him to buy more of the world's mightiest steel maker and less of the mom-and-pop underwriters. But he stuck to his plan and invested strategically rather than nostalgically. Nostalgia for America's smokestack heavyweights was hazardous to wealth: U.S. Steel stock topped out in 1954 and then began a 40-year descent.

CHAPTER 7

THE BULLISH 1950s

THE 1950s TURNED OUT TO BE THE BEST DECADE for stocks since the 1920s. The Dow nearly tripled, rising from 235 to 679, while a wider selection did better. Ten thousand dollars hitched to the S&P 500 in 1949 became $67,000 by 1959, a whopping 21.1 percent annual increase. There wouldn't be a comparably enriching stretch until the 1980s.

In the demoralizing yo-yo of the 1930s and the 1940s, every advance was reversed, but during the extended and consistent bull run in the 1950s, buying and holding lived up to its former good reputation. Setbacks were temporary. War in Korea spooked investors in 1950, but Mr. Market's losses were quickly recouped. Similarly, a brawl over the Suez Canal, combined with the Russians rolling tanks into Budapest and launching a manned satellite into orbit, gave stocks another fleeting case of jitters in 1957. These two selloffs were accompanied by brief recessions, but both times, the economy was easily resuscitated. Corporate earnings grew, and price-earnings multiples expanded. The investment game was easy to win.

In typical fashion, during the best time for stock holding, people were the most reluctant to hold them. While the mathematical bottom in prices was reached in the 1930s, it took much longer to hit a psychological bottom. Into the 1950s, the masses continued to doubt the wisdom of equity ownership.

Stocks were cheap in 1950, there was no doubt. The Dow hadn't yet surpassed its 1929 high. With few exceptions (Standard Oil of New Jersey, Chrysler), the average blue chip was chronically depressed. GE sold for less than it fetched during the Coolidge prosperity. Anaconda Copper and RCA were down 50 percent. A 1952 issue of *Barron's* magazine identified 35 of the leading 50 U.S. companies as long-term losers. An entire generation had grown old waiting for capital gains.

At this point, most people owned stocks for their dividends, not their earnings, and the IRS continued to take the unkindest cut: 80 percent on income in the highest bracket. Mutual fund promoter John Templeton recommended that clients sidestep this cruel levy by owning fast-growing companies that offered low dividends or no dividends. Whenever investors needed money, he advised, they could sell a few shares and pay a much lower capital gains tax. His idea—using shares as a source of income—never caught on with the public.

Even after an impressive rally in the early 1950s that made Davis a millionaire, the masses were skeptical. In 1954, *Fortune* magazine, reflecting popular sentiment, wondered on its cover, "Is Wall Street Obsolete?" While the business of America boomed, the stock exchanges remained sleepy outposts. Only four out of every 100 Americans owned shares.

On the NYSE, trading kept the same syrupy pace (one million shares a day) that had persisted in the mid-1930s. Traders, brokers, and underwriters were baffled and frustrated by the public's inaction. To fight the lethargy, the NYSE launched a snappy promotion: "Own Your Share of American Business." NYSE President G. Keith Funston, who'd rented a summer cottage to the Davises, instigated a new sales campaign that targeted the nonstockholding middle class. Small investors were invited to buy shares on the installment plan, the way they bought cars, furniture, and appliances. Though the NYSE called the initial response "promising," only 28,000 people took advantage of Funston's invest now/pay later offer. In its first year, the program attracted a paltry $11.5 million in new investment.

It turned out that the public wasn't needed to stage a bull market. The population at large was reluctant to buy, but existing shareholders had become reluctant to sell. With fewer sellers to drive prices down, a relatively small clique of buyers could drive prices up.

Even as the business boom began to allay depression worries, inflation warnings crept in. During and after the Korean War, inflation stirred on cue. The military buildup was financed, as usual, by an overactive printing press. Consumer prices rose at a double-digit clip in 1950 to 1951, and, by raising short-term rates, the Fed applied the classic cure. The cure had the customary side effect: the mild recession mentioned earlier.

In 1951, the Fed also lifted the lid it had clamped down on the long-term bond yield a few years earlier. Loosed from regulatory repression, long-term rates ascended in the inflationary updraft. Few people realized that bonds were in the early stages of an impoverishing rout. In fact, the 1957 bear market in stocks drove investors back into the "safety" of Treasuries—on margin, no less.

After 1929, tough new rules were imposed to foil giddy stock speculators—for example, no more buying on 10 percent down. But nothing was done to deter giddy bond speculators, who could buy Treasuries on 5 percent down. In 1957, high and middle rollers gambled with gusto, snapping up the latest supply of government paper with bank loans. To satisfy demand, the Treasury issued a glutton's supply—$1.7 billion in new debt, maturing in 1990 and paying 3.5 percent annual interest. Noting the 1990 maturity date, Wall Street wags called these bonds the "Gay Nineties."

"People lined up to buy," James Grant reported on the Gay Nineties bond rush. But as soon as they did, the bond market tanked. Absent the margin buyers, the losses might have been less drastic, but rampant speculation produced a brutal mark-down. Soon after the speculators took their losses, the Fed's medicine (higher short-term rates) quelled the inflation rate and restored calm to bond trading. Inflation rose at 2 percent or less during the next six years.

Davis didn't care about bond gyrations. He stuck with in-surance stocks—especially the small, aggressive variety—and by 1954, after seven years of self-employment, he became a wealthy man. Every sector in the market was profitable, but Davis staked out the sweetest and least popular spot. Without fanfare, life insurers grew their earnings at a pace later associ-ated with computers, data processing, pharmaceuticals, and celebrated retailers like McDonald's and Wal-Mart. The math was inspirational. In 1950, insurance companies sold for four times earnings. Ten years later, they sold for 15 to 20 times earnings, and their earnings had quadrupled. Let's say Davis acquired 1,000 shares of Insurance USA (a fictitious example) for $4,000 when the company earned $1 a share. He held on until the company earned $8 a share and a crowd of camp fol-lowers pounced on the opportunity. What he'd bought for four times $1, they bought for 18 times $8. His $4,000 was now worth $144,000 in Mr. Market's estimation. In terms of profit, he made 36 times his initial outlay, plus whatever divi-dend checks had landed in his mailbox during the waiting pe-riod. Davis called this sort of lucrative transformation "Davis Double Play." As a company's earnings advanced, giving the stock an initial boost, investors put a higher price tag on the earnings, giving the stock a second boost. Davis got a third boost from his margin loans.

He never borrowed for personal consumption. To him, going into hock for a new car or refrigerator was an insult to money. On the other hand, going into hock to make more money was a chance he eagerly took. Insurance companies enjoyed some terrific advantages, as compared to manufacturers. Insurers offered a product that never went out of style. They profited from investing their customers' money. They didn't require expensive factories or research labs. They didn't pollute. They were recession-resistant. During hard times, consumers delayed expensive purchases (houses, cars, appliances, and so on), but they couldn't afford to let their home, auto, and life insurance policies lapse. When a sour economy forced them to economize, people drove fewer miles, caused fewer accidents, and filed fewer claims—a boon to auto insurers. Because interest rates tend to fall in hard times, insurance companies' bond portfolios become more valuable.

These factors liberated insurers' earnings from the normal business cycle, and made them generally recession-proof. Meanwhile, the income from bond-heavy portfolios continued to rise.

Davis didn't buy insurers indiscriminately. In his short career as a regulator, he'd developed a method for separating winners from losers, which he described in a speech to the Greater New York Insurance Brokers Association in 1952. The topic was "How Healthy Is Your Insurer?" but, between the lines, the audience got a tutorial in savvy stock selection.

First, he crunched the numbers to find out "whether a company was making money or losing its shirt." This required a working knowledge of the accounting tricks that were in widespread use in the industry. Once he'd assured himself that a company was profitable, he turned his attention to the portfolio where the assets compounded. Here, he separated reliable assets (government bonds, mortgages, blue-chip stocks) from iffy assets. He was about to invest in an apparently attractive insurer when he noticed its portfolio was loaded with junk bonds. Later, several of these risky issues defaulted, and the insurer collapsed. Davis had sidestepped a total loss.

In step three, he made a rough guess at the private market value of any apparent opportunity. In other words, what would a company be worth if a larger company decided to acquire it? For Davis to buy any insurer, his guesstimated value had to be far greater than the amount Mr. Market said it was worth at the moment. Putting his own price tag on the business gave Davis conviction and staying power.

Investors who had no idea of the private worth of their holdings were susceptible to being scared out of them. Their only measure of value was the stock price, so the more the price dropped, the more they were inclined to sell. Davis was panic-proof. Wall Street's daily, weekly, monthly, and yearly ups and downs didn't alter his strategy. He held on to shares through demoralizing declines, knowing that the market had misjudged the true attractiveness of the contents of his portfolio. Bear markets didn't rattle him.

Gyrations in stock prices were the least important of Davis's indicators, but he still kept an eye on the tape. A "prolonged sinking spell" in a specific company was, to him, a sign of possible trouble behind the scenes. Most likely, a swoon occurred when knowledgeable insiders dumped their shares. "It probably means, as they used to say in 'Ol' Man River,'" he told an audience, "somebody 'must know something.' It doesn't just keep 'rolling along.'"

Once he grasped a company by its numbers, Davis turned his attention to management. He was constantly on the road, meeting with executives, quizzing CEOs on everything from the sales force to the claims office to the company's strategy for fending off competitors and luring new customers.

A full investigation didn't always uncover a company's fatal flaw. To illustrate this point, Davis cited a reputable auto insurer that became a Korean War casualty. The war and its aftermath produced a "fresh outburst of reckless driving" in the United States, along with the usual inflationary outbreak, making it more expensive to fix cars and settle accident claims. Thanks to carefree underwriting, the insurer was caught in a double whammy and landed in bankruptcy court. The moral? Own enough stocks so your unpleasant surprises are outnumbered by your pleasant surprises.

Davis was a complex character. He was a maverick who liked to drop names. He was chummy with the lunch-pail crowd, but behind his hail-fellow-well-met lurked a confirmed anglophile who spent hours studying the family's "black books" of genealogy and reveling in his genetic linkage to Jamestown and Plymouth. He joined an array of patriotic organizations: Colonial Wars, Sons of the American Revolution, the Pilgrim Society, and Mayflower. He managed to get a membership in the Sons of Cincinnati, though he lacked the primary qualification: He didn't descend from the first son of a military officer who had served under General George Washington.

On Wall Street, he cultivated analysts and knew their opinions, but didn't value them and never acted on them. He was a loner who avoided trends and ignored group think, yet he was miffed when he couldn't attract customers to his brokerage and underwriting business. He was a strict disciplinarian who taught his children the work ethic by example and by edict. He permitted no nonsense in the office, and upbraided his staff for reading the paper at their desks instead of in their homes. He didn't swear or tell dirty jokes, and he disliked hearing them. Yet he enjoyed parties, galas, dinners, celebrations, and male smoking-room banter.

He had no use for fancy clothes, yet delighted in outfitting himself in tails and cocked hats, draping his chest with sashes festooned with medals and ribbons, and carrying flags in parades and patriotic ceremonies sponsored by his numerous organizations and clubs. He rose to the top rank of every club he joined. The rosters were all-male and, except for an occasional co-ed dinner bash, so were the meetings. Once, Davis traveled to London for a Pilgrim Society event and discovered he'd forgotten his ceremonial sash. Kathryn searched the London costume shops for several hours before she found a replacement.

Davis was already famous in the life-and-casualty circles. Insiders began calling him "the dean of American insurance," though he'd never worked for an insurer. He was a walking Rolodex or Who's Who of industry notables; an almanac of underwriters small and large; an encyclopedia of actuarial trivia; a database on earnings, assets, and liabilities; an appendix of footnotes and sources. He had photographic recall for names and faces. He was adept with numbers, yet he didn't pick stocks on numbers alone. "You can always learn accounting on the side," he told his son, "but you've got to study history. History gives you a broad perspective and teaches that exceptional people can make a difference."

A constant stream of invitations flowed into his mailbox: to attend industry powwows; to speak at conferences; to hobnob with CEOs at their annual outings at home and abroad. His office manager and minority partner, Ken Ebbitt, always knew where the boss was by the phone calls that came in from attendees at Davis's latest lecture in Zurich, Paris, Rome, or London, wanting to buy shares in companies Davis had touted. Wherever he spoke, the dean of insurance drew a crowd. Wall Street investment houses sent moles to catch what Davis said and to ask him for stock picks in the question-and-answer sessions. Davis enjoyed the attention.

Sometimes, while Davis hobnobbed, Kathryn traveled. In 1953, she toured India with her mother, Edith. The two

Wasserman women had tea with Sir Edmund Hillary at his house in Darjeeling, soon after he descended from the skull-cap of Everest. Hillary, Kathryn recalls, was proud of his effort, but prouder still of his all-American kitchen, complete with magic stove and deep freeze—a victory trophy from the Indian government. Edith never saw the kitchen. She sat outside the house and refused to enter because she was afraid of Hillary's dog.

Mountaineering attracted new converts worldwide, including Kathryn's nephew, Steve Wasserman. At age 15, Steve scrambled in the French Alps. Two years later, in 1957, he took his climbing skills to California. He and a friend worked in a mine to cover expenses (Steve's father Wild Bill was part owner), and spent their free time on the slopes. One weekend, they scaled the tough east face of Mt. Whitney. Steve fell to his death.

Davis and Kathryn attended the annual insurance bash at the posh Greenbrier resort in West Virginia. This event was off-limits to outsiders, and though Davis was excluded from the meetings, he was invited to share in the meals and the festivities. He trolled for industry gossip, learned of promotions and demotions, met new executives and formed opinions about whether they were doers or bluffers. He worked the room like a reporter, getting the scoop before it was leaked to the Street.

Though Davis was well connected and highly regarded, his broker-dealer business attracted few customers. He was constantly annoyed that people bought stocks he recommended but used other brokers to make the trades. People who took his advice, he believed, owed him a commission as a form of respect.

His firm competed for the underwriting jobs that helped insurance companies "go public," but Davis lacked the clout and the funding to play the role of lead underwriter in these transactions. He deferred to Morgan Stanley and other high-octane investment houses whose names always appeared at the top of "tombstones"—the newspaper ads announcing the latest deals. Davis often had to settle for his firm's name appearing at the bottom of a tombstone, but once in a while the firm name appeared on the right side of the tombstone as a junior comanager.

He opened small branch offices (each was manned by a single employee) in six cities. He spent almost nothing on this effort, hoping his brokers would generate enough commissions to pay the overhead and then make a living on top of that. His cut-rate brokerage sputtered. In fact, his stock shop resembled an insurance company where the sales commissions paid the monthly overhead, and the real profits came out of the investment portfolio. The inactivity in his office allowed Davis to tend his own portfolio without distraction.

By owning insurance stocks, he enriched himself far more than highly paid executives who'd made insurance their career. By the mid-1950s, his net worth had soared. His stake in 32 insurance companies was worth $1.6 million, so Kathryn's original $50,000 had multiplied thirty-twofold.

All the names in his original portfolio were gone. After six years of jockeying and maneuvering, he'd found companies he felt comfortable owning for extended periods: Continental, Commonwealth Life, et al. From here on, he stuck with his holdings, adding new names with the cash he borrowed on the rising value of his assets. By 1959, he was riding on $8 million in leverage. So his net worth was probably $8 to $10 million.

Around this time, an Austrian, Dick Murray, befriended Davis and introduced him to the reinsurance game. To reduce their exposure to huge claims in future hurricanes, earthquakes, and similar calamities, European insurers paid reinsurance companies to cover some of the risk. Murray was promoting the concept in the States. He and Davis often ate lunch together at Davis's favorite club, the Downtown Association. When Davis invited him to his summer house in Maine, Murray quickly learned he was dealing with a wallet hugger.

"The two guest rooms shared a bathroom," Murray recalls. "You had to knock to see if it was in use. Once, when I was in there, a woman from the other guest room knocked, then advised in a loud voice: 'If you need hot water, forget the sink. It hasn't worked in three years. Try the tap in the bathtub.'"

Back in New York, Murray arranged for Davis to meet the CEO of a French insurer that planned to list its shares on the NYSE. "The three of us got together in Davis's one-room office on Pine Street," Murray said. "Davis sat at his desk in the middle of the room, and his small staff worked around him. There was no privacy and it was hard to carry on a conversation. The Frenchman and I both noticed Davis's banged-up shoes. Later, the Frenchman asked me to pass along some advice: 'Put some walls around your desk, and while you're at it, buy a new pair of wingtips.'"

Whenever they talked, Davis peppered Murray with questions about reinsurance. Murray led Davis to several outstanding foreign prospects, which started Davis thinking about investing abroad. A "philosophical Quaker" with no interest in big bucks, Murray never took advantage of his own stock tips.

During the 11 years since Davis had launched his portfolio, the dividend from the typical stock was more generous than the yield from the typical government bond. Throughout the twentieth century, whenever dividends outpaced bond yields, stockholders had prospered.

Bond yields caught up with dividends in 1958, halfway through the postwar bullish rampage. The Dow was selling at 18 times earnings, a price tag that seemed rich at the time, but a decade of gains had turned skeptics into believers. Signs of the revival were obvious. The AT&T pension fund bought equities for the first time since 1913. Sales of a newly launched Lehman Brothers mutual fund ran far ahead of expectations. Stocks were going up because the public was buying, and the more the prices rose, the more the public bought. The rally persisted in spite of bearish news: rising interest rates; threat of war in the Middle East. Pundits tagged this latest advance an "Indian rope trick"—stocks levitated for no apparent reason.

A *Life* magazine reporter, Ernest Havemann, reflected on this curious phenomenon in a 1958 article entitled "The People's Stock Market: Optimistic and Unpredictable Buying Baffles Wall Street's Professionals." "We live today under genuine people's capitalism," Havemann wrote. He described how the reckless 1920s investor had gambled on margin, but noted that the 1950s investor "usually buys stocks as he would buy insurance or make regular deposits in a savings account. He is in the market for the long pull and temporary setbacks don't discourage him."

Old hands weren't impressed with this sudden and mass conversion to born-again buying-and-holding. They'd seen bear markets turn professed long-term investors into panicky sellers overnight. But echoing the arguments made in the Roaring 20s, Havemann described the 1950s as an enlightened "new era" in which companies and their shareholders would benefit from the emerging "science" of corporate management. Beyond that, he said, Wall Street had become more conservative, better regulated, and more honest in its dealings with individual investors. "Buyer beware" was passé.

Yet danger lurked. While the United States prospered, its consumers ran up a worrisome trade deficit; their purchases of foreign goods exceeded foreigners' purchases of U.S. goods.

Routinely, the United States paid its trading partners in dollars, but Britain, Belgium, Switzerland, Italy, and others began to doubt the dollar would hold its value. They demanded payment in gold, and, based on the modified gold standard still in force, the United States was obliged to comply. The U.S. Government had more gold on deposit than all other nations combined, but at the end of the decade, large quantities were shipped abroad. The nation's reserves were declining fast.

Economic soothsayers and money experts figured the United States soon would be forced to raise the price of gold, so it could settle its debts with smaller amounts of the precious commodity. A higher gold price automatically cheapened the dollar, because it took more dollars to equal an ounce of the metal. By making foreign goods more expensive to buy, a cheaper dollar was inflationary. Runaway inflation was bad news for stocks and for the economy, but those ugly consequences weren't felt until 1971, when President Richard Nixon formally devalued the dollar, and gold enjoyed a triumphant revival. "The monetary aircraft," said James Grant of the 1950s trade deficit, "was indeed flying straight into a mountain, but the pilot's miscalculation was so slight and the distances involved so great that no collision would occur for years."* In the glacial pace of financial upheaval, a future calamity often is spotted years before it does real damage.

---

*Quotes from and references to the 1952 *Barron's* article, the 1954 *Fortune* article, and the 1958 *Life* magazine article cited in this chapter, as well as details on the New York Stock Exchange share ownership program and the Gay Nineties bonds appeared in James Grant's *The Trouble with Prosperity,* Times Business/Random House, 1996.

CHAPTER 8

DAVIS SHOPS ABROAD

T HE BULL MARKET OF THE 1950S CONTINUED into the 1960s. Some people built bomb shelters in their basements and fretted over a possible nuclear holocaust. Many feared and loathed the Russians, and investors started a nationwide romance with mutual funds. Once-lethargic trading turned frenetic; a billion shares changed hands on the Big Board in 1960, the busiest year since 1929. Investors paid more to own the stocks that they held for shorter periods.

The bull was knocked off stride, but only momentarily. A 10-month recession in 1960 slowed but didn't stop the onward-and-upward trend. Even the botched invasion of Cuba in 1961 didn't faze the Street; stocks were up sharply the week after Fidel Castro's communist guardians repelled the invaders. President John F. Kennedy's spat with the steel industry in 1962 led to a bear attack, and U.S. Steel tumbled to 38, a long way off its record high of 109. Once again, stocks rallied and the bears were quickly banished.

Mr. Market shrugged off bad news—even the Kennedy assassination was bullish. Investors were briefly unnerved on

November 22, 1963, the day the president was killed, but when trading resumed during the following week, prices took a carefree leap. Electronics and other high-tech issues went on a speculative binge that caught the attention of the NYSE's president, G. Keith Funston. Davis's former summer landlord issued a public warning about the "unhealthy appetite for new shares of unseasoned companies just because they are new."[1] Most of these prized hatchlings soon disappointed their financial backers, but Polaroid, Xerox, Litton Industries, and a few others distinguished themselves.

Davis's portfolio had the constancy of a dowager's living room. If a company he owned failed to meet his expectations, he disposed of it. If it merged with or was acquired by a larger company, he'd sometimes take his profit and invest elsewhere. But these were exceptional cases. Mostly, he bought and held. Year after year, he stuck with the same names. His biggest positions (Continental, Commonwealth Life, et al.) stayed on top.

In his corporate ledger, Davis's stocks were carried at cost, making it impossible to calculate his net worth, but his margin loans provided a useful clue. He borrowed roughly half the market value of his portfolio, so if he owed $10 million to various banks (as he did in 1962), we can figure he was sitting on $20 million in stocks. By 1965, his bank debt had doubled to $20 million, so his stocks were probably worth $40 million, a 100 percent appreciation in three years.

The Dow was up fivefold since Davis had begun investing in 1947; his hand-picked insurance companies were up 200-fold. The Davis Double Play had worked its magic: Insurance earnings had quadrupled across the industry, and eager investors paid three times more for those earnings than they had paid in 1947. Add a terrific boost from leverage plus Davis's unusual talent to pick stocks that go up, and investing became as rewarding as baseball and writing Harry Potter books, 40 years later.

Part of Davis's advantage came from owning stocks for the full postwar ride, whereas typical investors hadn't opened their wallets until the mid-1960s, when the ride was nearly over. By then, Davis was less enthusiastic than he'd been during the period of prevailing pessimism. U.S. stocks had exited the bargain basement. After seeing his favorite insurers rise far beyond the "buy low" stage when he acquired them, Davis found new chances to buy low beyond the borders. He went shopping abroad.

Again, he was far ahead of the crowd. The last hurrah for foreign investing had been silenced in the 1930s, when the U.S. public lost huge sums in Latin American bonds sold nationwide by zealous brokerage houses. Thirty years later, foreign stock exchanges were terra incognita to Wall Street money managers. Emerging markets hadn't emerged. There were no global mutual funds, no country funds, and hardly any talk of diversifying abroad.

Then, in 1957, a troop of New York security analysts flew to Europe on a fact-finding mission that was inspired by the opening of the Common Market in 1956. The analysts visited companies in London, Amsterdam, Paris, Milan, and Düsseldorf. Their impressions were positive overall, though they lamented the murky and unreliable financial data released by European enterprises. Some corporate executives they interviewed had never heard of security analysis. Nevertheless, as a result of this trip, several European stocks were listed on the New York Stock Exchange for the first time. Nobody paid much attention.

Davis didn't go to Europe in 1957, but he was aware of the analysts' junket. His study of history and his earlier globetrotting in Europe, Russia, and the Middle East had cured him of parochial myopia, so he was receptive to putting money to work offshore. On this subject, he'd been talking with his friend Richard Murray, the Austrian immigrant and an expert in "reinsurance" (one insurer lays off risk by paying another insurer to cover part of its claims, should disaster strike). Murray also served as an informal roving ambassador for U.S. companies, which often faced endless shakedowns and harassment from anticapitalist regimes in Africa and Latin America.

Whenever Murray returned from a trip, he'd tell Davis about some great local insurer he'd discovered. Murray's favorites operated south of the border, but Davis refused to take chances there. "South of the border, you lose your shirt," Davis insisted, but the idea of investing abroad was beginning to percolate. He signed up for an analysts' trip to Japan in 1962.

At this point, the Japanese supplied U.S. consumers with miniature pot-metal Statues of Liberty and other tacky tourist fare. "Made in Japan" meant "This is junk." In the minds of many Americans, a nation that botched World War II, slept on floor mats, built doors out of rice paper, and bowed its way through life was no match for Western know-how and Yankee can-do. Who knew Japan even had a stock market?

Wives were invited on the trip, so Davis and Kathryn boarded a plane at Idlewild (now Kennedy International) Airport on Long Island. Kathryn's sister drove to the airport from Philadelphia to see them off. The plane stopped to refuel in Anchorage, Alaska. Through the cabin windows, passengers saw a grease monkey climb a tall ladder onto the wing and pour several cans of what looked like oil into a hole. They wondered: Should we be flying in a plane with leaky gaskets?

The group stayed at Tokyo's Imperial Hotel, which had been designed by Frank Lloyd Wright and was surrounded by Japanese gardens. The building was run down. "At least it didn't have rats," Kathryn recalls. The Japanese, she was told, had demolished numerous rat-infested buildings in the city. Tokyo was preparing to host the 1964 Summer Olympics, but the rubble of war was still in evidence. The spouses visited shrines, watched pearl divers, and hiked to the base of Mt. Fuji. Hostesses in native garb served them Coca-Cola. Their husbands sampled sushi, met with corporate VIPs, flirted with geishas. (Out of the 50 analysts who made the trip, 46 were male.) In the nightclubs, a geisha stood behind each analyst, lighting his cigarettes, refreshing his martinis, pulling on his tie. "Davis loved geishas," says Francis Haidt, who organized the junket. "He told me how they played a Japanese version of patty-cake. I asked if they played more exciting games. 'That's not what geishas are for,' he said. I laughed."

The group got a delightful reception and found the Japanese surprisingly polite to visitors from the country that had dropped two atom bombs on their cities. Davis felt a kinship with these Oriental Ben Franklins, who worked hard, saved for the future, spent as little as possible, and lived by the precepts of *Poor Richard's Almanac*. His fellow analysts were impressed with the factories they toured. At an eccentric company called "Sony," a brass band played "Yankee Doodle" while their host recorded the event with a hand-held minicam. He sat the Americans in front of a monitor and wowed them with an instant replay.

At a Toyota assembly line, they marveled at the snazzy automated machinery that produced the cars. But their enthusiasm was squelched by Japanese accounting, which was murkier, even than European accounting. "The Japanese hemmed and hawed and put up smoke screens around the numbers, so we never found out anything useful," Haidt recalls. "By the end of the trip, almost nobody wanted to invest in Japan." Nobody except Davis and a California money manager named James Rosenwald, an expert on Japanese number crunching. As the group traveled from venue to venue, he and Davis huddled in the back of the bus, intent on Rosenwald's calculations via his slide rule.

This minority of two soon broke away from the tour and made appointments to visit insurance companies. Neither Davis nor Rosenwald spoke Japanese, but, according to Davis's friend Richard Murray, a frequent traveler to Tokyo, linguistic ignorance was a plus. "The Japanese didn't like foreigners who spoke bad Japanese," Murray said, "and if a foreigner spoke good Japanese, it made the natives nervous. It was better to speak zero Japanese." In any event, translators were provided, and the more they found out, the more Davis and Rosenwald agreed they'd stumbled onto the bonanza of a lifetime. Japanese companies in general were protected by the state and by their culture, which spared them the rigors of free competition. Insurance companies got extra benefits, because authorities wanted to ensure that they never lacked for the yen needed to compensate victims of the next big earthquake—Japan's national fear.

As Davis and Rosenwald soon discovered, 20 Japanese insurers divvied up most of the property/casualty business, as opposed to 10,000 competitors in the United States. Of these 20 companies, five dominated and enjoyed guaranteed market share, coddling by the Ministry of Finance, and permission to charge customers two to five times what U.S. customers paid for insurance. Victims of car accidents and other mishaps were subjected to prosecutorial grilling and were challenged to prove that their claims had merit. Frequently, their claims were denied, keeping payouts to a minimum. The wondrous insurance-friendly atmosphere in Japan wasn't lost on the inquisitive Americans.

With Rosenwald's help, Davis found Japanese numbers were easily crunchable, and the more he crunched, the more excited he got. The entire insurance sector was "overwhelmingly cheap," as Rosenfeld later wrote. Fail-safe companies were selling for a fraction of the value of their investment portfolios, and, in some cases, for less than the value of their headquarters. Large chunks of the income thrown off by their portfolios were allowed to compound tax-free. This yen buildup, called the "catastrophe reserve," was an irresistible hidden asset. The reserves were set aside to pay future claims after earthquakes, but they'd been built up to an amount that far exceeded the damage estimated by the most pessimistic forecasters.

For example, a casual review of Nissan Fire and Marine's balance sheet showed the company's equity at 47 yen per share. This figure didn't include a catastrophe reserve of 228 yen per share, plus other hidden assets amounting to 545 yen per share. With Nissan's stock selling at 450 yen—a niggardly two times earnings—a buyer got 800 yen worth of stocks and bonds in Nissan's portfolio, plus a thriving insurance company. These assets were carried on the books at cost, so the hidden part was much larger than it appeared at first glance.

One night, when the rest of the group went out for dinner, Davis sat in his hotel room, sipped a Japanese beer, and shared his findings with Kathryn. He explained that Japan didn't have mutual funds, but local insurance companies, with their vast portfolios, offered a convenient way to invest in a Japanese recovery. The trip convinced him that Japan would overcome its postwar malaise, just as the United States had overcome its 1930s malaise. "Since I believe in the Japanese people," he asked his wife, rhetorically, "why don't I invest in them?"

On the route home, the analysts stopped to shop in Hong Kong. Davis used the time to continue his insurance shopping. He went to lunch with a top executive at American Insurance Underwriters (AIU), a company he'd heard about in Japan. AIU had been founded in Shanghai, China, 30 years earlier, and its American-born CEO, Cornelius Van Der Starr, had done a remarkable job of selling policies throughout the Far East. In fact, AIU was one of the only U.S. corporations, insurance or otherwise, allowed to compete in Japan. It gained a foothold during the Allied Occupation period in 1946, when the Emperor was taking orders from a higher and quite cantankerous authority, General Douglas MacArthur, the Supreme Commander of the Allied Powers.

By 1952, AIU was selling more auto and personal accident policies than any other company in Japan. Its continued prosperity throughout the region caught the attention of insurers back home, and AIU was captured in a takeover by a similar abbreviation—AIG, the American International Group.

Another U.S. insurer, American Family, now AFLAC, broke through the Japanese resistance in 1974 and established a thriving business selling cancer policies. Japanese authorities let AFLAC into the country because they couldn't imagine anybody buying a cancer policy. It turned out they misjudged their own consumers, who craved cancer insurance. As one wag explained, "The Japanese are hypochondriacs."[2]

Davis bought shares in AIU after his Japan trip, so he automatically owned shares in AIG after the takeover. Two other U.S.-based insurers in his portfolio, were also bought by AIG, so he received more shares in that busy acquirer. When AIG went public in 1969, Davis added to his position, even though he was absorbed in his ambassadorial duties and not in his portfolio.

Davis and Kathryn landed in New York, after what proved to be the most important trip Davis ever took. His colleagues returned unenthusiastic, but he and Rosenwald were eager buyers. Their timing was perfect. The yen began to strengthen and the Japanese economy kicked into high gear. Three other prominent American investors who weren't on the trip also bought into Japan: Oliver Grace, Al Hettinger, and John Templeton, founder of the Templeton Funds and later knighted by Queen Elizabeth. Grace and Hettinger used Rosenwald as their Japanese broker. Along with Templeton, each made more than $50 million on their Japanese holdings.

Rosenwald continued to serve as "mission control" for U.S. buyers in the 1960s and beyond. He published a newsletter that did for Japanese stocks what Davis did for insurance stocks. Like Davis, he was a confirmed long-term investor. He advised people who purchased shares through him to buy and hold Japan. Davis bought with gusto. Soon after his return in 1962, he made sizable bets on four of Japan's big five insurers: Tokio Marine & Fire, Sumitomo Marine & Fire, Taisho Marine and Fire (it later became Mitsui), and Yasuda Fire & Marine. A year later, Davis added to his Sumitomo stock and loaded up on Tokio ($700,000 worth), making it his biggest holding. Japan had captured 10 percent of his total assets.

Davis's Japanese holdings soon sent his net worth soaring and made him a confirmed international investor. Now he was on a constant lookout for insurance prospects in South Africa, Europe, the Far East, and even Russia. (He studied the Russian insurance scene on the far-sighted theory that someday the country might turn capitalistic. His prophecy was correct, but three decades premature.) Before long, he had assembled a United Nations of insurance stocks: 35 Dutch, German, French, and Italian holdings were purchased to complement his Japanese holdings. As his portfolio expanded, his margin loans increased. He borrowed $17 million in 1963, and $22 million in 1965–the year he scrapped his "Just Say No to Latin America" policy and picked up four Mexican insurers plus one Irish, and one South African.

Richard Murray met with the CEO of the South African insurer, not realizing that Davis was already a shareholder.

Murray made a mental note to tell Davis about this latest opportunity, but changed his mind when the CEO informed him the stock already had advanced 100-fold. Out of curiosity, Murray asked the CEO if any foreign investors had bought early enough to profit from this huge move. "As a matter of fact, yes," he said. "An American guy named Davis."

CHAPTER 9

WALL STREET A GO-GO

I N THE SUMMER OF 1965, FED CHAIRMAN William McChesney Martin spoke of "disquieting similarities between our present prosperity and the fabulous Twenties." Martin elaborated as follows: "Then as now, many government officials, scholars and businessmen were convinced that a new economic era had opened, an era in which business fluctuations had become a thing of the past, in which poverty was about to be abolished, and in which perennial economic progress and expansion were assured."

Martin's misgivings were ignored as the Dow slogged toward the magic 1000 pinnacle. Though the most dyspeptic fortune-teller wouldn't have predicted such an uninspiring future performance, Dow 1000 wasn't exceeded for good until the early 1980s. A sharp but abbreviated decline in 1966, precipitated when U.S. planes bombed Hanoi, was a warm-up for trouble ahead. The Fed raised rates twice, and a credit crunch stalled the home builders. The Dow wheezed to a geriatric halt. President Lyndon Johnson demanded that G.K. Funston, president of NYSE, and SEC Chairman Manuel F. Cohen do something about falling prices—as if the trend could be reversed by decree.

Many non-Dow stocks raced ahead, as so-called "go-go" investors jumped on hot issues for a quick lift. Go-go mutual funds (more on these in a minute) posted gains of 40 percent or better in 1965, thanks to "new era" companies like Applied Logic; nursing-home chains that stood to benefit from Medicare (Four Seasons Nursing centers, United Convalescent Homes), and aggressive fast-food outfits such as Kentucky Fried Chicken. If you bought (and held) Fairchild Camera in early 1965, you tripled your money in four years. If you bought Boise Cascade in early 1967, you quadrupled your money in two years. If you bought blue chips, your portfolio went nowhere.

Sluggish blue chips, in the face of vigorous public buying, meant veteran shareholders were vigorously selling. A mass transfer of assets from the smart money crowd to the naïve money crowd was called "distribution." Never was there more spirited and widespread distribution than in the era of drugs, free love, and rock-and-roll. The floor of the New York Stock Exchange was roused from its lassitude. Two million shares changed hands during a typical session in the 1950s; 10 to 12 million shares traded daily in the late 1960s. On June 13, 1968, a 21-million-share day caused the NYSE to gag on its paperwork and shut down operations. As Wall Street reveled in hyperactivity, U.S. cities burned in summer race riots. "The great garbage market," one pundit called the final buying spree in the twilight of the second great bull market of the century. Merrill Lynch opened 200,000 new accounts in five months in 1969.

Americans had flipped over mutual funds, which now controlled $35 billion in client assets, 35 times more than they'd handled a generation earlier. One quarter of the value of all stock transactions was effected by fund managers. An appealing aspect of funds was their apparent buoyancy in a market undertow, as they'd exhibited in the 1962 sell-off. Alas, one triumph didn't make a trend, as subsequent undertows would reveal. Paul Samuelson, the MIT professor whose popular textbook made him the Benjamin Spock of economics, appeared before the Senate Banking Committee to discuss the fund craze. He noted with alarm the hastily recruited sales force, 50,000 strong, that trolled the suburbs, selling managed portfolios as though they were Avon products. Moonlighting lawyers, clerks, secretaries, and teachers spent weekends and evenings ringing doorbells. For every 70 potential investors nationwide, there was a Willie Loman flogging the merchandise. The main attraction for the sales force was the up-front commission of 8.5 percent. Customers gladly paid it, and why not? They were buying a professionally chosen lineup of stocks on a permanent rise. Greed had replaced fear as the market's prevailing emotion.

Go-go managers, also known as gunslingers, jumped on smaller issues that shot up the fastest, and then jumped off as soon as the prices stopped rising. They bought high-tech wonders and quickly replaced them with higher-tech wonders. A long-term investment lingered in the portfolio a few weeks. Gunslinging Gerry Tsai, a Fidelity defector who launched his own Manhattan Fund, became America's first celebrity stock jockey. At his Fifth Avenue corporate bivouac, Tsai reportedly kept the thermostat at 55 degrees Fahrenheit to "keep his head clear." The press played him as inscrutable and suggested that his Oriental background gave him a built-in knack for sage investing. Where Tsai had hoped to raise $25 million, he ended up with $247 million.

Fred Alger cowed the competition and wowed the public with his Security Equity Fund in New York. On the West Coast, ex-broker Fred Carr of the Enterprise Fund mixed the past with the future by filling his office with antique furniture and op art. Carr's investing was more op-arty than anti-quated: He bought flashy start-ups that most of his colleagues had never heard of. In May 1969, *Business Week* flattered Carr by saying he "may just be the best portfolio manager in the U.S." Another Fred, Fred Mates, weighed in with a buy-no-evil approach in 1967. The Mates Fund portfolio kept itself free of military contractors, cigarette companies, and polluters, so clients could make a guilt-free return. Mates called his staff the "flower children." After a year in operation, the feel-good fund caused clients to feel even better, with a 168 percent gain. Mates closed the sales window to keep from being over-whelmed with cash, clients, and paperwork. To "make poor people rich," he planned to offer a minimum investment of only $50 and market his product in urban ghettos and other disadvantaged areas.

By 1969, mutual funds controlled $50 billion worth of stock and were replacing their inventory at a rate of 50 percent a year, a frenetic pace when compared to the 20 percent turnover in 1962. Taking a cue from the professionals, fund clients switched funds as readily as managers switched their holdings. Fund surfing was in vogue, and investors moved in and out of top performers, trying to catch the latest wave. The surfers paid big commissions at every turn, but if a Mates or a Carr could double their money in a year, who cared?

Only old stock hands were appalled at the gold-rush impa-tience, the breathtaking price tags, and the fatuous promoting by cheerleaders of the New Era. The cheerleaders argued that the new computer and data-storage industries would revolu-tionize commerce and rewrite the rules of business and fi-nance, so what went up was no longer destined to go down. It was hard not to catch the New Era fever. Shelby had suc-cumbed to it in 1965. In a letter to clients, he advised: "Such a highly respected authority as the National Industrial Confer-ence Board believes that the 'normal markets of the late 1960s and early 1970s should be off the scale of anything yet experienced, even in the cyclically advanced prosperity of the present.'" He cited "new product development" and "exciting new industries such as nuclear power, salt water conversion, and space communications" as powerful bullish catalysts. He correctly mentioned two spoilers—Vietnam and the balance of payments problem—but downplayed the damage they might cause.

"We believe too that a downward stock market spiral is just about as unlikely as a downward economic spiral. Let us recognize that in as diversified and affluent a country as ours, with all its built-in checks and balances, we have freed ourselves from the fear of a 1929-type stock market spiraling depression."

As go-go was about to become no-go, an obscure but extremely rewarding money manager and New Era disbeliever named Warren Buffett quietly distinguished himself with a non-go-go portfolio. Investors in his private partnership enjoyed a 59 percent gain in 1968, while the Dow rose a mediocre 9 percent. Having triumphed on the upside, Buffett shocked his financial peer group by doing the unthinkable. He liquidated his investments and sent back his partners' money, along with a letter informing them that his supply of "promising ideas" had been exhausted; with stocks selling at Tiffany prices, he could find nothing promising to buy. He parked his own assets in boring municipal bonds. A shortage of promising ideas didn't stop Wall Street experts from continuing to recommend the priciest issues. Merrill Lynch flogged IBM at 39 times earnings; Bache pushed Xerox at 50 times earnings; Blair & Company touted Avon at 56 times earnings. McGeorge Bundy, president of the Ford Foundation, needled his fellow fiduciaries for being too conservative with their endowments and trusts, and urged them to throw money at stocks.

In a frenzied search for the "next Xerox," investors bought shares in anything with "electronic" or "data processing" in its name. Companies bought each other just as readily, and Wall Street played host to merger madness. Clumsy conglomerates such as ITT, Litton, and Ling-Temco-Vought got bigger and clumsier. Davis wouldn't have touched such stocks, but, as you'll see in Chapter 12, Shelby did.

In 1968, a giddy Mr. Market had high-stepped over and around the Martin Luther King and Robert Kennedy assassinations, jack-booted cops pummeling protesters at the Democratic national convention in Chicago, widespread campus riots, and foreign banks shunning the dollar. As John Brooks wrote, "The silly market had gone its merry way, heedlessly soaring upward as if everything were okay. . . ."[1]

"A new-issues craze is always the last stage of a dangerous boom," noted Brooks, and, in 1969, new issues abounded. The most popular of these debutantes were called "shooters" because their prices shot up, often doubling during the first day of trading. Nursing homes and other health-care issues that expected to benefit from Medicare were standouts in the shooting range.

In spite of the cult of personality that developed around the go-go managers, a study of the 1960 to 1968 period, published by the Twentieth Century Fund, concluded that dumbly buying the market at large was more rewarding than paying a professional to pick the stocks. It was a moot point. Soon after this study appeared in 1969, the rewards vanished. A three-month drubbing left the Dow clinging to 800 points by the spring of 1970. Economists were confounded by the co-existence of inflation and recession, which they called stagflation. The country had sunk into a grand funk—"one of the deepest moods of gloom to darken any American April since the Civil War," said Brooks.

Vanishing assets were as much effect as cause, though a lingering Vietnam War, bloodier campus riots (four Kent State University students were killed by Ohio National Guardsmen), and upheaval along the racial fault line contributed. A venerable railroad, Penn Central, collapsed in bankruptcy. The dollar sank lower, and home builders were idled; on Wall Street, 100 firms faced extinction or merger. The NYSE motto, "Own your share in American business," was dropped without explanation. By May 1970, Brooks reported, "A portfolio consisting of one share of every stock listed on the Big Board was worth just about half what it would have been worth at the start of 1969."

As usual, the high flyers fell harder than the Dow, which was down 36 percent. Investors who owned overhyped stocks like Data Processing, Control Data, Electronic Data Systems, or anything else with "data" in its name, did worse. Ten prominent conglomerates lost an average of 86 percent apiece; tech stocks in general lost 77 percent; and computer and computer leasing stocks lost 80 percent. The computerized Nasdaq[2] market made its debut in 1970, just in time for Nasdaq-type stocks to wreak havoc.

When Electronic Data Systems fell from 164 to 29, its principal owner, H. Ross Perot, lost $1 billion on paper. Years later, Perot would run for president and capture the public's fancy with his no-nonsense approach, until he exhibited Captain Queeg traits and self-destructed as a candidate. But in 1970, he got international attention for having experienced the first $1 billion personal wipeout in the history of finance. Average investors were wiped out in smaller denominations. Nearly half Perot's damage was done on Earth Day.

As performance stocks underachieved, so did the gunslingers who owned them. Gerry Tsai had timed his exit well. Two years earlier, in the nowhere market of 1968, his Manhattan Fund earned a minus 6 percent, dropping his ranking to

299th among 305 competing funds. Tsai promptly sold his company for $30 million-plus and retired from active management. He wasn't around to take the real punishment.

The Freds stayed in business long enough to ruin their reputations and traumatize their clients. Fred Carr's Enterprise Fund lost half its value. Carr resigned nine months after he was lauded in *Business Week*. At least he had the consolation of having kept up with the dartboard; the typical stock on the NYSE was cut in half as well. The NYSE's new advertising slogan, "Own your share in American business," was quietly shelved. To stop frantic shareholders from fleeing his fund, Fred Mates persuaded the SEC to let him freeze the fund's assets. This was a controversial maneuver at best, and the Omega fiasco made it worse. Mates had bought a large block of "restricted shares" in that company. There was a required waiting period before the shares could be sold on the open market. Many funds trafficked in restricted issues, paying a low price and carrying the shares on the books at a much higher price, creating instant gratification. For example, having bought the restricted version of Omega for $3.25, Mates put a $16 valuation on his purchase. This "gain" helped his fund rise to the top of the performance charts in 1968.

A year later, when $16 Omega had lost its plausibility, a crowd of Mates's clients rushed to exit his portfolio. With Omega restricted, Mates had trouble selling the quantity of stock needed to raise enough cash to reimburse the defectors. That's when he appealed to the SEC to halt the reimbursement.

By the time he was ready to accommodate the defectors, Omega was a 50-cent product, and Mr. Market had depreciated considerably. Mates had hoped stocks would rally and his clients would rethink their decision to quit his portfolio, but stocks didn't rally and the clients didn't rethink. Eventually, the Mates Fund lost 90 percent of its former self. On a happier note, Mates never carried out his plan to let the less fortunate join his fund for as little as $50. Thus, the destitute avoided further destitution.

More than a third of the 31 million U.S. shareholders in 1970 were virgin buyers, having put cash into the market for the first time somewhere between 1965 (at around Dow 900) and 1970 (at around Dow 650). As Brooks writes, in *The Go-Go Years,* "People's capitalism had left at least 10 million American investors, or one-third of all American investors, poorer than it had found them, and poorer by an aggregate sum of many billions of dollars" (p. 353). Brooks called this "vintage 1929 stuff." Overpriced insurance issues weren't spared the markdown. Like most stocks, their lofty valuations weren't supportable, and their decline was accompanied by a barrage of negative publicity. A *Fortune* magazine reporter and a respected statistician both wrote convincingly that insurance had been a lousy business all along.

The statistician was Dr. Irving Plotkin. In 1968, this nervy 26-year-old ruffled the industry with a well-researched study that covered most of the period in which Davis had built his insurance portfolio: 1955 to 1968. Plotkin showed how insurers earned far less on their investment dollar than other types of companies earned on theirs. Not only were insurance earnings skimpy, they also were volatile and swung wildly from one season to the next.

That Plotkin's work was commissioned by the industry he debunked and distributed by his employers at Arthur D. Little, an eminent accounting firm, added credibility to his salvo. Insurance honchos cobbled together a rebuttal, arguing that the industry's "true" earnings were twice as high as Plotkin had claimed. Plotkin had no trouble rebutting their rebuttal, and, in the end, the doubters were forced to agree with his conclusions. "[Nothing will] change the fact that the insurance business is currently a low-profit business," said the vindicated gadfly.

One reason for the low profits was the tight regulatory collar under which all insurers chafed. Companies endlessly sought permission to charge more for their products, and regulators routinely refused to grant it. In the regulators' view, insurers had squirreled away heaps of valuable assets in their portfolios, so they could afford to charge less and give their customers a break. In the insurers' view, their assets were constantly threatened by escalating claims and future disasters. A case in point was auto insurance, a main subject of the *Fortune* cover piece that hit the stands in December 1970: "Why Nobody Likes the Insurers." Since the late 1950s, according to the reporter, Jeremy Main, the cost of insuring a car had risen twice as fast as the cost of living. In spite of this apparent windfall, the typical insurance company struggled.

According to Main, the entire property/casualty sector had lost a cumulative $1.5 billion since 1955, a year of record profits. This chronic underachievement, said Main, was caused by dull management, too many agents feeding at the commission trough, and a litigious population.

Bigger cars on more highways had produced more crashes, more victims, and more damage awards. Student riots, psychedelic drugs, and urban guerrilla warfare added to the damage tab. Whenever insurers tried to raise rates to cover their escalating expenses and liabilities, state regulators balked and customers fumed.

Insurance had always been stuck with an insoluble public relations problem. This was the rare industry in which a popular brand name wasn't particularly valuable. Consumers were partial to Coca-Cola or Kleenex or John Deere tractors, but not to State Farm auto policies or Prudential life policies. Smart shoppers looked for insurance companies that had earned decent scores from the rating agencies, and then compared their rates to get the best coverage at the lowest price.

Whether it came from GEICO or Travelers, Metropolitan or the Equitable didn't matter. Often, they bought whatever their local agent wanted to sell them. Generally, they distrusted and resented *all* the contenders. Customers got their money's worth when something bad happened, in which case they were dead, in pain, or anguished. When nothing bad happened, they complained about being overcharged for the protection. Companies that raised rates were always accused of greedy gouging, when their profits were actually sporadic at best.

In the property/casualty area, a string of fat years was followed by a string of lean years. The fat years began after a monster calamity—hurricane, earthquake, flood, or similar catastrophe—produced claims totaling billions, wrecked balance sheets, and drove poorly capitalized firms out of business. Better capitalized companies survived to regroup, raise rates, and start another cycle of fickle prosperity. Insurers could economize, but cost-costing was often unenthusiastic, especially among the high-salaried thumb twiddlers in redundant home offices. Three thousand separate companies employed 1.4 million workers in the early 1970s, and on the efficiency scale, insurance ranked as low as government. Overall, the typical underwriter charged $2 in premiums to deliver $1 in benefits. In 1969, property/casualty companies spent $3 in salaries and overhead for every $7 they paid in claims.

As Main pointed out, if a freelance gadfly named Ralph Nader could pester Detroit into making safer cars, why hadn't the powerful insurance lobby done Nader's work long ago? In a resounding vote of no confidence in their own profession, leading insurers funneled excess cash into unrelated businesses. Aetna bought a hotel chain; Aetna and Travelers dabbled in real estate; INA, founded during George Washington's presidency, set up a holding company to diversify its interests. As fast as insurers gobbled up noninsurers, noninsurers gobbled up insurers. American Express acquired Fireman's Fund, ITT swallowed Hartford Fire, and so on, and this maneuvering did little to improve the bottom line.

An insurance investor couldn't rely on longevity and a trusted brand name to produce worthwhile results. A few bad decisions, and even the world's most famous insurer—Lloyd's of London—faced extinction in the 1960s. Lloyd's was unprepared for the surge in costly claims, brought on by Hurricane Betsy, airline hijackings, and other mishaps and catastrophes. In 1965, Lloyd's ran a $106 million deficit.

These well-publicized negatives made Davis's accomplishment all the more impressive. How did an apparently lousy industry provide an exceptional reward to the astute investor? There were several reasons. Insurers hid their true profitability, so the aforementioned lack of profit may have been, at least in part, an actuarial illusion. Davis bought when insurers were cheap, especially the mom-and-pop kind in his original portfolio. When these small companies were acquired by bigger companies, Davis reaped a windfall. He caught the post-World War II boom in home, auto, and life insurance policies. He avoided investing in chronic underachievers—Aetna, for example—that punished shareholder loyalty. He sought out aggressive, low-cost compounding machines like the Japanese insurers, Berkshire Hathaway, and AIG, which steadily enhanced shareholder value for decades. A well-managed technology company could always be toppled by a clever competitor or the latest scientific eureka from a rival. A well-managed insurer could outfox and outlast the competition, and never had to worry about becoming obsolete.

CHAPTER 10

SHELBY GETS FUNDED

I N 1969, THE YEAR WHEN NEIL ARMSTRONG strolled on the moon in his Michelin suit, the Davis era gave way to the Shelby era. The dividing line is somewhat arbitrary. Shelby already had been working on Wall Street, and Davis's investing career was only half over. But Shelby, along with sidekick Jeremy Biggs, took charge of the New York Venture Fund in 1969. For the first time, Shelby was picking stocks in the public arena and being audited by the SEC. Davis wasn't around to witness his son's debut. He'd left the country for an ambassadorial appointment in Switzerland. President Richard Nixon had offered the post, and Secretary of State William Rogers, a Davis crony since the Dewey days, brokered the deal.

Davis, at age 60, was the beneficiary of 20 uplifting years. This entire stretch had been fruitless to bondholders and fruitful to stockholders of all stripes. It was hard *not* to make money on equities. During this extraordinary run, the Dow was up fivefold while Dow earnings had merely doubled. The gains had depended on the public's willingness to pay escalating prices for earnings. Investors' presumption regarding future corporate profit had boosted stock prices more than actual corporate profit. Moreover, the actual profit was enhanced by borrowed money; corporate debt expanded fivefold over the 20-year period.

Years before, Davis couldn't have started investing at a better moment. He got in when the buying public was distrustful and stocks had nowhere to go but up; Shelby couldn't have joined Venture at a worse moment. He entered in the thin air of valuation, when the public was euphoric and prices were fantastical. Davis started investing in a sweet spot: the typical stock sold at six times earnings and carried an 8 to 10 percent dividend; interest rates were low; and a Treasury bond paid less than 3 percent. Shelby started investing for Venture in a sour spot: stocks were selling at 20 to 25 times earnings and carried a 3 to 4 percent dividend; and a Treasury bond was paying 5 to 6 percent. The aging bull was in its death throes. The Dow had hit a top it wouldn't see again for another 15 years. The immediate future was treacherous for bondholders *and* for stockholders. Being out of bonds or stocks was more rewarding than being in them. Gold and the lowly money market triumphed in the early years of Shelby's tenure. He had entered at the most dangerous entry point since 1929.

Returning to the scene of their courtship, Davis and Kathryn moved into the ambassador's manse in Bern. Davis was delighted to serve in a country full of tightwads like himself, where insurance was a glamour industry. Refusing to let a sleeping asset lie, Davis rented the family house in Tarrytown. One month's rental income exceeded what the Davises had paid for the place three decades earlier.

Swiss diplomats were amazed at Davis's knack for remembering names. At one gathering after another, he stood up and introduced every person in the room without consulting the guest list. His experience at the patriotic societies' functions–

wearing sashes and medallions, presiding at ceremonial dinners—served him well in Bern.

For his ambassadorial garb, Davis upgraded to tailored suits and high-end shoes. "I'm representing my country," he told his wife, justifying his sartorial reformation. Every day, at public functions, he wore a red carnation in his lapel. "One person is sure to miss me when I leave Switzerland," he joked. "The person who provides the flowers." He assumed they were plucked from the ambassadorial garden, but near the end of his tenure was annoyed to discover the embassy bought them at a store. Had he known earlier, he would have dispensed with this "waste of taxpayers' money."

Davis left his second-in-command, Ken Ebbitt, to run the office in New York and to baby-sit his portfolio. Ebbitt was a bond trader and had no feel for stocks, but his boss wasn't overly concerned. The ambassador immersed himself in his duties: improving Swiss-American relations and coaxing Swiss bankers to abolish secret accounts where the world's biggest crooks stashed their ill-gotten gains. His aversion to capital gains taxes kept him from selling holdings back home, so he was fully invested for the wealth reduction to come. Being out of the country didn't stop the losses, but it removed him from the tumult and the fallout, the finger-pointing and the despair the bears soon would bring to Wall Street.

Shelby had prepared for his opportunity—such as it was— his entire pre- and postadolescent life. A self-taught investor, Davis had cobbled together his maxims and his modus operandi from a variety of experiences and sources. Shelby had the whole program hammered into him from the start. Shelby's childhood was his MBA. He'd grown up on dinner-table stock talk, fact-finding missions to Hartford, and annual reports strewn about the house. He absorbed finance the way a musician's child absorbs syncopation or the diatonic scale.

From the time he was 9 or so, Shelby and his sister Diana, then 7½, served as their father's part-time clerical department. "If you work hard," Davis told the children, "maybe you'll get to like it." Every other Sunday afternoon, they cranked out copies of Davis's biweekly insurance letter on the office mimeograph, collated pages, stuffed and sealed envelopes, and affixed stamps.

"Dear Fiduciary," each letter began. The children wondered what a fiduciary was. They also wondered whether anybody read the letter, and why they weren't getting paid in cash, instead of in dinners at local restaurants. "Better than my cooking," Kathryn said, but the children would have preferred cash.

Shelby was coached on the basics of investing. Around the dinner tables of America, circa 1950, families traded opinions on the McCarthy hearings, the Korean War, the invincible New York Yankees. In parks and backyards, other fathers taught sons the three balls: base, basket, and foot. Davis taught his son about insurance companies: how they paid claims, what could ruin them, how they grew their assets. His passion was infectious.

Along with the popular homilies of the day—"Honesty is the best policy," "A penny saved is a penny earned," and so on, Shelby learned more sophisticated lessons of business and finance:

- Don't be a bondholder. Bondholders are lenders. Be a shareholder. Shareholders are owners. Owning shares in a successful company is far more rewarding than owning its bonds.
- The more wisely you invest, the faster your bankroll will expand. If you know the rate of return on your investment,

the Rule of 72 tells you how long it will take to double your money. The greater the return, the faster the compounding, which is why an extra percent or two makes a huge difference. A 10 percent return over 21½ years turns $100,000 into $400,000. At 12 percent, the payoff is $595,509.

In the summer of 1950, the Davises had driven west on the Pennsylvania Turnpike. Their destination was Springfield, Illinois, headquarters of Franklin Life Insurance. Franklin Life didn't attract many tourists, but visiting an insurance company was Davis's idea of a good time. On separate trips, he'd taken the family to the home offices of Glens Falls Insurance in Glens Falls, New York; Lincoln National in Fort Wayne, Indiana; and Businessmen's Assurance in Des Moines, Iowa. Usually, Kathryn and the children killed time in local parks and museums while Davis hobnobbed in boardrooms with CEOs and CFOs, reviewing future plans and critiquing past performance. Upon arriving at each corporate enclave, Davis checked the executive parking lot for empty spaces—evidence that the leadership might be working harder to improve a golf score than to increase the return on shareholders' capital.

He also liked to nose around the hallways and waiting rooms, looking for signs of waste, inefficiency, designer furniture, and other expensive froufrou. Shelby, at age 13, had sat in on an interview at Franklin Life. Looking around at the high ceilings, dark wood paneling, and gilded trim, he decided there was a lot of money in this place. The same thought, "That's where the money is," launched Willie Sutton's career as a bank robber. If only Sutton had been taught the Davis method of extracting wealth by owning shares, the quotable felon could have spared himself a lot of jail time. In any event, Franklin Life impressed Shelby enough that he bought shares with his own money. This was the first stock he ever owned, and the price increased tenfold before Franklin was bought out by American Tobacco in the 1980s.

The Springfield trip was also Shelby's introduction to the downside of stocks. In the June swelter, as the family cruised the Pennsylvania Turnpike with the radio on, they heard President Harry Truman (the surprise winner over Davis's ex-boss, Thomas E. Dewey, in the 1948 race for the White House) declare war on North Korea. Stock prices dropped after Truman's announcement. It was the first notable reversal since Davis had started his firm, yet he seemed to welcome the sell-off. "Out of crisis comes opportunity," Shelby remembers him saying. "A down market lets you buy more shares in great companies at favorable prices. If you know what you're doing, you'll make most of your money from these periods. You just won't realize it until much later."

The following summer, the Davises rented a summer cottage in Madison, Connecticut, which, in ascending order of importance, offered woods, shoreline, and daily train service to New York. The latter was the main attraction for Davis. The landlord was G. Keith Funston, head of the New York Stock Exchange and mastermind of an unsuccessful campaign to coax the masses to buy stocks. It was from Funston's house that Shelby joined his father on the three-hour daily commute to Wall Street. Father and son rose before dawn, dressed, gobbled breakfast, walked to the Madison station, caught the 6:00 A.M. local to Grand Central (the earliest train available) transferred to a subway line, and arrived at the office on Pine Street at 9:00. This regimen gave Davis a chance to work undistracted before the market opened at 10:00. In those days before 24/7 trading, the New York Stock Exchange kept leisurely bankers' hours.

After 3:30 P.M., when the market closed, they'd retrace their route. On the train ride back to Madison, Shelby wrote "confirmation slips"—receipts of the day's trades that were then sent to clients who had bought or sold shares through his father. "The hard part," Shelby recalls, "was calculating the tax on each trade—the government imposed one in that period. The pocket calculator wasn't invented yet, so we did the math by hand. I stuck the slips in preaddressed envelopes. When the train stopped in New Haven, I jumped off and tossed the envelopes in a nearby mailbox."

They returned to the cottage in Madison by 7:00 or so—in time for the obligatory cold dunk in Long Island Sound before dinner. Between the commuting and the working, Davis's relaxed summer schedule took up 13 out of every 24 hours.

After two summers in Madison, the Davises rented a cottage in a Maine summer colony—Northeast Harbor—far beyond the commuter lines, and a 10-hour drive from Manhattan. By the mid-1950s, they'd bought their own vacation home on a ridge above the village. Built by a Cabot (from Boston) railroad magnate, the rambling wooden retreat provided a magnificent view of the harbor and the ocean beyond. Davis yo-yoed to Wall Street by plane from a nearby regional airport.

Except for this real estate purchase, the family's escalating net worth had no noticeable effect on the household budget or routine. Around the house, Davis wore moth-eaten sweaters and tattered pants. On family hikes, he led the way with his soles flapping. When Kathryn tossed the old shoes out, he'd rescue them from the trash, reattach the soles with glue, tape, or rubber bands, and return them to the closet. One summer, the family's hired cook reported a gas smell coming from the old stove, which was so rusty that metal flakes sometimes fell into the food. Poking at a rust hole below the main burner, she suggested her boss buy a new stove. Davis sniffed the air around the burner and patted the ancient appliance. "We don't need a new stove," he insisted. "Just paint the old one."

Kathryn knew the money was piling up but, to her, paper wealth was a mirage. The summer house, the airlift from Maine to Wall Street, and Davis's obvious delight with his career change signaled prosperity, but at a time when millionaires were scarce and didn't live next door, the children had no clue their father had become one. There were no plans to abandon the main residence in Tarrytown—their Sparta in the suburbs—for more elegant digs. The family drove an economical Chevy, flew tourist, and stayed in cut-rate lodges on ski trips. The children weren't allowed to order lobster in restaurants. The only lobster they ate was bought in fish stores or at the local dock in Maine.

Davis passed along his conviction that frugality was more than idle virtue. In his view, a dollar spent was a dollar wasted; a dollar unspent could be sent off to compound. He taught the children not to squander pecuniary resources. At home or on the road, they treated money the way desert tribes treat water—using as little as possible for any given task. Inside an investment account, which was where it belonged, money was a joyous and nourishing substance. Outside an investment account, in the hands of spenders, money was worrisome and potentially toxic. It sapped self-reliance and subverted the work urge of its possessors.

Near the end of third grade, Diana asked her father to send her to a summer camp where her favorite classmates were enrolled. After Davis nixed her request, Diana sent a letter to John D. Rockefeller, who lived in the Tarrytown area, asking him to buy insurance shares from her father. She figured that commissions on Rockefeller's purchase would cover the camp fee and then some. Rockefeller never responded. This anecdote was typical. Economizing and preserving the bankroll were, in the Davis household, part of a training mission to prepare Shelby and Diana for an independent adulthood that was free of toxic subsidy. They could then live on their own earnings (preferably below their means), invest the rest, and begin the compounding process anew.

The rudiments of investing weren't taught in the typical high school or college classroom. To many academics, capitalism was legalized larceny, and Wall Street was where the thieves hung out.

In 1958, when Shelby turned 21, John Kenneth Galbraith published *The Affluent Society,* a literary sneer against the bustling U.S. economy that produced an acquisitive, hard-working middle class. In this best-seller, the disapproving Harvard economist expressed his preference for an economy directed by social engineers, devoted to less production and less consumption, particularly by the masses. Galbraith was convinced that people would be healthier and happier living at a Spartan level of subsistence rather than working to own cars, appliances, and fashionable clothes. While the snobby old-money class could handle enrichment, he worried that the brash new-money class should be thwarted for its own good. His was a popular viewpoint: Investing in companies was evil as well as risky, and consuming too much corporate merchandise was tawdry and disgraceful.

Davis would have disagreed with Galbraith about the perils of capitalism, and he espoused a Spartan existence for a different reason: to free up capital for further production to create wealth for the very masses that Galbraith wanted to protect from wealth—supposedly to make them better human beings.

From chats with their peers, the Davis children discovered that they got smaller allowances and were saddled with tougher chores: raking leaves, stacking wood, shoveling snow. School chums who slept over on weekends were handed rakes and shovels and conscripted into the Davis cleanup crew. When Shelby was 8 or so, he and Diana lobbied their father for a swimming pool, pointing out that there was plenty of room for one next to the tennis court (a rare

Davis indulgence). Davis gave tentative approval: The family had to agree to dig the hole by hand, to avoid an expensive backhoe rental. The children couldn't believe that Davis was serious about a do-it-yourself excavation measuring 15 by 40 feet with a depth as much as 8 feet, but they went along with Plan A because there wasn't any Plan B. Kathryn was smart enough to stay indoors while the others picked and shoveled during two exhausting weekends. The results were: a small pile of dirt and several large calluses. On the third weekend, the amateur excavators hit bedrock. As Shelby and Diana struggled to contain their glee, their father called off the dig. He hired bulldozers to finish the job.

Shelby and Diana brought home good grades and generally stayed out of trouble, except for the Halloween when they spattered red paint on the porch of an unpopular neighbor. The police were called, and they caught the culprits red-handed. The story made the local newspaper's front page.

Diana, then 10, was convinced she and Shelby would be hauled off to jail. They weren't, but Davis paid for a new paint job on the porch, and sentenced the children to installing wallboard in the upstairs attic and writing an essay on the history of vandalism.

Davis's genealogical obsession grew with his bankroll. Several years running, he gave Shelby a membership in one patriotic society or another as a birthday present. The teenager had no interest in playing dress up, parading with flags, or listening to long-winded speeches about heritage. "I never could figure out why my father was so attracted to these groups," Shelby said. "It was curious how he invested in the future, but was emotionally tethered to the past. There were some interesting people involved, but that wasn't the attraction. Maybe it was his way of living history, his favorite subject in college. Or maybe he played up his ancestry to protect my mother from the social stigma that narrow-minded people still attached to hers."

On paper, Shelby was his father's clone. Like Davis, he'd prepped at Lawrenceville and attended Princeton. He majored in history, not accounting, and chose not to pursue an MBA. He worked in his father's office on breaks from school. He wrote for the college daily (his father had been an editor of the same paper, the *Princetonian*). He helped produce the "Careers in Insurance" supplement, which involved selling ads to his father's business contacts and writing about the various facets of the industry. He interviewed Russian scholars (his father's friends) for an article on Soviet politics (his father's academic specialty) that was published in the *New York Times*. He considered pursuing an insurance career (his father's investment specialty) but he already fancied a career on Wall Street (his father's bailiwick).

Shelby met his wife-to-be during a summer tour of Europe after he had completed his junior year at Princeton. His best friend in college, Keith Kroeger, picked the cities, and the two Princetonians met up with two Vassarians in Rome. Shelby had girlfriends back home—his mother preferred one named Pamela. But when in Rome, he fell for Wendy Adams. Again, he followed in his father's footsteps; Davis, too, had found his future bride during a trip to Europe. Kathryn came from a wealthy Philadelphia family; Wendy from a wealthy Boston family. During Wendy's first visit to the Davis summer house in Maine, Shelby took her on an easy climb up a local mountain. She passed a Davis test for prospective brides: Were they as pleasant at the end of the climb as they had been at the outset? Shelby proposed. He was 21; Wendy was 20. They married the next summer, after graduation. They never climbed another mountain together, but the marriage lasted 17 years.

Shelby's relationship with Davis was cooler than Shelby's flattering imitation might have suggested. Davis had resented that Shelby never answered his letters during Shelby's four years at Princeton. Davis saw letter writing as a duty and the lack of a response annoyed him. Shelby saw formal correspondence as a waste of time, especially when the telephone was readily available. The letters were more formal than chummy, full of epigrammatic advice and parental rhetoric. Starting when he was at Princeton, Shelby received an annual accounting of his father's latest investment triumphs. This document arrived in the mail without comment. Shelby took it as his father's challenge to do well. Their relationship deteriorated further after a family squabble made the front page of the *New York Times,* as described in the next chapter.

During Shelby's senior year at Princeton, his father hinted at a job offer. Shelby ignored the overture. He wanted to work on Wall Street but preferred to be a stock analyst. He'd concluded long ago that Davis was "hard to deal with" and "would pay me next to nothing." Having heard Davis compliment the research department at the Bank of New York, he signed up for an interview with one of the bank's recruiters. The recruiters promised him a chance to start researching companies right away, without having to waste time at a teller's window or interning in the appraisal or loan departments. Shelby was enthralled. The bank hired him forthwith, at $87 a week.

Shelby and Wendy moved into a Manhattan apartment. He and his new father-in-law, Weston Adams, quickly developed mutual admiration. Adams was a successful financier who had served as president of the Boston Stock Exchange and also founded a well-known investment house: Adams, Harkness, and Hill. He was also a sports-loving bon vivant whose family had owned the Suffolk Downs Racetrack. His purchase of the Boston Bruins brought Canadian-style hockey to America. Shelby impressed him with his work ethic, modesty, and business savvy. He chose Shelby as treasurer of the Bruins. He took Shelby along on the occasional scouting trip, looking for young hockey talent. On weekends, they watched games together in the family box. They explored Boston occasionally, drank Bloody Marys at noon, and sometimes ordered lobsters for lunch. Davis would have disapproved.

Davis was famous in insurance circles, but in banking circles and around Wall Street in general, a mention of his name was likely to elicit a quizzical "Who's he?" Unlike the sons of movie stars, literary celebrities, or famous restaurateurs, Shelby was spared any demoralizing chatter about his father's brilliance. He was free to make his own reputation in his father's profession and to carve out his own lifestyle.

Research analysis was still an obscure trade, and brokerage houses gave their analysts only lukewarm support. The typical write-up on a company or an industry ended up in the hands of investment professionals. The average investor rarely saw a research report. Information that's readily available in today's market was esoteric in the late 1950s. Realizing there was a demand for reliable data, the Bank of New York maneuvered to fill that demand and sell its research to pension funds, mutual funds, bank trust departments, and other institutional types.

Shelby's first boss, Peter LeBay, was an amiable number cruncher. LeBay didn't ask Shelby to cover the industry Shelby knew best, because, in spite of the fantastic run-up in stock prices, insurance was considered a marginal and sleepy prospect. Instead, Shelby was assigned to the heavyweights of U.S. industry: companies with staying power and economic clout; companies that would have been voted most likely to succeed in the future. "Just like being in college," Shelby said, referring to the stack of term papers he produced on the makers and sellers of steel, rubber, aluminum, oil, copper, and cement.

1938 Shelby Davis, age one.

Early 1940s Shelby with sister, Diana, outside Tarrytown Homestead.

1947 Shelby Cullom Davis, now with his own firm, becomes president of the New York Society of Security Analysts.

Mid-1950s Kathryn W. Davis photographed for her 25th wedding anniversary.

1972 Ambassador and Mrs. Shelby Cullom Davis returning to Switzerland from a trip to the Soviet Union.

1970s   Shelby Cullom Davis appearing in white tie at a Mayflower Society function.

1993 The two Shelbys, father and son, near the family retreat in Maine.

1995 Shelby and sons, Andrew and Chris, meet in New Mexico to discuss transfer of Davis operations to the third generation.

1995   Chris, Andrew, and Shelby (after a bike accident) at Davis Investment Seminar.

1996   Chris and Shelby being photographed for a *Forbes* article.

1993   Andrew and Chris outside Chris's Fifth Avenue office soon after both became Davis fund managers.

Each term paper included charts and tables, so the reader could compare profit margins, earnings, sales, and so on, going back several years. "You'd notice if a company had lowered its costs, raised its profits, and accelerated its growth," Shelby says. "If a company performed better than its peers, you'd see why. Once you had this data, it was easy to question management about the company's future. Would a favorable trend continue? What were they doing to make things happen?"

Lingering at the bank after hours, Shelby thumbed through financial magazines, newsletters, and reports by other analysts, looking for unusual angles. The generic viewpoint didn't interest him, and crunching numbers didn't satisfy him. He realized he couldn't judge a company's prospects by sitting at a desk with a slide rule and an adding machine (calculators weren't readily available). Soon after his arrival, he lobbied his boss to let him make corporate house calls, where he could meet managers and quiz them in person, the way his father had. Most analysts didn't stray far from their desks, and few actually visited companies on their research lists. With no chance to rate the leadership, how could they separate doers from bluffers? The bank wasn't wild about Shelby's plan to turn analysis into investigative reporting, but he got a tentative go-ahead and a modest travel budget.

Investor relations departments didn't exist yet, and companies were as unprepared for Shelby's visits as his bank was unsure of the benefits of sending him. At age 22, Shelby found himself sitting in executive suites, talking directly to CEOs his father's age.

In his role as tire-and-rubber analyst, he flew to Akron, Ohio—the Detroit of the tread trade—to meet with the industry's Big Five (Goodyear, Firestone, General Tire, Cooper, and UniRoyal). These competitors were headquartered within a

10-mile radius, and Shelby saw them all during one trip in 1959. The tire business was cyclical; its profits rose and fell with the economy, and tire stocks rose and fell accordingly. The gyrations of cyclicals contributed to the widespread conviction that stocks were untrustworthy.

The midpoint of the bull run that carried Davis's net worth into eight figures was 1959, but hadn't attracted Main Street buyers. The public, by and large, still owned the "prudent" investment: bonds, but the sorry performance of bonds mocked their prudence. Bond investments continued to disappoint; stock investments were pleasant surprises. Stocks had been the losing assets at the zenith of their popularity in the late 1920s; they became unpopular winning assets in the 1950s.

The Dow was dominated by the big shots of heavy industry on Shelby's research list—rubber, autos, cement, aluminum. (Most are much smaller shots today.) Companies in these industries were touted as high-quality, low-risk, and good for the long haul in any portfolio. Already, the Reynolds Metals and Alcoas had begun to falter, but even the most pessimistic analysts didn't foresee the abandoned refineries and shuttered factories left to rust, or how gritty industry would never recover its profitability and would disappoint investors for the rest of the century.

Fast-food restaurants, shopping malls, and chain stores would soon spread from coast to coast, but who knew then that McDonald's, Dunkin' Donuts, and Kentucky Fried Chicken would someday become more valuable and more rewarding to shareholders than almighty U.S. Steel?

Shelby quickly advanced through the cubicles and became head of equity research at the Bank of New York. At age 25, he was named a vice president—the youngest since Alexander Hamilton. After his promotion, he was told he had a shot at bank president if he stuck around for 30 years. That prospect became less and less appealing, the more he thought about it. "I saw myself attending one formal dinner after another. Basically stuck in a glorified public relations job. I realized I'd rather review 100 financial statements and quiz 100 CEOs than host a cocktail party with the bank's preferred 100 clients."

Shelby made many good research calls and a few bad ones. When asked about the latter, he replied: "Analysts always remember their mistakes and try to learn from them. I've never forgotten Hertz Rent-A-Car. It was a hot stock when it came public, selling at 30 to 40 times earnings. I gave it a thumbs up, which was a boneheaded call. The company was okay, but the stock was too expensive." A lot of the annual earnings came from selling used cars—much less reliable than rental income because used car prices could gyrate widely.

He never forgot Reynolds Aluminum, either. Forty years after the act, Shelby still wishes he hadn't recommended it in a 1960 report. Reynolds was one of aluminum's "Big Four," along with Alcoa, Alcan, and Kaiser. This foursome dominated the world market. Alcoa enjoyed a monopolistic lock on production before World War II, but, to create competitors for Alcoa, the government built aluminum plants and sold them to Reynolds and Kaiser. To increase the odds of survival, the government gave the two new companies zero-interest loans to pay for the plants. "Certificates of necessity," the loans were called. Meanwhile, an antitrust action forced Alcoa to spin off its Canadian subsidiary, Alcan, creating the third rival.

Aluminum was in high demand, so there was plenty of business for all four companies. They worked overtime to handle the orders during the Korean War.

In his May 1960 "Survey of the Aluminum Industry," Shelby noted that aluminum companies were expensive to operate and, after a vigorous run-up in the 1950s, their stocks had gotten expensive (25 to 40 times earnings). Yet he ignored these defects and gave a buy signal based on aluminum's

147

bright future. He put it in Wall Streetese: "Current high stock market valuations of present earnings are justifiable on a long-term basis."

His favorite was Reynolds, selling below its 1956 all-time-high price. A visit to the Reynolds headquarters in Richmond, Virginia, got him excited. He and his fellow analysts were routed through a giant hangar where full-scale models of products "soon to be made from aluminum" were displayed from floor to ceiling. Everything from cars to furniture, locomotives to bridges, could be sculpted from this lightweight metal, and it promised huge potential sales to the aircraft manufacturers.

Back in the office, Shelby wrote a rave review and recommended Reynolds at 40 times earnings. He fancied that it could double its earnings every three years, thereby turning an expensive proposition into a screaming bargain. A terrific growth stock, he thought. After all, Reynolds had been growing fast ever since it was launched.

This was one case, in which visiting a company and chatting with management led Shelby astray. While he was in Richmond marveling at what he'd seen in the hangar, unsold aluminum was piling up in company warehouses. Analysts were unaware of this backlog because the warehouses weren't part of the tour.

In spite of the exciting new uses for aluminum, the supply had far outdistanced the demand. Prices fell, profits collapsed, and the stocks took a bungee. Four decades later, Reynolds and other metals stocks are selling for less than they did when Eisenhower was president and Johnny Mathis was a teen idol. Shelby had witnessed the peril of buying high-priced growth. He'd also learned that typical corporate managers emphasize the positive and, if they can get away with it, neglect to mention the negatives.

Davis tended his insurance portfolio from his office at 110 William Street. Once in a while, his son dropped in for some perfunctory shop talk, but Davis had no interest in aluminum, rubber, auto, or concrete companies. Manufacturers such as these required expensive factories, and repairs and upgrades depleted their cash. They tended to lose money in recessions, so their earnings were unreliable. They were always vulnerable to some new process or invention that could put them out of business. The entire history of manufacturing had produced few long-term survivors, and only companies that had reinvented themselves had escaped obsolescence. Several insurance companies had celebrated their 200th birthdays, and were still selling essentially the same product they sold when the Founding Fathers were alive. They profited from investing their customers' money; manufacturers never got that chance. Shelby didn't follow the insurance industry, but his stint at the Bank of New York had taught him that banks had a lot in common with his father's favorite sector. Banks and insurers tended to operate out of marble, filigreed headquarters that resembled jumbo mausoleums. Banking never went out of style because money never went out of style. Shelby's own employer was proof of this. Bank of New York had been founded in the eighteenth century.

Along with its longevity, banking had developed a stodgy reputation. Because banks were never trendy, investors were never inclined to pay scalpers' premiums to own them. Ergo, you could always buy bank shares at bargain rates relative to other types of shares and invest in a bank's growth on the cheap.

A bank profited from other people's money, but only if that money was prudently deployed. Reckless lending was an occupational hazard, but the risks were minimized by skilled managers who did not let their greed strangle their caution.

It would take more than a decade for Shelby to fill his mutual fund portfolio with banks and other financials, but the Bank of New York gave him an insider's familiarity with the group.

Davis's reinsurance friend and colleague, Richard Murray, visited the Maine compound soon after Shelby's promotion to vice president at the bank. In spite of his long-term friendship with Davis, Murray had no idea Shelby was making a living on Wall Street. In years of chitchat with his friend, Murray recalled, "Davis hardly mentioned his children. Somehow, I got the impression Shelby was a playboy and a trust-fund welfare case. That he was off to a quick start in his father's field never crossed my mind."

CHAPTER 11

THE
INHERITANCE FLAP

O N THE INHERITANCE SUBJECT, DAVIS AND Buffett were in full agreement. Both opposed trust funds. Both decried the indolence, drug addiction, and low self-esteem prevalent among trustafarians. According to his biographer, Roger Lowenstein, Buffett had planned for his children to inherit a token of his appreciation. For his part, Davis had screwed up his planning by opening small trust accounts for Shelby and Diana. In the early 1940s, he funded each account with $4,000—surely not a sum that would sap anybody's future self-reliance. By 1961, as the New York *Daily News* reported, each "$4,000 acorn had grown into a $3.8 million oak."

At his most optimistic, Davis never imagined that ferocious compounding in his children's trusts would put them near the top of the national wealth heap soon after they graduated from college. He wished their acorns had sprouted at a slower rate. The twin oaks, particularly Diana's oak, became the spoils in a vicious legal and public relations battle.

Davis's knack for maximizing profit collided head-on with his conviction that a large inheritance corrupts the recipient.

He couldn't stand the thought of 21-year-old Diana getting control of the initiative-smothering fortune that already had her name on it. His father had mainly lived off of his mother's inherited wealth, and he was determined not to give his daughter a lifetime functional exemption. In theory, Shelby's $3.8 million was just as objectionable as Diana's but, for the reasons explained below, Davis only objected to hers.

About the time he began stewing over the trust predicament, Davis decided to give a sizable sum to a worthier cause: the history department at Princeton. He felt indebted to his alma mater, where he'd spent four stimulating years learning how great men create great civilizations. Applying history to finance, Davis invested in the great CEOs who made great insurance companies, and gave Princeton credit for this enriching experience. He attended reunions, hung a Princeton banner in the living room at the summer house in Maine, hobnobbed with his ex-professors, and agreed to endow a chair in memory of his father, George Henry Davis, Princeton, 1886. He also agreed to provide a few fellowships and scholarships for the "deserving but needy."

Yet, when it came to signing a check to Princeton, Davis suffered severe writer's block. "Money," said Shelby, "was my father's way of keeping score, and he hated to give up any points." After several months' hemming and hawing, the reluctant donor hatched a scheme to satisfy Princeton without losing points, save Diana from her trust fund, and restore her "thrill, joy, and satisfaction" at the prospect of a trust-free adulthood. He'd donate Diana's money to Princeton.

Neglecting to inform Diana that she was the source of his largesse, Davis instructed his lawyers to draw up the transfer papers on her $3.8 million. (Not consulting women about financial matters, even when the finances belonged to them, was standard operating procedure at the time.)

Davis scheduled a meeting in downtown Manhattan, at which Diana would sign over her wealth in a roomful of lawyers, trust officers, and emissaries from the university. He instructed Kathryn to invite Diana to attend his mandatory "afternoon tea."

Smelling a rat in the tea, Diana stayed put in Massachusetts, where she was interviewing for a teaching job. Back at the tea party, paid experts and invited guests (including Princeton president Robert Goheen and the chairman of Chemical Bank/New York Trust) sat around an antique maple table and made small talk. Sublimating his fury, Davis fiddled with the ceremonial pen and speculated about train delays. By late afternoon, it was obvious Diana was a no-show.

Diana and her mother saw a darker motive to Davis's ploy than a noble attempt to support a worthy cause. There was a suitor in the wings. Diana had fallen for a prep school history teacher, John Spencer. Her father disapproved. He argued that Diana, at 21, was too young to marry anybody, especially a low-octane academic. Davis had footed the bill for her two coming-out parties—the Debutante Cotillion in New York and the Westchester Cotillion in Rye. She'd met numerous budding tycoons with high-octane ambition. Why hadn't she fallen for one? Though Spencer was a distant relative of Winston Churchill and his family was "old Hartford"—both pluses in Davis's ledger—the pluses were outweighed by the minuses. Spencer was four years older than Diana; he taught at a rural school and spent summers on his family farm (Davis was convinced Diana would be happier living in or near a city); Spencer's insistence on rushing to the altar made Davis suspect he wanted to stake a quick claim on his girlfriend's assets.

Spencer and Diana ignored her father's demand that they delay the marriage, and announced their formal engagement over his objection. Their defiance infuriated Davis; Kathryn sided with her daughter. Both women were convinced Davis had concocted the Princeton deal to keep Diana's money out of Spencer's pocket. Shelby offered behind-the-scenes support to his sister. Shelby owned an identical trust, and the siblings hired a lawyer to protect their joint interests. That Davis hadn't tried to divert Shelby's millions gave the anti-Spencer theory credence.

The evening of Diana's no-show, she called her father at home to wage peace. She told him she'd defer any decision about whether to hand over her trust until after the upcoming wedding. Davis hung up on her and hired a public relations firm. The firm sent out a five-page release. On June 2, 1961, readers of the *New York Times* opened their paper to photos of the multimillionaire and his rebellious daughter under an intriguing headline:

"Girl Refuses to Yield $3.8 Million to Princeton as Father Planned"

Davis flew to Scotland on a business trip, and lobbed long-distance insults. He chided his daughter for "unreasonable selfishness." He lamented her absorption in the "unrealistic materialism prevalent among American youth today." Diana's selfishness was all the more reprehensible, he said, in light of the "assured" $30,000-a-year income he'd provided her and the $100,000 cash wedding gift he'd promised. "Diana has always been a good girl, but money seems to encourage greed," Davis confided to the world, "We were far happier when there was less."

Diana launched a public relations defense from a Manhattan apartment owned by a Spencer relative. Since her fiancé's brother recently had died of cancer, she told reporters she was inclined to support cancer research with her trust—not Princeton. "Dad threatened me on money matters," she confided in a phone interview. "I suspected ever since my engagement this was going to be his weapon. After John and I are married, we plan to live . . . modestly. Please understand, money isn't important to us. We're not going to be pretentious. But what John and I do is up to us and not up to Daddy."

Diana insisted she'd never heard of the $30,000 annual income or the $100,000 wedding gift her father claimed to have promised her. She was distressed at his bitterness and embarrassed by his public attack. "Now I don't know what I'll decide to do. He's doing all this for his own glory, anyway." Davis retaliated by trans-Atlantic telex, while his flacks dutifully passed along his latest jibes to the news hounds. "Stubborn, that's what she is, just plain stubborn," he said. The lead flack added his own two cents: "You may find this hard to believe, but Mr. Davis fervently believes that young people should not have too much wealth. He believes it is bad for them."

"The deplorable record of the past week proved conclusively to me that too much money goes to the heads of young people," Davis amplified. "Since Diana has not so much as lifted a little finger to earn the $3.8 million, she has no moral right to its disposition. I fear what Diana needs is a good spanking."

"Father Says Girl Needs Spanking Over $3.8 Million," trumpeted the headline in the New York *Daily News*. "I hate to say this about my own father, but he is inclined to be somewhat authoritarian," Diana shot back.

Reporters swarmed this story, pursuing every angle. In the Chrysler Building, they talked to Diana's attorney, Julian Bush, who'd found no documentary evidence of the alleged $30,000 annual stipend. They talked to Diana's mother, who described herself as "very unhappy about all this publicity. It's gotten ridiculous. My daughter is a generous, warm-hearted girl and has no desire at all to keep the money." They talked to

Diana's fiancé, who said he'd taken a "frightful ribbing" from his friends over the fund flap. They talked to Princeton, where a spokesman denied Davis had proposed a gift, even though all parties to the discussion already had acknowledged the fact. The spokesman promptly changed his response to: "This is a family affair and the university does not wish to become involved." They pressed Davis for details on the $30,000 stipend, and he admitted the stipend wasn't coming from him and might not materialize for several decades. She'd get it from her mother's estate, but only when Kathryn died. Apparently, Davis had recast the story in the present tense to make Diana appear as greedy and selfish as possible.

They tried to talk to Diana's brother, Shelby, but he was sailing off Cape Cod. When they finally reached him, Shelby had no comment at first, but then he commented. They asked his reaction to his father's wishing out loud that Shelby would cede his trust fund to a philanthropic foundation that Davis was planning to establish. "I don't know what my father's talking about," Shelby said.

For more than a week, the *New York Times,* the *Daily News,* the *World-Telegram,* and other New York dailies relayed these details on their front pages. Headline writers had fun with "Heiress Gives Dad What For," "Heiress Puts Foot Down on Handout," "Donor Daddy: 'Heirbrush Her,'" referring to the spanking threat. Reporters had fun pitting "willful" Diana ("113 pounds of shapely spunk") against a "Victorian-minded, emotionally buffeted, *Mayflower*-descended" Daddy Warbucks. Sometimes, they took Davis's side (benevolent father versus selfish daughter); more often, they took Diana's side (young love thwarted by old fogie; dutiful daughter versus tyrannical tightwad), and once in a while, they showed practiced objectivity by skewering both sides (fat cat Indian giver embarrassed by ingrate debutante).

From the *Times* to the tabloids, they played up the big bucks angle and the society angle: Diana's double debut, Davis's colonial ancestors; the Spencer-Churchill connection. "In socialite circles, there was some conjecture yesterday on what Diana's ancestors would say if they just knew," wrote the *Times's* Sidney Kline, playing on the theme. "They include, on her paternal side, John Alden and Francis Cooke (from the *Mayflower*) and Thomas Warren, a member of the original Jamestown settlement in 1607." There was scarce mention of the source of the big bucks—the bull market in U.S. stocks, which, in 1961, still offered considerable upside. That Davis's fortune was largely self-generated, that he was an ex-state bureaucrat made wealthy by clever stock picking, that any astute investor of modest means could also have turned $4,000 into $3.8 million was omitted from the reportage. The New York press could have presented Davis as an example of capitalist meritocracy; instead, they focused on the debutante angle and the Davis pedigree. This reinforced the notion that America was a clubby re-creation of Europe, where the rich got richer and snobs got snobbier.

Davis, still in Scotland, was too angry not to keep up the front-page cat fight that was bad for business and devastating to his daughter. As a show of motherly solidarity, Kathryn and Diana took a room in a motel in Westchester County. Davis was offended that his wife had sided with the children. After he returned to the States, the family gathered at the Maine summer house. In stereotypical Davis fashion, they feigned cordiality, taking their morning dips together in frigid Maine water, while their lawyers haggled in New York.

Seven days after Diana's no-show, a truce was declared. "Diana, Dad, and Dollars End Family's Feud," the New York *Daily News* reported on June 9. Diana and Shelby got to keep $1 million apiece from their trusts. The balance was left to Davis to disburse as he chose. "Harmony has returned to our home," said the cause of the dissonance. "Diana is an intelligent and sensible young lady." "Everybody is happy now," echoed Kathryn. "Our family storm is over."

Diana and John Spencer were married June 24, 1961, at a Presbyterian church in Scarborough, in front of a crowd of 150. Several reporters witnessed the event. "The wedding was gay," noted the *Daily News,* using an adjective that still belonged to heterosexuals. "Mr. Davis appeared gayest of all as he handed over his daughter who was clad in a white gown and carried a bouquet of yellow roses." Everything ran smoothly until the guests overstayed their welcome and the caterers ran out of food.

Davis's check for $5.3 million was turned over to Princeton at a ceremonial dinner on campus three years later, on the 100th anniversary of his father's birth. Higher stock prices, including a huge run-up in the Japanese insurers, more than made up for the $1 million lost to Diana. Davis's father had died a decade earlier, but Davis's brother George attended, along with Kathryn, Shelby, and Diana (who wasn't acknowledged as a benefactress). Davis felt the university never gave him proper credit for his exceptional gift. At the least, he'd expected to be added to the Princeton investment committee, and at most, to be named a university trustee. Neither offer materialized. It irked him that he never got a thank-you or a sales commission for the insurance stocks he'd touted to the Princeton endowment fund, after the fund benefited from taking his advice. He maintained close ties to the history department, where several Davis Chairs were established, and funded an annual lecture series on colonial history, because he never cessed to admire the coverage of American pioneers.

The front-page squabble was a constant source of embarrassment for Shelby, already installed at the Bank of New York. For years thereafter, friends and business associates needled him about the "heirbrush" and his father's pompous harangue. His relationship with his father, distant before the flap, now got more distant. Having felt the shame of foolhardy publicity, Shelby avoided interviews and press agents, which explains why his exceptional mutual fund record remained obscure for many years.

CHAPTER 12

COOL TRIO RUNS HOT FUND

S HELBY'S ESCAPE FROM THE BANK OF NEW York was hatched at a Christmas party in 1965. Having downed a few eggnogs, he and Guy Palmer, a Yale grad and a fellow bank vice president, decided to open their own freelance investment firm. Once again, Shelby had flattered his father by imitation. He abandoned a paying job in favor of insecure self-employment. Davis had done the same 20 years earlier.

The two escapees tried to recruit Jeremy Biggs, a portfolio manager at the $1 billion U.S. Steel pension fund, as a third partner. They'd met Biggs through his father, a much-admired executive at the bank Shelby and Palmer had left behind, and a helpful ally to Shelby. Biggs saw no point in quitting U.S. Steel to join a rookie enterprise. "You're crazy," he told Shelby. "You don't have any accounts."

After opening a small office, hiring three employees, and attracting a few accounts, Shelby approached Biggs with a second offer. In 1968, Biggs accepted, jilting U.S. Steel. His banker father was skeptical; his mother was supportive. "Nobody in the family ever had his name on a business before," she enthused, referring to the Davis, Palmer and Biggs moniker. Neither Biggs's father nor Shelby's gave their sons any money to manage.

These three musketeers of finance were all in their early thirties. Shelby was short and spare; Palmer, short and chunky; Biggs, tall and lanky. Palmer was the organizer and front man, a prodigious eater and a good talker. He and Biggs enjoyed schmoozing clients; Shelby hated schmoozing. Biggs and Shelby handled most of the stock picking, and both worked overtime, especially in the March rush when companies released their annual reports. But where Biggs was reasonably devoted (he chose dinner with his family over staying late at the office), Shelby was fanatical (he chose the office).

Shelby quizzed as many analysts, investor relations officers, and CEOs as he could cram into a 16-hour schedule. When he wasn't asking questions, he was reading reports to prepare more questions. If he didn't gather every fact, challenge every statement, and, pursue every angle, he felt like a slacker.

In their third year, the trio moved to roomier midtown digs, where they tore down walls to "facilitate communication." At this point, they were handling $100 million in clients' money—some invested in stocks, some in bonds, depending on the client. Shelby put his father on the advisory board for window dressing, but the musketeers later dropped the board altogether. Trophy boards, they realized, didn't win clients. Performance did.

They advertised their services in an old-fashioned brochure with sepia photographs and print that looked like handwriting. This gave the impression of tradition, folksiness, and prudence. In the text, they reversed the image, describing themselves as "imaginative," "objective," and "aggressive."

"Since each account represents different financial circumstances," they wrote, covering all the bases, "we view each client separately and tailor-make investment decisions to coincide with the particular situation. However, no matter how divergent the client's needs may be, one of the primary objectives for our clients is maximum long-term capital appreciation commensurate with reasonable safety."

The mission statement, called "Basic Investment Philosophy," owed a lot to Davis, and though the main points sound obvious today, they were far from obvious to the U.S. investing public in the mid-1960s:

- Stock prices ride on a company's earnings. Eventually, earnings, or the lack of same, determine whether the shareholder wins or loses.
- Earnings ride on the U.S. economy. The reason to be bullish on stocks is that the U.S. economy has a habit of doubling in size every 16 to 18 years, going back more than a century.
- If history repeats itself, the economy will expand eightfold during the adult life of an average investor. Thus, at minimum, an investor can expect a portfolio to generate at least an eightfold gain during his stock-picking career. In periods when stock prices rise faster than earnings, he'll possibly do better. Meanwhile, he'll also benefit from dividends.

This was bedrock logic for steady compounding, and understanding and believing it was all the education required for successful investing. You could win the game with a sensible, diversified portfolio of stocks or mutual funds, and the critical ingredient, time. You didn't need luck, hot tips, or knowing somebody who knew somebody. You didn't need to dodge bears by switching in and out of your holdings. If you thought successful investing depended on luck, hot tips, knowing somebody, or nimble switching, you were a cinch to lose money. Chronic losers often misunderstood the cause of their losses. They thought they were jinxed. Without a solid grounding in the bedrock logic of compounding, it was hard to invest sensibly.

The sepia brochure tells us how Shelby went about picking stocks in this early phase of his career. He was attracted to companies "whose earnings and/or price-earnings ratios are likely to show above-average expansion," which sounded a lot like the Davis Double Play. But the fact that he didn't put a limit on how much he'd pay for earnings was a departure from Davis. Shelby watched for "industries that are changing their characteristics," and he kept track of "the shifting of investor interest among various industries" just as he'd done as an analyst. He and Biggs didn't specialize in certain types of companies, and they showed no particular interest in insurance or banking. They readily revamped their clients' portfolios to take advantage of trends. Davis never cared about trends, but in the go-go era of the late 1960s, trendy high-tech stocks ruled the market. Investing in high-tech soon gave the musketeers their comeuppance.

In the meantime, Davis, Palmer and Biggs served their clients well and continued to attract new capital. Biggs was put on hospitality detail, driving or flying to various cities, where he took the firm's biggest clients (mostly corporate pension funds) to dinner and gave them updates on the firm's thinking. He and Shelby were surprised to discover that enriching a pension fund wasn't necessarily in their best interest. "Talk about being punished for good deeds," Biggs recalls. "The more money we made investing for an institution, the less money its bosses gave us to manage. They funneled cash to managers who did worse than we did, figuring last year's underachievers would work harder to improve their results the next year."

Biggs still remembers the confusing reception he got at Rohm & Haas, a chemical and plastics supplier. After thanking

Biggs repeatedly for brilliant performance on behalf of Rohm's pension fund, a company mouthpiece told Biggs the fund was slashing $10 million from its stake with Biggs' firm. "Hearing news like that made you want to tear your hair out," Biggs said.

In 1966, Shelby and Biggs bumped into Hugh Bullock: a devout Anglophile, snazzy dresser, president of the Pilgrim Society, and friend of both their fathers. Bullock ran a conservative investment house based in London. A young salesman in Bullock's New York office, Martin Proyect, had convinced his boss to launch an "aggressive" mutual fund to go with the stodgier offerings in Bullock's lineup.

Bullock doubted an aggressive Bullock fund would amount to much, so he gave his enthusiastic underling, Proyect, controlling interest in the management company. Because this was a venture from New York, Proyect called it the "New York Venture Fund." After a year-long in-house dry run conducted in private, Venture had failed to impress. Bullock noted the failure, remembered his chance encounter with Shelby and Biggs, and asked Proyect to recruit the young money managers to run the portfolio. To avoid paying a fee, Bullock gave the musketeers his stake in the management company. Proyect handled sales and promotion; Bullock's office took care of the paperwork. Shelby's two partners saw Venture as a sidelight to their real job—investing for wealthy individuals, corporate pension funds, and so on. Shelby saw it as a chance to test his stock-picking skills.

Shelby and Biggs began their active management in February 1969. America was bogged down in Vietnam, inflation was on the rise, and the almighty dollar was losing both its buying power and the respect of the rest of the world. Stocks had rallied after a short bear market back in 1966, but another decline was in progress. Taking charge of a fledgling fund near the latest bear bottom was lucky timing—at least temporarily.

New investors supplied Venture with $2 million in fresh cash—a pittance for most mutual funds, but enough to double Venture's assets. Shelby and Biggs put their cash to work buying depressed shares, while most of their competitors had no cash on hand.

Bears don't honk horns to announce their arrival, and even if the typical fund manager believes a selloff is probable, he or she can't afford to switch out of stocks and wait to buy them back at a discount. Unless the timing is perfect, the manager will lose customers when stock prices continue to rise, and that loss will cause the fund to lag its fully invested rivals. The manager's job security depends on keeping up with the crowd, so the manager would rather suffer with the crowd than prepare for a downturn that can't be precisely predicted. When the crisis materializes, a cash shortage forces the manager to liquidate key holdings to repay fickle clients who opt out of the fund and demand the return of what's left of their original investment. This punishes loyal shareholders because the fund has ditched attractive holdings at unattractive prices. Plus, there's no money left to buy bargains.

Starting in February, Shelby and Biggs were acquiring what their colleagues were unloading. "You're buying with your fingers crossed," Shelby later told *Institutional Investor* magazine. "Your chances of picking the bottom of the market are very slim, but if you're within five or ten percent, your gains can be extraordinary."

Venture's portfolio was limited to 30 issues because, as Palmer explained, "The easiest thing in the world is to buy the latest good idea. This is very inefficient, and it doesn't help your performance . . . you can end up with 200 names, but none of those 200 is big enough to do you any good." With fewer stocks, Biggs noted, it was easier to play defense during a further decline. "Sell a couple of things, and you've got 20 percent of your assets out of the market." Owning fewer stocks, Palmer added, made a fund manager more cautious about purchases. "It's not so easy to sweep a bad idea under the rug if a big lump of your assets is wrapped up in it."

It was hard to see the Davis influence in these initial maneuvers. Shelby and Biggs bought an array of small, fast-growing companies—everything from McDonald's and Dunkin' Donuts to nursing home franchises, medical suppliers, real estate developers, and a couple of oil refiners. Shelby bought four of his father's favorite insurance names, including AIG and GEICO, but less than 10 percent of the portfolio was riding on insurance and financials. Fannie Mae, the dominant player in the mortgage business, was already in the fund when Shelby and Biggs took over, and they promptly sold it. More than a decade later, Shelby bought it back, and Fannie became one of his most rewarding ideas.

Their biggest positions were high-tech. With Palmer out trolling for clients, Shelby and Biggs decked the portfolio with Memorex, Digital Equipment, American Micro Systems, and Mohawk Data. "Data" and "systems" were the buzzwords that attracted investors to the technology hive, where prices were steep and expectations buoyant, in spite of the latest market setback. Financial pundits declared this a New Era of American Ingenuity, repeating a phrase coined by their predecessors in the late 1920s. Shelby was attracted to the "high earnings visibility" of the New Era companies. To be successful, a writer must find a voice and an investor must find a style. In his impatience to prove himself, Shelby lost sight of his father's maxims and was carried away by the go-go drumbeat. It was hard not to do otherwise.

Biggs and Shelby visited the Memorex corporate headquarters one afternoon and, using the Davis technique, they counted empty spaces in the executive parking lot. An empty space was circumstantial evidence that a company VIP had left early to play golf, but whatever the excuse, unless it was a medical emergency, the absentee had put a trivial errand ahead of what should have been his or her real purpose in life: working for the betterment of Memorex shareholders. Biggs was happy to see a full lot. "People work 20 hours a day here," he marveled. He and Shelby made Memorex their top position.

The results from the first year were indeed extraordinary, just as Shelby had suggested in the interview with *Institutional Investor.* While 144 competitors had reported a loss, New York Venture was up 25.3 percent. Of his rookie success, Shelby said, "We all thought we were geniuses." "Cool Trio Runs Hot Fund," gushed *Business Week* in a congratulatory piece that appeared on February 7, 1970. In the photo that ran with the article, Shelby has sideburns and looks very mod. Biggs and Shelby denied they were go-go investors, or "gunslingers," although Memorex and several other tech picks were clearly go-go stocks. "Buy a good company," Biggs said, defending their strategy, "and even if it's overpriced, you know it's a good company."

Shelby elaborated. "We guarantee that we will never be number one in a roaring speculative bull market. We eschew the go-go philosophy that last year made instant winners of funds that favored new issues and hotshot over-the-counter securities." Yet their holdings were considerably more hotshot than Davis would have tolerated.

By March 1970, the Cool Trio had attracted $55 million in new capital. As soon as the capital arrived, and with the *Business Week* plaudits fresh in investors' minds, Memorex dropped 20 percent in a single day on a bad earnings report. Shelby and Biggs bought more. Halfway through Memorex's swoon from $168 to $3, they bought again. They bailed out at $20, taking a big loss.

Memorex was a fast grower with a fancy price tag—a fatal combination when the profits disappear and investors fall out of love. Then, the Davis Double Play goes into reverse. Let's say a beloved faster grower sells at 30 times earnings and earns $1 a share, creating a $30 stock. If the earnings drop by half and disenchanted investors decide to pay only 15 times earnings, the $30 stock suddenly becomes a $7.50 stock. When further disenchantment drops the price to 10 times earnings, a $30 investment is whittled to $5. The "Cool Trio Runs Hot Fund" article marked the end of the hot streak.

"Memorex wounded us all," said Biggs, but it wasn't the only high-tech flop in the portfolio. Computer Tape was another. Venture went from champ to chump. The number-one fund in its rookie year landed in the bottom 10 percent in the year that followed. The math was discouraging.

To devote his full attention to bringing Venture out of its tailspin, Shelby declined an invitation from Bill Wasserman to join the board of the Wasserman family trusts in Philadelphia. With his usual edgy humor, Wild Bill had cracked, "We could use some more of your half-baked ideas." Shelby couldn't entirely disagree. His confidence was shaken, and more shakes were to come. "My father had five years of glory at the outset of his investing," Shelby recalls. "I was about to experience five years of hell at the outset of mine.

Venture's third annual report arrived in clients' mailboxes in July 1971. A "V" for Venture monopolized the cover space. Below the "V" was a photo of three bespectacled men staring at a piece of paper. "A mutual fund whose investment objective is growth of capital" was the tag line. In a photo montage on the inside pages, male staffers (all wearing glasses) stared at each other or into the camera. Female staffers, all visibly younger than the men, were shown cradling their phones. It's always a challenge for Wall Streeters to make growth of capital look exciting.

Venture hadn't given investors much to be excited about, after the hot hands of the cool trio cooled off. A share worth

$10.22 in 1969 regressed to $8.06 in 1970, and by 1971, share-holders had only $10.88 to show for their patience. The entire portfolio was worth $29 million. If Davis and Biggs had run the fund and nothing else, they'd have to find another job.

The immediate future was bright, or so thought Martin Proyect, chairman, president, and chief organizer for the fund. In the letter to shareholders, he enthused: "In terms of . . . future outlook, the indications we have are all very positive." Confident consumers were spending at a brisk pace. Inflation advanced, but modestly. Economic problems, he said, were "temporary in nature." Proyect was correct, but only temporarily.

The sharp decline of 1969 to 1970 had been quickly for-gotten. While Watts burned, Main Street America fought with its hippie offspring, and more GIs died in Vietnam, Wall Street regained its swagger. There were bullish developments on the trading front. In 1971, the Nasdaq market made its debut, with computers taking the place of screaming and flail-ing in a pit. A year later, the Chicago Mercantile Exchange launched its financial futures contracts, turning stocks and bonds into commodities—the pork bellies and soybeans of the paper economy. A sure sign of renewed optimism: Donald-son, Lufkin, and Jenrette went public. As reported by James Grant in *The Trouble with Prosperity,* the DLJ offering broke a centuries-old tradition of Wall Street firms raising money from their partners. They'd taken other companies public, not themselves.

Buyers returned to stocks with gusto, but they'd lost their affection for the washed-out tech variety. The money tide had shifted; it flowed out of the go-gos and into larger, safer, wondrous blue chips that comprised the so-called Nifty Fifty. These were established brand names: Avon, Polaroid, Gillette, Coca-Cola, IBM, Xerox, McDonald's, and others. During the first half of the twentieth century, the economy

Original Nifty Fifty[a]

Company	Stock Price[b]	P/E Ratio
Polaroid	$ 63	97
Simplicity Pattern	54	50
Disney	6.50	82
Avon Products	68	63
ITT	60	16
Schlitz Brewing	58	37
Xerox	50	47
Hueblein, Inc.	58	31
Coca-Cola	3	44
McDonald's	3.75	75
JCPenney	22.50	31
Gillette	4	25
American Express	16	38
Sears	58	29
Chesebrough-Ponds	44	40
Eastman Kodak	66	44
Anheuser-Busch	4.50	33
Kmart Corp.	16	49
General Electric	9	25
PepsiCo	1.60	27
IBM	80	36
American Hospital Supply	33	50
3M	21	40
Squibb	26	34
Louisiana Land and Exploration	48	25
Digital Equipment	15	61
AMP Inc.	7	47
Emery Air Freight	30	55
International Flavors and Fragrances	14	72
Black & Decker	36	51
Baxter International	14	73
Johnson & Johnson	5.40	60
Revlon	36	25
Burroughs	37	46
Bristol-Myers	4.30	27
Procter & Gamble	14	33
Citicorp	19	21

Original Nifty Fifty[a] (Continued)

Company	Stock Price[b]	P/E Ratio
Texas Instruments	15	42
Merck	5	45
Schering-Plough	8.50	48
Pfizer	5	28
Upjohn	7	41
Philip Morris	4	25
American Home Products	10	38
Eli Lilly	10	43
Lubrizol	11	34
Halliburton	23	37
Dow Chemical	17	25
Schlumberger	12	46
MGIC Investment	N/A	
Average P/E	$42.7	

Source: Montgomery Securities.
[a] As of December 31, 1972.
[b] Rounded to nearest whole number.

lurched from boom to bust, and people didn't expect companies to provide steady, consistent profit growth. Starting in the 1940s, the busts were less busty, and owning growth companies became fashionable. By the early 1970s, it had become wildly fashionable. At their priciest, many Nifties sold for 40 to 50 and a few higher than 70 times earnings, but the Street's analysts pronounced these "one-decision stocks" worth owning at any price. They were applauded by analysts, who touted the group as fast growers for the long haul, and much less risky than the fly-by-nights in the computer arena. Buy them, forget them, and in a few years, whatever you paid, you'll be glad you paid it.

CHAPTER 13

THE WORST DECLINE SINCE 1929

SHELBY FELT A CERTAIN LIBERATION WHEN THE ambassadorial absence took his father more than 3,000 miles away from Wall Street. From Bern, Davis sent him letters with the latest news on the insurance front. Shelby didn't bother to answer. As usual, father-son relations were more dutiful than enthusiastic, though Shelby visited his parents on an annual ski trip to Switzerland. They took a ride through the countryside together. Davis brought a picnic lunch: a few rolls he'd squirreled away from a restaurant car on a train.

Meanwhile, Davis's friend and fellow Nippophile, James Rosenwald, gave a prescient spiel to a gathering of security analysts at San Francisco's St. Francis Hotel in May 1972. Too bad more people didn't act on his message: Flee U.S. stocks and buy the Japanese version. The U.S. version had rallied into 1972, recovering nearly all the ground lost during the 1969 to 1970 retreat. Optimists assumed the worst was over. Rosenwald disagreed, and offered an exit strategy. The theme of his lecture was "The U.S. Market Isn't the Only Game in Town."

176

He began by describing the malaise in the Dow. Only nine of its 30 companies had made new highs in the rebound. The biggest losers in the group—Alcoa, International Paper, Bethlehem Steel, and U.S. Steel—sold for lower prices than they'd fetched in the 1950s. Shares in AT&T, Texaco, General Motors, DuPont, Union Carbide, and Standard Oil—some of the other notable laggards—were worth less in the early 1970s than in the mid-1960s.

"Who in this room," Rosenwald challenged, "doesn't remember the bullish articles written on DuPont at 261 (now 164), General Motors at 114 (now 77), or U.S. Steel at 108 (now 32)? When we talk about beating the averages (meaning the Dow), aren't we really talking about beating a former world champion who happens to be 100 years old and in a wheelchair?"

"It has more than once occurred to me," he continued, "that a sign should be posted over the entrance to the New York Stock Exchange: 'Abandon hope all ye who enter here.'" From this demoralizing recap, Rosenwald went on to explain how labor had hobbled U.S. companies: Striking steelworkers had won fat contracts that were paid for with sticker shock in the auto showrooms. Detroit priced itself out of the car market, and the Japanese attacked with lower prices and higher quality. Union resistance made it harder for Detroit to modernize its plants by switching to Japanese-style computer-guided assembly lines. Without spending billions, U.S. steelmakers had no hope of competing with their modernized Japanese competitors.

Rosenwald had toyed with the idea of advising clients to bear-proof their portfolios by investing in U.S. multinationals (he was ahead of his time with this suggestion), but he rejected the strategy as problematic. With unions pressuring the government to keep jobs at home, who knew what pernicious tax might be levied on profits made abroad? Beyond U.S.

borders, multinationals faced the constant threat of having their factories confiscated by anticapitalist regimes. A less risky way to invest globally, Rosenwald concluded, was to buy shares in non-U.S. companies, as he and Davis already had done in Japan.

On the domestic front, Rosenwald expected Washington to continue its big spending and predicted that inflation would rise accordingly. He doubted the government would impose price-and-wage controls or take other drastic measures to avert higher prices. Given these unfavorable portents, Rosenwald urged his audience to take a leave of absence from U.S. equities, and buy Japanese equities.

The Toyko Dow had more than doubled, from 1,400 to 3,400, in the decade since Rosenwald and Davis had invested in Japan. During that period, a sizable crowd of Americans had done the same, helping to cause foreign ownership of Japanese stocks to jump from $185 million to $3.9 billion. Notwithstanding the impressive gains to date, Rosenwald predicted that the biggest advances were yet to come. Japan was emerging from a long recession. It did a lively export business. In spite of the nuclear umbrella held over its head by China, Japan had extended its influence into Communist Asia. Its auto companies were outsmarting Detroit, and its TV manufacturers were poised to do the same.

With stocks on the rise in the United States, neither pundits nor the public shared Rosenwald's somber forecast. The high-profile marketeers on the *Barron's* annual roundtable were bullish. Bears already had struck twice, in 1966 and 1969. That they wouldn't strike three times in six years was a popular illusion about to be dispelled. The third strike did the most damage. This 1973 to 1974 rout was the worst decline since 1929 to 1932. We've labeled that bygone sell-off, with its intervening rally, Bear I. The entire period from the late 1960s down to the 1974 bottom can be labeled Bear II.

There were several catalysts. The Vietnam War lingered. Nixon's dirty tricksters were caught bugging the Democrats, and the President was captured on tape subverting justice. With impeachment proceedings in full swing, he was forced to resign. The Israelis clashed with Arabs in the Yom Kippur War, and the Arabs' oil cartel called an embargo, which pushed the price from $6 to $23 a barrel. Queues of nervous drivers waited to fill their gas tanks at quadruple the pre-embargo price.

Beyond the political negatives, stocks were undermined by the sagging dollar, which rapidly lost favor abroad. Since the late 1940s, the dollar had played the role of the world's most reliable currency. By the early 1970s, the government had subverted its appeal with an overactive printing press. With the money supply up nearly 60 percent from 1959 to 1971, consumer prices had risen 40 percent. U.S. trading partners lost their appetite for Uncle Sam's money and demanded gold as payment. Facing a run on the national gold cache, the Nixon Administration "devalued" the greenback. As public debt expanded, corporate profits declined. Inflation stirred, then exploded.

Stocks were not priced to reflect so many problems—in fact, they weren't priced to reflect *any* problems. After its quick recovery from the two prior declines, the S&P 400 peaked in 1973 at a utopian 30 times earnings. Companies in that index, however, paid a stingy collective dividend of less than 2.5 percent. Earnings were looted by inflation. In fact, when inflation is added to the equation, from 1968 to 1982, the real return on stocks (judging by the S&P index) was negative. The stock-holding masses had shrugged off the rising inflation of the 1960s on the theory that inflation was ruinous to bonds, but healthy for equities. For years, the steady inflationary uptick hadn't stopped the bull market, strengthening the popular conviction that inflation was no threat to portfolios. The assumption that companies could raise prices in lockstep with

179

inflation, and thus preserve their profit margin, proved fallacious in the 1970s, and once Mr. Market realized this, equities were repriced accordingly.

The Street capitulated. A skittish Biggs convinced Shelby that they should lighten up on stocks before the bears launched a third attack. Venture moved 30 percent of its assets into cash. As a rule, attempted timing is a chump's gambit, and Shelby never tried it again. Here, it saved the fund because, without it, Venture might have perished in the pecuniary apocalypse that began in January 1973 and ended in December 1974.

A large contingent of victims, from the 1969 to 1970 warm-up to this stunning finale, had taken what was left from their high-tech wagers and redeployed the proceeds into the fail-safe, blue-chip Nifty Fifty group. The "buy Nifties" strategy came undone almost as soon as Main Street adopted it. Shareholders who went to sleep with Polaroid, Disney, or Avon in their portfolios woke up to a wealth-wrecking nightmare—a 79–85 percent decline from peak to trough. The top 20 losers in the average stock in Nifty Fifty dropped 50 to 85 percent. Investors who paid Tiffany rates (for instance, a 75 multiple for McDonald's growth in 1973) suddenly were unloading shares at Woolworth rates (McDonald's growth now fetched an 18 multiple, shrinking the stock price by 61 percent). There was nothing wrong with McDonald's, the enterprise; the valuation was the rub. Similarly, the profits mounted at Ross Perot's EDS. It wasn't a Nifty, but that stock couldn't support its 500 multiple and shrunk from $40 to $3. Multiple contraction took Avon down from $68 to $14, Polaroid from $63 to $9, and Xerox from $50 to $17.

At the 1974 bottom, the entire Dow was selling for six times earnings. Investors didn't have to look hard to find excellent companies stacked up in this thrift shop. The same S&P 400 that had fetched 30 times earnings a few months

Fallout from the Nifty Fifty

Company	Stock Price 12/31/72	P/E Ratio	Stock Price 12/31/74	P/E Ratio	Change in Price
Polaroid	$ 63	97	$ 9	22	−85%
Simplicity Pattern	54	50	9	15	−83
Disney	6.50	82	1.25	14	−81
Avon Products	68	63	14	14	−79
ITT	60	16	14	4	−75.5
Schlitz Brewing	58	37	15	9	−75
Xerox	50	47	17	12	−65
Hueblein, Inc.	58	31	20	8	−65
Coca-Cola	3	44	1	16	−64
McDonald's	3.75	75	1.40	18	−61
JCPenney	22.50	31	9	17	−60
Gillette	4	25	1.60	9	−60
American Express	16	38	6.50	12	−60
Sears	58	29	24	15	−58
Chesebrough-Ponds	44	40	18	13	−58
Eastman Kodak	66	44	28	16	−58
Anheuser-Busch	4.50	33	2	17	−57
Kmart Corp.	16	49	7	25	−55
General Electric	9	25	4	10	−54
PepsiCo	1.60	27	.75	11	−53
IBM	80	36	42	13	−48
American Hospital Supply	33	50	17	20	−47
3M	21	40	11	17	−46
Squibb	26	34	14	14	−46
Louisiana Land and Exploration	48	25	24	8	−45
Digital Equipment	15	61	8	13	−45
AMP Inc.	7	47	4	19	−44
Emery Air Freight	20	55	16	21	−44
International Flavors and Fragrances	14	72	8	28	−43
Black & Decker	36	51	21	19	−42

(continued)

Fallout from the Nifty Fifty (Continued)

Company	Stock Price 12/31/72	P/E Ratio	Stock Price 12/31/74	P/E Ratio	Change in Price
Baxter International	14	73	9	27	−39
Johnson & Johnson	5.40	60	3	28	−38
Revlon	36	25	24	13	−35
Burroughs	37	46	25	21	−31
Bristol-Myers	4.30	27	3	13	−27
Procter & Gamble	14	33	10	21	−26
Citicorp	19	21	14	11	−26
Texas Instruments	15	42	11	17	−25
Merck	5	45	3.60	23	−25
Schering-Plough	8.50	48	6.50	22	−23
Pfizer	5	28	4	17	−23
Upjohn	7	41	5.80	22	−21
Philip Morris	3.70	25	3	15	−19
American Home Products	10	38	8.30	23	−18
Eli Lilly	10	43	8.50	27	−15
Lubrizol	11	34	9.80	16	−13
Halliburton	23	37	22	18	−2
Dow Chemical	17	25	18	9	8.3
Schlumberger	12	46	14	27	19
MGIC Investment	N/A				
Average P/E	$42.7			16.76	−43.6

Source: Montgomery Securities.

earlier now fetched a disparaging 7.5 times. The sweetener for the deal was a 5 percent dividend. The Dow, which had flirted with 1000, settled in at a wallflower's 570. "Be fearful when others are greedy, and greedy when others are fearful," Warren Buffett had advised. In 1974, fear was in oversupply. The President resigned in disgrace, the economy fell into recession, and inflation continued apace. The novel predicament of rising prices in a sluggish economy confounded economists. They called it "stagflation." While consumers delayed big purchases, their cash was losing buying power by the day. Headlines in the 1974 business pages ran from negative to ghoulish: "Whistling Past the Graveyard" (*Business Week*), "Why Buy Stocks?" (*Forbes*), "The Sickening Slide" (*Barron's*), "Running Scared" (*Forbes*), "The Gloom is Deepening" (*Fortune*).

The best investment on Wall Street during this period was the lowly money market fund. It had been invented just in time to be put to good use. To compete with the money market, banks and S&Ls offered competitive rates on savings accounts. For decades, the savers of America were shortchanged on their passbooks when all banks were obligated to offer the same low interest rates. Now, they were liberated.

There were flops in the Venture Fund. Its shareholders lost 20 percent in 1970, 1973, and 1974. Pioneers who had bought at the outset and held on for five years had zilch to show for their loyalty. Cash hidden under a mattress provided a far superior return. With $50 million in assets, Venture was a minor irritant to the Bullock group that owned it. Otherwise, Bullock might have disbanded the fund or fired Shelby and his bear-battered colleagues. Chris Davis was age 8 during this crisis. He remembers that it was a tense time for his father. "There was a graph Dad clipped from a newspaper, framed, and hung on the wall. It showed the Dow Jones average heading down a steep slope. Over the graph, someone had scrawled: "Screw the Dow Jones."

In 1974, as the bears finished mauling the market, Shelby flew to La Jolla, California, to talk to Ben Graham, Buffett's teacher and a major influence on Davis. Graham was living with his mistress in an ample but modest apartment overlooking the Pacific. He'd just celebrated his 80th birthday. At a party thrown by friends, he gave a speech about beauty and the meaning of life, never mentioning balance sheets, price-earnings ratios, or book value.[1]

On weekdays, Graham sat in his broker's office in La Jolla, reading the latest analyst reports from Standard & Poor's. He hadn't divorced stocks entirely (unfortunately, he still owned GEICO; see Chapter 14) but he had cut back before the markdown. In the late 1960s, he had warned whoever would listen that stocks were overpriced and should be avoided. Bullish critics dismissed him as a fuddy-duddy—a pecuniary killjoy who was too busy checking pricetags to notice the crowds of customers who continued to take home the merchandise. The back-to-back bear markets of 1969 to 1970 and 1973 to 1974 proved Graham right and brought bargains back to Wall Street. In typical fashion, eager buyers in the extravagant phase avoided buying in the bargain phase. Prevailing opinion was so negative that even Shelby was discouraged.

"Don't despair," Graham told Shelby over a pot of tea in his apartment. "Sonny boy, you're looking at one of the great buying opportunities of your generation. Do your homework." Graham left Shelby with a misguided stock tip: Buy GEICO. Fortunately for Venture investors, Shelby didn't listen.

The big sell-off was the latest proof that trendy growth companies can be hazardous to wealth. Popular can't-miss propositions, many of America's most reputable enterprises, were Nifty Fifty casualties. Shelby surveyed the wreckage and revamped his strategy. From this point forward, he would shun high-priced fast growers and embrace lower-priced moderate growers. Companies that were nobody's darlings when stock prices rose, he decided, were less likely to disappoint when the market fell. Why risk a pole vault when you could take the stairs?

Table 13.1 illustrates the advantages of investing in low-key companies that can deliver steady, if unspectacular earnings at a modest price. Under "High Expectations," we see what can happen to a spectacular earner with a hefty price tag. This company puts together an impressive five-year run,

Table 13.1 High versus Low Expectations

High Expectations

A 30 Percent Grower for Five Years becomes a 15 Percent Thereafter

	1994	1995	1996	1997	1998	1999
Earnings	$0.75	$1.00	$1.30	$1.69	$2.10	$2.52
P/E	30×	30×	30×	30×	30×	15×
Price		$ 30				$ 38

Result: Stock Price Goes from $30 to $38
Performance: A 6.7 Percent Annual Return on Investment

Low Expectations

A 13 Percent Grower Selling at 10 × Earnings for Five Years Finally Sells at 13 × Earnings

	1994	1995	1996	1997	1998	1999
Earnings	$0.88	$1.00	$1.13	$1.28	$1.44	$1.63
P/E	10×	10×	10×	10×	10×	13×
Price		$ 10				$ 21

Result: Stock Price Goes from $10 to $21
Performance: A 20 Percent Annual Return on Investment
"The Davis Double Play"

increasing its profits 30 percent per year over the stretch. Then, in the sixth year, the profits increase only 15 percent. Investors are somewhat disenchanted and begin to pay only 15 times earnings for the stock. The company was very successful, but the shareholders who paid $30 five years earlier, left with a $38 asset and a subpar return on their investment.

Under "Low Expectations," we've got a more mundane enterprise that increases its profits 13 percent per year, which bores Wall Street and causes investors to pay only 10 times earnings to own this stock. Then, after six years of watching the company live up to modest expectations, investors are inclined to up the ante and pay 13 times earnings for the shares.

185

Now, shareholders who paid $10 five years earlier are left with a $21 asset, doubling their money in a Davis double play.

Their first tussle with failure also taught Shelby and Biggs to sell quickly whenever there was reason to believe a company's earnings would falter. "You tended not to want to believe it," Biggs said, "but if you waited until a decline in earnings was a matter of public record, it was too late to sell. The price had already collapsed." As the economy fell into recession, Shelby and Biggs abandoned their tech wrecks and replaced them with reliable names like Philip Morris and Capital Cities broadcasting. They figured cigarettes and TV stations would fare well in a weak economy and would attract investors who'd also had it with go-go. "While you work your way through a recession and a market slump," said Biggs, "some dark old blue-chip Dow Jones kind of company can do very well, over a relatively short period of time, and have a better short-term earnings outlook than a Digital or a Memorex or Mohawk."

On the rebound, Shelby became a "counter puncher." He bought shares after temporary bad news about an attractive company had depressed the price. He looked for chances to grab predictable earnings at a discount–the opposite of the strategy that had gotten him into trouble. On the other hand, in the aftermath of Bear II, he saw it was dangerous to buy stocks just because they were cheap. He came to realize that many cheap stocks deserved to be cheap because they were attached to mediocre enterprises. He forced himself not to be swayed by an attractive price tag, and to fully inspect all gift horses. Like his father, he fancied himself as a part owner of every holding in the portfolio. He refused to buy "obsolescence" or to traffic in fads. He kept the Venture fund free from coffee bars, discount retailers, or high-tech hopefuls whose survival hung on a single gizmo or gadget. He studied management as much as he studied numbers. "If something goes wrong," he said, "you want to know the people." Strong balance sheets and strong leadership helped him sleep at night.

"Money never becomes obsolete" became one of Shelby's mottoes. Banks, brokerage houses, and other players in the money business wouldn't wake up one day to discover money was obsolete, the way high-tech companies wake up to find that their most profitable inventions have been trumped by somebody else's invention. He increased his holdings in banks and insurance, and reduced his exposure to retail and electronics. A well-managed retailer may thrive for a generation and then face extinction in spite of its best efforts, he reasoned, but it's hard to destroy a well-managed bank.

He also bought shares in natural resource companies. Here, Shelby applied theme investing, something he'd come to appreciate when he studied industry groups at the Bank of New York. In the mid-1970s, the obvious theme was rising inflation, which favored oil, mining, forestry products, and other hard assets. By sticking to the resource theme and looking for not-so-hot stocks and modest growers that produced occasional double plays, Shelby made Venture a consistent top performer. He kept the downside to a minimum. He cut the portfolio's annual turnover to a sleepy 15 percent per year, while the standard mutual fund replaced its holdings at a 90 percent clip. Less buying and selling meant lower taxes and lower transaction costs. Many companies, as well as the U.S. Government itself, wallowed in deep debt, and rising interest rates made debts harder to pay. Aware that rising rates threatened to put debtors out of business, Shelby vowed never to subject his fund to companies with debt problems.

More lessons were learned as Venture adapted. On the rebound off the 1974 bottom, small stocks outran their more seasoned brand-name counterparts. This is where Shelby distinguished himself, along with another young fund manager, Peter Lynch. Both avoided the fallen Nifties because, after bear markets, companies that fall the most are often slow to rise. They filled their portfolios with lesser names that offered better prospects. For the next nine years, small stocks continued to outperform the rest. Though 1975 to 1980 was not a bull market era (averages were going nowhere), a nimble stock picker could triumph, and Shelby did.

Near the end of 1976, the already beaten-up Nifties took another beating. After Disney shares were marked down from $5.50 to $1 in 1974, bargain hunters came to the rescue and pushed the price to $3. Two years after that, profit takers drove it down 33 percent to $2. This was a great buying point. The entertainment giant sold for 10 times earnings as it continued to expand.

Cheap steel imports, galloping interest rates, and a weak dollar (even the Mexican peso rose against it!) continued to pester the Dow and the other blue chips. Small stocks were undeterred and rose to new highs in 1977. To make money in this period, you had to think small. Wall Street itself was having internal problems. In 1975, the SEC did away with fixed commissions on stock trades. Like banks, brokerage firms in the belly of free enterprise had been granted a long-standing exemption from free market competition, and commission rates were set high enough to guarantee a continuous and ample profit. Now the gravy train was upended; the fix was off, the cost of trading dropped fast, and brokers and investment houses lost a reliable source of easy money.

Davis's brokerage operations were marginal to begin with, but he responded by closing all six one-man offices he'd established in major cities such as Cleveland, London, and San Francisco. These offices had never cost him anything— the emissaries he installed paid their own overhead and made a living on their commissions when they were able to persuade clients to buy insurance stocks through Davis. Now, their reduced commissions weren't enough to keep them interested. In the lingering malaise on Wall Street, seats on the NYSE could be had for $35,000, only $2,000 more than Davis had paid 30 years earlier.

An original share in New York Venture, bought for $10.64 in 1969, was worth $14.64 by mid-1978. In a bull market, a 43 percent increase over nine years wouldn't deserve mention, but in the stingy market of the 1970s, it deserved a standing ovation. The S&P 500 index, a proxy for the average stock, was down 1.7 percent over the same stretch.

The Dow had bottomed at 577 in 1974, then promptly soared to 1014 by the end of 1976, but could never mount a consistent advance. It rose and fell between 740 and 1000 for the balance of the decade. By 1981, it had regressed to 742, a level it had first reached in 1961.

While the economy flourished during the 1970s, corporate profits were hampered by inflation, which the government fought to no avail. The Ford White House ran a fanciful anti-inflation campaign, handing out Whip Inflation Now (WIN) buttons, which foiled inflation about as much as Nancy Reagan's "Just Say No" campaign foiled drug traffickers a decade later. Prices for everything continued to rise—even the WIN buttons were bid up by collectors. In theory, companies pass along their higher costs to their customers; in practice, they couldn't raise prices fast enough to counteract the price increases their suppliers were charging them. In 1976, gold bugs thrived as $35-per-ounce gold became $100 per ounce and climbed to $700 per ounce by 1979. Powerful Chrysler required a government bailout, Paul Volcker became Fed chairman, and Iranian zealots seized the U.S. Embassy in Tehran and took hostages.

Davis, Palmer, and Biggs had sold their money-management company to Fiduciary Trust in January 1978. Shelby and

Palmer favored the sale; Biggs was opposed but he went along with it. They'd all witnessed the ruination of many secondary firms like theirs, and though they'd attracted $650 million in clients' money, there was no guarantee that the owners of the money would stick with them. The three musketeers had grappled with the "harsh realities" of competing against Wall Street's bigger names. Fiduciary paid an attractive price, gave the trio a lucrative five-year employment contract, and made them all vice presidents and multimillionaires.

There were several snags and delays in the deal, which took several months to close. According to Shelby, Palmer expected to be named president of Fiduciary, and as soon as he realized it wouldn't happen, he bolted Fiduciary for the General Motors pension fund. His premature exit rankled Shelby and Biggs. Both were slated to earn bonuses if their clients stuck with the firm after the Fiduciary takeover, but that was less likely with the defection of Palmer, who handled customer relations.

The orphan in this merger was New York Venture, about to celebrate its tenth anniversary. Legal constraints kept Fiduciary from acquiring the mutual fund, but the musketeers were allowed to continue to operate the fund only as a side business. Martin Proyect, who'd convinced Hugh Bullock to launch Venture in the first place, was majority shareholder in the side business, and Shelby and Biggs were minority partners. Shelby was delighted that Venture had survived. Biggs left the stock picking to Shelby, who was now free to operate without other voices in his head. He celebrated by adding to his schedule more visits to companies and meetings with CEOs.

No longer formal collaborators, Shelby and Biggs took a corner office together at Fiduciary headquarters on the 97th floor of the World Trade Center. The bronze nameplates on their desks ("Mr. Biggs" and "Mr. Davis") looked like they belonged in a countinghouse in a Dickens novel. Both

190

nameplates were mementoes from the Bank of New York, where Shelby had served his apprenticeship and Biggs's father was a prominent vice chairman and chief investment officer. The Venture collaborators lunched together, pondered the markets together, and often spent weekends together. "Our marriage," said Biggs of his friendship with Shelby, "has lasted through two wives apiece."

CHAPTER 14

DAVIS ON
THE REBOUND

DAVIS HAD RETURNED TO AMERICA IN 1975 with Kathryn in tow. They landed in Hartford and headed for the nearest soda fountain—what they'd missed most in six years in Switzerland was milkshakes. The Tarrytown house, Davis's investment firm, and his portfolio all had seen better days. The house suffered a fire and a succession of careless tenants; the firm, such as it was, suffered a reduction in commission revenue that followed the SEC's Mayday edict; the portfolio suffered the twin bear markets of 1969 to 1970 and 1973 to 1974.

When he arrived in Switzerland in 1969, the ambassador's net worth hovered around $50 million. Six years later, he returned to the United States $30 million poorer. His stocks had failed him, as they had failed everybody in the bear market of 1973 to 1974. The caretaker of his portfolio, Ken Ebbitt, had presided over the wreckage in his absence, but Davis didn't blame his stand-in for the market's mischief. Even if Ebbitt had advised Davis to sell, it's unlikely his boss would have listened.

Absorbed in his ambassadorship, a night of jet lag away from Wall Street, Davis was spared the remorse and second-guessing of active investors who'd kept track of their plummeting net worth in the daily stock tables or on their Quotrons. Insurance didn't hold up well in this pecuniary quicksand. In fact, many insurers were mired deeper than the typical manufacturer in the S&P index. Figure 14.1 is a graph of property-casualty (provided here by the Securities Research Company) and shows that group down from $150 to $60. Life and health insurers (Figure 14.2) went down from $280 to $120 before Wall Street found a bottom. These graphs are based on only a handful of companies, so they're not fully representative of the insurance group as a whole. Still, these declines were typical for the period.

Some insurers turned a market problem into a fundamental problem via managerial bungling. USF&G, a stalwart with a two-century pedigree, pulled off a triple bungle. By investing in bonds and cash in the early 1960s, its operatives missed the run-up in stocks. To correct this error, they scuttled caution and moved into stocks just in time for the 1973 to 1974 bear market. Near the bottom in 1974, they panicked, dumped their losing equities, and bought bonds. Stocks went up and bonds were trampled in the inflationary breakout.

Equivalent mistakes, not in the portfolio but in the underwriting department, left the Government Employees Insurance Corporation (GEICO) a few bucks away from being the biggest insurance failure in history. The near collapse of the great GEICO was a powerful reminder that no company was foolproof. Of the thousands of choices in the firmament of equities, GEICO had attracted Davis and Buffett, plus their guru, Ben Graham. All three value nabobs owned a heap of shares. All three admired GEICO's no-frills approach to auto coverage. Graham, who had introduced Buffett to this sure bet in his class at Columbia University in the ancient

Figure 14.1 Insurance (Property–Casualty) (SPC.I). Used by permission of Securities Research Company.

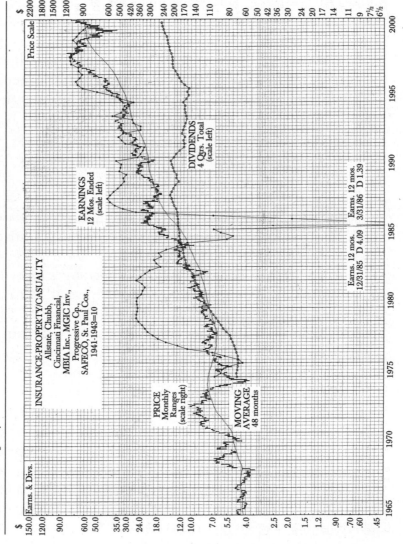

Figure 14.2 Insurance (Life/Health) (SLI.I). Used by permission of Securities Research Company.

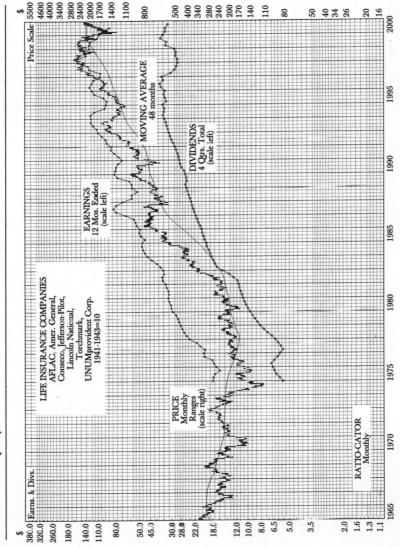

1950s, marveled at GEICO's return on equity, which he called a "sight to behold." At one point, the celebrated author/professor had served as company chairman.

GEICO was a Texas brainstorm from the 1930s. Its creator, Leo Goodwin, added two brilliant features that distinguished this auto insurer from the white bread version. GEICO sold policies by mail, cutting out the expensive sales brigade. It only sold to government geeks. Goodwin once read a study that showed federal, state, and local bureaucrats caused fewer car wrecks than blue-collar or corporate types. A bureaucrat might be boring as a date, but he or she was a dreamy client for an insurance company.

Lower expenses and fewer accident claims formed a winning combination for GEICO. Ben Graham figured this out and bought half-ownership in the company in 1947. GEICO soon went public, so anybody could buy the stock by 1951, the year Buffett got interested in it. One Saturday that year, Graham's star pupil hopped a train from New York to Washington to behold GEICO in person. Finding the place locked, Buffett banged the door and roused the janitor. The 23-year-old grad student talked his way around the janitor and into a four-hour interview with the CEO.

As Buffett discovered during his visit, GEICO's profit margin was five times that of the average insurer, and profits were rising fast. Wall Street analysts rated GEICO overpriced; Buffett disagreed. That he was a mere student disputing seasoned professionals didn't sway his opinion. "You are neither right nor wrong because the crowd disagrees with you," Graham had taught.

Buffett even rejected Graham's advice to wait and be able to buy GEICO for less. (The market had enjoyed a snappy advance, and Graham expected a retreat.) The tyro from Omaha bought immediately, sinking most of his savings ($10,000) into this appealing find. The market and GEICO moved higher. In 1952, Buffett sold too soon and booked his 50 percent profit. For several years thereafter, GEICO continued to rise twice as fast as the S&P 500. Davis was 52 when he discovered GEICO in the early 1960s. His research led him to the same lode Buffett and Graham had already worked. Davis was impressed with GEICO's ability to pay claims out of customers' premiums, leaving the investment portfolio untapped.

With its investments merrily compounding, GEICO was a cash cow on speed, and Davis took a sizable chunk of the ownership. GEICO put him on the board. Then came the 1970s, when fast cars, generous juries, and fraudulent claims bedeviled the most reliable earner in the industry. The U.S. population had never been younger, and teenage drivers swarmed the roads. Extra horsepower and flashy fins encouraged reckless hijinks. "Severity"—the industry code word for accident rate—was on the rise. More than it had in the late 1960s, inflation jacked the cost of rehabilitating cars and accident victims. Juries were more generous than ever, and turning stiff necks into lawsuits became a lucrative pastime.

Insurers staggered through a blizzard of dubious awards. CEO Ralph Peck picked the worst time in company history to relax its rules and sell policies to nonbureaucrats. These newer, more exciting customers caused more expensive wrecks, catching GEICO with its claims up and its reserves down. Through 1974 to 1975, the company lied about its problems to the press and to its own board, including Davis. An outside auditor hired by the board delivered the bad news. Claims on assets exceeded assets. The company announced a staggering $126 million loss for 1975. After hitting a high of $42, the stock took a 90 percent header, landing at $4.80.

As the biggest shareholder, Davis was the biggest loser. Ben Graham wasn't far behind. Now in his eighties and splitting his time between California and France, Graham had the largest chunk of his life savings wrapped up in this sinking enterprise. Davis had returned from his ambassadorship in mid-crisis. In 1976, more than 400 angry shareholders jeered company officials at a meeting held at Washington's Statler Hilton. A month later, Peck was ousted. Davis was on the search committee that picked a replacement: Jack Byrne, a veteran of Travelers. Byrne quickly shut down 100 GEICO offices and dismissed half the payroll. Still, the company teetered on the edge of bankruptcy, and the stock took another dive, to $2.

An acquaintance of Byrne's, *Washington Post* publisher Kay Graham (no relation to Ben Graham) called with a mysterious offer. If Byrne was amenable, she said, an unnamed friend of hers was willing to volunteer expert advice. Byrne declined until somebody suggested the mystery adviser might be Buffett, Graham's business partner at the newspaper. Byrne rang Graham back, and they set a date to meet at Graham's house. When Byrne came through the door, Buffett was already in the living room. The ex-GEICO shareholder and the new CEO blathered into the night. Buffett wanted to know whether GEICO was still a low-cost operator; Byrne said it was. Byrne insisted that if the company survived, its legendary profitability would return. Based on these assurances, Buffett bought 500,000 shares at $2⅛ and left a standing order to buy millions more. Meanwhile, he urged Byrne to raise more capital. Byrne accomplished that by selling 27 million new shares (18 million of the common variety plus 9 million "preferreds" that paid an attractive dividend).

The Buffett-Byrne bailout plan polarized the board. Davis opposed the stock sale on the grounds that an oversupply of new shares would "dilute" future profits and depress the future stock price, to the shareholders' detriment. Hank Greenberg, the cantankerous chairman of AIG (shares of which Davis owned in vast quantities), wanted to save GEICO first and sweat the details later. Who cared about dilution, he argued, if there was nothing left to dilute? After a raucous tête-à-tête, Davis stormed out of the meeting, returned to his office, and promptly sold his entire GEICO stake. By then, the price had quadrupled from $2 to $8, thanks in large measure to Buffett's heavy buying. Customarily, Davis never let his emotions sway his investing, but this time he was too angry to admire GEICO's future profitability and Buffett's million-dollar vote of confidence. To the end of his life, Davis regretted selling.

A few months into the Buffett-Byrne bailout, the company bought back some of the shares Byrne had issued to raise emergency cash. The buyback was solid evidence that GEICO had survived the worst. Davis called Byrne. "Jack," he said, "if I'd known you were going to reverse the dilution, I wouldn't have sold."

All along, Davis was free to make a new investment in GEICO, but he could never bring himself to do it. Graham died in Aix-en-Provence, France, at age 82, when GEICO's recovery was still in doubt.

In a separate transaction, Byrne tried to capture all the shares of a GEICO subsidiary—the Government Employees Life Insurance Company (GELICO). Unlike its parent company, GELICO never lived up to its promise. During the GEICO crisis, Byrne invited Shelby to sit on the GELICO board, after Davis had resigned the GEICO board. Byrne knew Shelby was a talented investor in his own right, and by involving Shelby in GELICO, Byrne hoped to remain in the family's graces.

Davis opposed the GELICO buyout as vehemently as he'd opposed the GEICO deal. The sticking point was price. Byrne offered $13 a share; Davis demanded $21 for his stock and never budged. Soon enough, the Byrne proposal was scrapped, and a British life insurance company acquired GELICO for $32 a share. Shelby helped negotiate this lucrative sale, and his father profited from his holdout. Davis had correctly predicted hard times for auto and casualty–though not necessarily GEICO–at the start of the decade. "Insurance is in a down cycle," he'd told Shelby. Yet, given Davis's appetite for margin, his 60 percent loss (from $50 million to $20 million) was well contained. Without Japan and without changing the mix in his portfolio, 1973 to 1974 might have wiped him out.

He held onto the life insurers and the Japanese holdings that were his biggest winners in the bull market, but he jettisoned some of his U.S. casualty and auto insurers. He upped his stake in AIG, the global insurance conglomerate he'd discovered in Japan. The company was multifaceted, creative, international, and parsimonious, just like its autocratic CEO, Hank Greenberg, who lived on a fraction of his wherewithal. Davis's AIG stake had already increased through AIG acquisitions. Every time Greenberg bought a mom-and-pop insurer Davis already owned, Davis got more AIG stock.

Neither the GEICO squabble nor his losses put a slump in Davis's work habits. He attacked his job with his usual gusto, arriving early and leaving late with his briefcase crammed with reports. In the small conference room down the hall from his office, he decked the walls with political photos and ambassadorial memorabilia. A hand-painted scroll celebrated his induction into the Baronial Order of the Magna Carta, a social club with a 750-year life span. He would eventually receive the Order's annual award, earlier bestowed on three ex-presidents (Hoover, Eisenhower, Nixon), and two famous generals (MacArthur, Omar Bradley). Hand-painted scrolls (including one souvenir of a blimp ride, the "Diplome D'Ascension En Dirigeable") shared wall space with handshake photos with Ronald Reagan and Gerald Ford.

He liked people to address him as "Ambassador." Kathryn, a minimalist when it came to jewelry, wore a gold pin issued to ambassador's wives. "It wasn't expensive," she recalled, "but it was the most expensive piece anybody ever gave me."

Why shouldn't Davis be enthusiastic? Stocks were cheap in 1976. Didn't Warren Buffett say he felt like an oversexed teenager at a dance hall? Bargains were as prevalent as when Davis began to invest a generation earlier. In June 1975, he wrote a special report to his newsletter subscribers, in case somebody bothered to read it: "The biggest improvement in fire-casualty earnings since the end of inflation after World War II lies ahead . . . interest in fire-casualty issues could well rckindle interest in life insurance stocks."

CHAPTER 15

SHELBY BUYS BANKS–DAVIS BUYS EVERYTHING

I N THE LATE INNINGS OF HIS INVESTMENT career, Davis strayed from his favorite industry and started buying everything. His new scatter-shot strategy baffled friends and family. They'd have been less surprised to see him join a Harley club and do wheelies on the lawn.

They date this curious development to Davis's being named to the board of Value Line, the research outfit that tracks nearly 2,000 stocks and rates them on timeliness, safety, and climbing ability. Value Line research was collected in a loose-leaf binder the size of the white pages in a metropolitan area phone book, and was updated monthly. Value Line was a popular item in local libraries, and the gamut of investors, from Joe Stockpick to Warren Buffett, relied on it. Buffett often raved about it.

Davis began to study Value Line in earnest. Instead of lugging around piles of annual reports and analysts' commentary, he could get all the pertinent data from this remarkable resource. Many excellent companies sported attractive price tags. He couldn't resist owning them all, especially the ones that got Value Line's top ranking: "1."

Many CEOs he had befriended had retired, and he didn't necessarily trust the information he got from secondary sources in investor relations departments. Sensing he was out of the loop, and lacking the confidence to make big bets, he made hundreds of small bets. For three decades, his portfolio had contained only 30 to 50 names; now, the roster grew into the hundreds. Even with Value Line's convenient reports, he exhausted himself keeping up with the latest data. His family suspected his investigative frenzy was an attempt to avoid facing the prospect of physical decline. Also, with his brokerage business all but defunct, he couldn't tolerate paying his in-house stock trader who had nothing to trade. His constant buying gave the guy something to do.

To further occupy the trader and add excitement to his life, Davis dabbled in day trading—another departure from the patient buying and holding that had made him wealthy. He established a special account for darting in and out of certain stocks at predetermined "target prices." For instance, he'd buy Aetna at $40, sell it at $45, and buy it back at $40, owning and disowning the same company repeatedly over several days or weeks. He never committed more than 3 percent of his capital to the quick turnover campaign, which was modestly profitable in a sideways market.

Wall Street was passing him by. His newsletter had never received much response, but now it got zero. Institutions no longer called on the dean of insurance for advice—they had younger sources of information. The latest crop of analysts had never heard of Davis. His day trading and voracious buying, plus the launch of his stock-lending program, brought excitement to a sleepy office.

His lending program took advantage of the "futures and options" on stock indexes that had begun trading in Chicago. Speculators could now place small to gigantic bets on where stock prices or bond prices were headed. Old-fashioned commodity futures were based on real agriculture: somewhere beneath the paper trades, farmers produced the soybeans, pork bellies, and other crops that connected the futures contracts to reality. Stock futures were no different. Somebody had to provide real shares as trading fodder. Generally, these shares were borrowed from common shareholders—institutions or wealthy individuals with an ample supply. Davis qualified. Once he learned the details, he was eager to lend his inventory to hedgers and speculators—mostly pessimists who bet against stocks by "selling short."

Short sellers paid interest on their temporary use of Davis's shares, which otherwise sat idle in his accounts. Moreover, the borrowers were obligated to return the shares at some point, or pay Davis the current market price. The risk of nonpayment was minimal because people who played this game were required to put up collateral, then add more collateral if their wagers went against them.

"Seven guys who thought the Ivy League was a garden club," Chris Davis jokingly described the group that pitched the lending program to Davis and handled the loans and the paperwork. "All well paid." For providing the raw material, Davis took 80 percent of the profit (about $10 million per year). The gardeners took the other one-fifth for providing the operating know-how. [This was the "hedge fund split" first devised by Alfred Jones in the late 1940s. An ex-*Fortune* magazine staffer, Jones started the original hedge fund (he called it a "hedged fund") that played stocks both ways—buying them or selling short, depending on conditions. Much less restrictive than a standard mutual fund, Jones's creation also allowed managers to trade commodities, bonds, or whatever else struck their fancy. Jones's own investors gained more than 750 percent between 1955 and 1965, a record that attracted many competitors. What started as a quirky notion later became an industry.

The 80-20 rule is still the standard today. A bankroll continues to be worth four times as much as the brains behind the strategy.]

Davis's insurance portfolio added $500 million to his net worth in the 1980s. Gains from his core holdings overwhelmed his profit from stock lending, from day trading, and from his hundreds of Value Line purchases. All this new stuff was incidental and diversionary.

Davis's financial life had three phases: learn, earn, and return. The learn phase lasted into his early forties, and the earn phase stretched from his forties into his late seventies. At that point, he tackled the return phase, turning his attention to the lucky would-be recipients of the money he'd hoarded and tended so devotedly. Earlier, he'd made the Diana donation to Princeton ($5.3 million for the history chair) and established professorships at Wellesley, Trinity College, and the Fletcher School of Diplomacy at Tufts. His generosity built and filled libraries at Lincoln Center, Bradley University, and New York's College of Insurance. Some of these bequests remained in his control so he (and, later, his grandson Chris) could handle the investing. He wasn't inclined to bestow more gifts on academia, and he continued to oppose any large giveaways to his family. Davis reiterated to Chris what he'd said decades earlier to Shelby and Diana: "You're getting nothing from me. That way, you won't be robbed of the pleasure of earning it yourself."

Davis's fortune had totally eclipsed the once-considerable Wasserman fortune, most of which was tied up in family trusts that were constantly losing ground to his portfolio. This occurred in spite of some amazing gains in the Wasserman trusts from stocks recommended by Davis and, later, by Shelby. Davis was, of course, a better investor than the surviving Wassermans, but there was another reason he got wealthier and they didn't. The typical trust operates at cross-purposes with the

goal of building wealth. It's based on a distrust of heirs by benefactors who fear their children and grandchildren will turn into
squandering trustafarians. The benefactors' lawyers fix it so the
heirs can't get their hands on the principal, but the trust is set
up to provide ample income to satisfy a healthy appetite for
spending. With that goal in mind, trusts tend to be heavily invested in bonds and dividend-paying stocks. The Wassermans
abandoned their all-bond strategy in the 1950s, but the portfolio was still income-oriented, as opposed to growth-oriented.

In most cases, an income portfolio can't reward its owners
like a stock portfolio, especially when the income is siphoned
off to beneficiaries who use it to pay bills and don't reinvest it
for further compounding. Between the siphoning and the
taxes levied on the withdrawals, an income-oriented trust is
destined to become a dwindling asset. What pluck, luck, ge-
nius, talent, enterprise (and in some cases, con artistry) create
in one generation, dependency, cash drain, and Uncle Sam destroy in the next two. Not in Davis's case, but if his offspring
weren't entitled to his spoils, and schools weren't getting them,
who was?

Warren Buffett intended to shunt his billions into zero
population growth, to help save the planet from the glut of humans, even though fewer humans meant fewer consumers to
buy products from his favorite multinationals: Coke, Gillette,
and AIG insurance.

When Davis turned 74, he prepared his exit strategy in a
similar fashion naming his favorite causes, though zero population wasn't the designated beneficiary. On a flight from Europe, in September 1983, he clarified his intentions in a memo:
"I am writing these lines on TWA's London–New York flight
703 economy," he began, after explaining he was sitting in
coach. "Always a believer in waste not, want not, I have set
aside this time to endeavor to answer the question." The question, basically, was: Who gets the money? The answer was:

Conservative causes. Whereas Buffett opted to invest his lump in a less crowded planet, Davis preferred to support the furtherance of the capitalism and free enterprise that allowed him to amass his lump. In his view, higher taxes, bigger government, and socialist ideologues threatened financial bounty.

"In recent years, I have begun to question whether our country . . . has already begun a slow decline into eventual servitude," he said. His advanced age contributed to his sense of urgency about federal metastasizing and a dispiriting hangover from the bumbling Carter Administration. Even with Reagan in the White House, he saw a nation in crisis. Funding chairs and libraries was useful, but funding the ideological resistance to liberalism was imperative.

To this end, he vowed to fortify the Heritage Foundation (a rightward think tank that counteracted the leftward Brookings Institution in Washington), the National Right to Work Foundation, Ethics & Public Policy Center, Accuracy in Media, Hoover Institution, and other advocates of limited government and a freer marketplace. Davis was always conservative, but since his return from Switzerland, he'd devoted more time and effort to politics. He'd served as Heritage Foundation chairman.

"What about all the limos they take?" Kathryn teased, referring to the lineup of stretch Mercedes parked outside Heritage functions. She didn't share his fervor about the liberal menace. "To be effective in Washington, they need those limos," Davis retorted.

Davis tapped Shelby, Kathryn, Diana, and the U.S. Trust Company as executors of the estate, and noted that Shelby could help U.S. Trust emissaries handle the investing if he wanted to.

In a multipage "final note," Davis asked himself why he hadn't provided "castles and plantations for the children and super-jets for the grandchildren." He answered as follows:

Where is the incentive if children and grandchildren start out with a trust fund which guarantees they never had to work? [He refused to condemn his offspring to a "life of ease" because] from my own experience and that of trust fund friends, I know such hapless (not lucky) recipients often if not usually become the victims of society, in the care of psychologists, psychiatrists and others. I believe in providing a "safety net" in case of emergency but, predominantly, I believe in the incentive to excel . . . and contribute to the common good.

As a postscript, he couldn't resist retracing his lineage: the two *Mayflower* passengers, John Alden and Francis Cooke on his mother's side; his namesake who served 30 years in the U.S. Senate; the Jamestown colonist and member of the Virginia House of Burgesses on his father's side. He exited the page praising his good fortune, his hard work, the common good, the national good, democracy, and a society that offers incentives to productive people: "Better Free and Alive than Red and Dead!"

He stuck this memo in a drawer at the office. His family never saw it, but the contents wouldn't have surprised them. Nobody in the Davis clan expected to inherit the Davis reward.

Ever since the Princeton flap, Shelby had lived and worked independently of Davis. His father's financial scorecard only interested him as a point of reference against which he could measure Venture's performance. Otherwise, he continued to keep his professional distance. His mutual funds didn't yet carry the Davis moniker. He worked out of Fiduciary Trust, a long cab ride from his father's office. His business card read "consultant" and provided no further details. His goal was to try to continue as the best-performing anonymous money manager on Wall Street.

Yet perhaps Shelby was more involved with his father than he wanted to admit. He owned a Tuxedo Park residence, a Florida getaway, and, in the early 1980s, he added a third property to his real estate roster: the house next door to his parents' house in Northeast Harbor, Maine. He remembered the fun he'd had as a child, tramping the Maine coast, cooking lobsters on the beach, swimming in teeth-chattering temperatures. He decided to give his offspring (Chris, Andrew, and Victoria, plus the younger trio of children he produced with his second wife, Gale) the same experience. Sharing this magnificent wooded aerie with his parents was proof he'd made a success of himself. His father would be reminded of that whenever Davis looked across his yard.

A neighborly dispute had led to Shelby's acquisition. The former owner had applied for a zoning variance to subdivide his property. Kathryn spoke against the variance at a town hearing. The application was rejected, the thwarted developer threatened to sue the Davises, and hilltop relations broke down. Soon, a "For Sale" sign appeared in the neighbor's yard, and an anonymous bidder made a generous offer. After the deal closed, the seller discovered that to escape from one Shelby Davis, he'd sold to another.

Shelby's abodes were far from rustic, but he expected to recoup the expenses, and then some, as his real estate appreciated. Aside from having more houses than Davis (later, he added two more retreats, in Jackson Hole, Wyoming, and Hobe Sound, Florida), he practiced Davis frugality. He bought his places furnished, kept the furniture, and never hired a decorator. He supplied his bathrooms with free soap squirreled from hotels. He hated buying cars, because they fell into a bear market the minute they left the dealership. He liked to hold on to a car until the motor failed or rust showed through the floorboards. He leased, because the down payment was minimal. He figured he'd pay for the car by investing the money he saved when he avoided a bigger down payment.

In a 1979 speech, "The '80s Are Coming," Shelby had foreseen the end to Mr. Market's doldrums. In spite of the pesky inflation, Shelby said, "The news could get amazingly good." Stocks were priced for amazingly bad news, and many companies were selling for less than their book value and at single-digit multiples.

On the economic front, the Fed's traditional inflation-killing tactic—raising short-term interest rates—had failed to produce the desired result, but cigar-chomping Fed chairman Paul Volcker led the fight into the 1980s with Churchillian aplomb. Volcker kept up the raises and strangled the money supply until the government's prime lending rate soared to $20\frac{1}{2}$ percent and 30-year Treasuries paid investors 15 percent to own them. A 15 percent coupon attached to Uncle Sam's IOU was the bond deal of the century—the riskier stock market returned only 10 to 11 percent over time. Yet mainstream investors shunned this glorious bond windfall just as eagerly as they had embraced 2.5 percent Treasuries—the sucker play of the century—a generation earlier.

Eventually, the financial law of gravity asserted itself. What went up for 34 years, came down. A sure sign of inflation's imminent demise was the gold and silver frenzy of 1980, when popular demand sent the gold price to $700-plus and the silver tab to $40-plus. Across the country, people scrapped their silverware, watches, chains, and trophies for the metal's value. Expert gold bugs predicted $1,000 gold and $100 silver, but prices quickly went south and never turned north.

Venture had its best year to date in 1980: up 31.9 percent, nearly doubling the gains in the S&P 500 and tripling the gains in the Dow. The fund passed a milestone—it was up more than 100 percent since its starting date 11 years earlier, while the S&P 500 was up only 18.8 percent and the Dow was down 0.3 percent! With dividends reinvested, an initial $10,000 put into Venture was now worth $23,524.

As the inflationary swell receded, bondholders and stock-holders were about to enjoy a 20-year fall in interest rates. But before stocks responded, they gave investors one last bear scare that kicked off what would prove to be the greatest bull market of the century. In 1981, the economy fell into recession and the Dow declined 24 percent. Sizable declines in companies involved in farm equipment (Harvester), metals (Inco), and asbestos (Manville) gave more hints that the hard-asset prosperity was over.

The signal for a momentous turnaround came when the Fed dropped rates. Shelby realized Volcker's anti-inflation crusade had succeeded in changing the Big Picture. In 1947, Davis had foreseen a prolonged period of rising rates. In 1981, Shelby foresaw the reverse. He began to specialize—cutting back on Venture's eclectic holdings and concentrating on fewer industries. He sold his oil and gas positions, figuring the gritty industries had had their run and would struggle as inflation abated.

The Reagan years added $1 trillion of debt to the federal balance sheet, equaling the prior IOU from the entire history of the U.S. Government. Consumers and companies alike followed Washington's lead. The entire nation had put itself in hock to the tune of $8 trillion by the late 1980s, up from $1.2 trillion in 1970.

With rates in reverse, the idea was to borrow as much as possible and buy whatever you could with it, including golf courses, major corporations, and high-priced art. The Pebble Beach golf course in California went for a hefty premium: $900 million. Van Gogh's *Irises* was auctioned at Sotheby's for $53.9 million, just before the 1987 Crash. Oil heiress Joan Payson Whitney had paid $84,000 for the painting in 1947, the year Davis started collecting insurance shares. The *Irises* price tag amazed the world, but the compounded return on this canvas was far less than Davis's return on stock certificates. His net worth had reached $386 million in 1987. That same year, one of Davis's Japanese holdings, Yasuda Fire and Marine, paid $39 million for Van Gogh's *Sunflowers,* a useless expenditure in Davis's view. That money could have been invested in Japanese stocks or bonds for further compounding, but the Japanese were bent on conspicuous consumption. They bought Rockefeller Center as well as Pebble Beach. Soon, they wouldn't be able to afford either one.

This was the heyday of the leveraged buyout, when Mike Milken and his junk-bond groupies held their famous gathering, the Predator's Ball. With access to Milken's magical pool of capital, small shots like Nelson Peltz of Triangle Industries captured large American corporations and sold them for parts. This chop-shop strategy held Wall Street in its thrall and led to a wave of so-called "hostile takeovers" that were sometimes overpriced and often ill-advised. Thanks to hell-bent leverage, the two largest department store chains in America became the property of a Canadian loon named Campeau.

Acting on a different theme—that falling rates favored paper assets and not brick, mortar, and baubles—Shelby populated Venture with financial stocks that had underachieved in the hard-asset prosperity of the 1970s. Besides being timely, bank shares were very affordable. They were selling at 10 times earnings, and their earnings were growing at a steady 12 to 15 percent. Banks' stodgy reputation caused investors to underrate their future prospects. This was a perfect setup for the latest Davis Double Play.

Shelby had learned the banking business during his apprenticeship at the Bank of New York. Banks had a lot in common with his father's beloved insurers. A bank didn't manufacture anything, so it didn't need expensive factories, finicky machinery, warehouses, research labs, or high-priced PhDs. It didn't pollute, so it spent zilch on pollution-control devices. It didn't sell gadgets or ready-to-wear, so it could avoid hiring a sales force. It didn't ship merchandise, so it had no shipping costs. Its sole product was money, borrowed from depositors and lent out to borrowers. Money came in different guises (coins, paper, blips on a screen), but was never obsolete. Banks competed with other banks, but banking itself was always in vogue. You couldn't say the same for horse-drawn carriages, oil lamps, passenger trains, telegraph machines, typewriters, gramophones, and a fat Rolodex of prominent industries undone by the next bright idea. An inspired nerd in Palo Alto might invent the next gizmo that puts half of Silicon Valley out of business, but banking lived on.

As mentioned earlier, several banks dated from the era of the Founding Fathers. Among them was the Bank of New York, where Alexander Hamilton was the youngest vice president on record until Shelby came along. Only a handful of manufacturers could match such longevity, and they survived only because their quick thinking CEOs got them out of outmoded activities and into new products.

Like insurance, banking bored most people. Racy novels about bankers were in short supply, although a bond salesman was a main character in *The Great Gatsby*. An exciting run-up in a bank stock was a rare event. Unless they were involved in a merger or a takeover bid, banks rarely made the list of daily big movers in the financial pages. Atlanta had its Coca-Cola millionaires; Bentonville, Arkansas, its Wal-Mart millionaires; and Seattle, Washington, was soon to be populated with Microsoft millionaires. But you didn't hear about clusters of millionaires who got that way by owning Wells Fargo, Chase Manhattan, or First Union.

The risky part of banking was its small margin for error. A bank made money on its depositors' money; it borrowed from Peter to lend to Paul. Normally, a bank had enough capital to cover roughly 5 to 6 percent of its outstanding loans. If more than 5 percent of its loans to the Pauls went sour, it had no way to pay back all the Peters. And if too many Peters withdrew their money at once, the bank was sunk.

In spite of their dark suits and their funeral-parlor demeanor, bankers could, at times, succumb to irrational exuberance and act like day traders. In a buoyant economy, they made loans to iffier projects and less reliable borrowers. Borrowers kept up with their payments in prosperous times, so banks had fewer defaults to contend with. With fewer defaults, they put less money aside to cover potential losses. This raised banks' earnings and generally resulted in higher stock prices.

In a sluggish economy, consumers hoarded cash and a happy chain of events could quickly turn unhappy. Bankers got pickier about lending to the next Paul because earlier Pauls had defaulted on their loans. As losses mounted, banks shored up their reserves with money that otherwise would count as earnings. As problems expanded, earnings contracted.

To escape from such a predicament, banks needed help. Usually, they got it when the Fed cut short-term interest rates. Falling short rates were manna to bankers, especially when long-term rates stayed relatively lofty. In that case, a bank borrowed for less and lent for more, boosting its profit on the wider "spread."

Whenever the economy hit a recessionary pothole, as it did in 1981, investors turned pessimistic and the prognosis for bank stocks was decidedly gloomy. Prices reflected the gloom, and canny buyers were rewarded. Knowing a few bank CEOs came in handy. From the horse's mouth, Shelby got status reports on the health of the rest of the horse. Often, a banker's informed appraisal was more optimistic than analysts' or journalists' appraisals, which already had created bargains. (When a CEO was hard to reach, Shelby sometimes waited and made a follow-up call from a vacation spot. His would-be source would be flattered, thinking that Shelby had interrupted his fun to pick his brain.)

By 1983, Shelby's strategy had combined his favorite banks, and some of his father's favorite insurers (Chubb, Lincoln National), with the strongest companies in other fields, especially computers (IBM, Motorola, Intel) and pharmaceuticals (Merck). He never found his Japan, but his father's success abroad caused him to invest in multinationals. He found appealing prospects in several global financial operators, including AIG and Morgan Stanley.

In the early stages of AIG's remarkable expansion, an earnest perusal of all the available numbers wouldn't have foretold this company's remarkable future as a high-octane compounding machine. It was the intangible quality of Hank Greenberg's leadership that made the difference. Shelby, who invested in Greenberg just as his father had, saw the same managerial knack in a more eclectic lineup of tough-minded, militaristic sticklers who had a distaste for excuses and a devotion to the bottom line.

Thanks to another charismatic boss, Andy Grove, Shelby took a rewarding ride on Intel. In his money management firm, he'd invested in the company before Intel was public. He dumped the shares for a sevenfold profit before the price was cut in half in 1973 to 1974. He'd already been burned by Memorex and other tech wrecks, and a submerging Intel intensified Shelby's aversion to tech stocks in general. Then a friend introduced him to Grove, Intel's new CEO. Here was another straight-talking workaholic who had a talent for one-liners. Shelby wrote down his favorite: "There are two kinds of companies—the quick and the dead." He was able to buy this wondrous enterprise at a single-digit multiple, and Intel has been a fixture in the Venture portfolio for more than a decade.

With Shelby on top of his game, Wall Street got the biggest boost in two decades: The Dow went up 48 percent; the S&P, up 58 percent, and Venture, up 68 percent. In one year, Shelby's fund bagged more profit than in the entire decade since the last bear market. Such surges were unpredictable. To avoid missing them, you had to stay in stocks permanently *and,* you had to reinvest your capital gains and dividends. This was and is a crucial and often overlooked factor in fundholder prosperity. Venture was typical. If you bought $10,000 worth of Venture at the outset and pocketed your gains, your investment grew to $17,902 by 1986. If you let the money ride, it grew to $75,074!

Many investors were too bored or too scared to let their money ride. They adopted a quick-in/quick-out strategy that hadn't been popular since Gerald Loeb's best-seller touted the practice in the 1930s. An array of market-timing newsletters met the demand in the 1980s. During the quick *in* phase, the market timers brought a lot of business to their chosen mutual funds, so funds tolerated the alliance. Then the money left just as readily, and managers were forced to keep a cash stash to cover the redemptions that were sapping their overall returns. "The market timing guys drove us crazy early in the decade," Shelby says. "We tolerated them for a while, but soon enough, their poor performance lost them popularity and credibility. We added extra fees to discourage frequent switching."

Bank stocks nearly tripled from 1981 to 1987, and the Dow also dazzled, hurtling past 2000 to reach a record top of 2722 in the summer of 1987. The Japanese Nikkei celebrated its all-time high as well, but from there it was all downhill in Tokyo and on Wall Street. A setback in bonds and a weaker dollar were the usual bearish portents.

This time, the wealth destruction was quick and vicious. By October, the Dow had shed 36 percent, including a panicky one-day drop of 508 points or nearly 23 percent—a bear market in a single trading session and the unkindest one-day loss in history. A sophisticated hedging system called "portfolio insurance" was designed to protect big investment houses from such air pockets, but, instead, the system aggravated the decline. The pundit majority was calling for Dow 3600, and they got Dow 1700 instead. Influential talking heads doubted the survival of the world financial system.

"One question on many people's minds is, 'How long can this outstanding American stock market keep going up?'" wrote Proyect and Davis, who'd cosigned the annual letter to Venture shareholders and sent it out a month before the crash. "The bull market has now had a life of approximately five years. But in spite of traditional thinking that says this . . . may end very soon, a number of economic and political factors indicate to us that this stock market could go substantially higher."

In their views about the future ups and downs of their merchandise, fund managers tended to be no more prescient than their clients, and just as susceptible to misjudgment. Had Shelby acted on his firm's market calls as described in Venture's literature, he might have avoided a few setbacks, but who could be sure he'd return to stocks in time for the important rallies? He kept his opinions and emotions out of the portfolio, and advised fundholders to do the same.

The fear persisted for months, and at the annual *Barron's* magazine roundtable, published in January 1988, the expert participants were gloomier than usual. "A bear market has started that will probably last several years," said dour Felix Zulauf. "We have had the first down leg."

"The questions to me," chimed in Paul Tudor Jones, "are not so much . . . will we have a bear market, but will we be able to avert a worldwide depression like we saw in the 1930s?"

"Most stock markets around the world," echoed TV commentator and motorcycle buff Jim Rogers, "are going to go up dramatically ... but no longer than six months, at which point we are going to have a real bear market. I am talking about a bear market that is just going to wipe out most people in the financial community, most investors around the world. And in fact there are many markets I would short but which I will not be short, because I think they will probably close them down."

As it turned out, there was no worldwide depression and no multiyear bear market. The market stayed open, stock prices rose, and loyal investors were rewarded. Venture had lagged the S&P 500 going into the crash, then lost far less than the index during the crash. Few of Shelby's investors had panicked and sold, so he wasn't forced to ditch future winners to raise cash. The most traumatic day in modern Wall Street history was a distant memory by the fall of 1988, and Venture's latest annual report didn't mention it.

The previous report was distributed before the event, so any clients who got financial news from Venture alone didn't know a Crash had happened. They saw only that Venture was down 6 percent for the year, the Dow lost 17 percent, and the S&P 500 lost 15 percent.

At Davis headquarters, the crash was a thrilling opportunity for Shelby's father. He'd always said a bear market helps you make money, and this was a wondrous example. With TV commentators pondering whether 1987 was 1929 all over again, Davis went on an acquisitive romp. His office manager, Arnie Widlitz, tried to restrain the boss by hanging up the phone while Davis placed his orders to the trading desk, but Davis grabbed the receiver and dialed again. Several times, Widlitz ended the call, and several times, Davis redialed. "Mr. Davis, you must stop," pleaded Widlitz, who believed his boss was tossing his bankroll at an undertow. "I'm not stopping," groused Davis. "Keep away from that phone."

After the market closed on that infamous "Black Monday," Widlitz had the unpleasant task of telling the boss he'd lost $125 million. The news didn't shake him. "Losing $125 million in the market he could tolerate," said Widlitz, "because a pile of bargains had landed in his lap. Losing $125 out of his wallet would have driven him crazy."

In a post-Crash inspection, the New York Stock Exchange checked the solvency of its member firms, and Davis passed the test, as usual. Though his firm was one of the smallest, according to the Weiss rating agency, it was always one of the strongest. The market value of Davis's assets (the stocks in his portfolio) was 1.5 times greater than his actual capital, reflecting the fact that Davis invested on margin. Merrill Lynch, to compare a pumpkin to a peanut, controlled assets with a market value 20 times greater than its own capital. Large investment houses typically operated much closer to oblivion than Davis did.

Davis made the *Forbes* 400 list of richest Americans on November 14, 1988. *Forbes* pegged the old man's net worth at $370 million (a lowball estimate) and mentioned he'd been named head of the Heritage Foundation. Shelby quipped: "My father's in *Forbes,* unfortunately," meaning this sort of attention was more embarrassing than flattering. That same year, Shelby made the *Forbes* Honor Roll for exceptional fund handling in good markets and bad. His decade-long stretch of 19 percent returns beat mediocrity (the S&P 500) by 4 percent a year and put Shelby within breathing distance of Peter Lynch. His performance was threatening his anonymity. "My father's certainly done far better than I have," conceded Shelby, then 51. "But I've done okay."

One of Shelby's best picks in this period was Fannie Mae, formally known as the Federal National Mortgage Association. In the savings and loan (S&L) debacle of the late 1980s, he looked for an investment angle. In his "Crisis Creates Opportunity" mode, he found an obvious beneficiary in Fannie Mae, a buyer and processor of home mortgages.

In cities and towns across America, the same buccaneer spirit that inspired corporate raiders bankrupted hundreds of local thrifts. The S&L wheeler-dealers lacked a Michael Milken to supply other people's money, but they raised it themselves by selling certificates of deposit at irresistible interest rates. CD buyers didn't fret about the solvency of their investment because Uncle Sam guaranteed it. Meanwhile, the CD sellers diverted the proceeds to borrowers for high-risk and grandiose ventures such as Versailles-style hotels and glossy condos. Price was no object, and the recipients of the construction loans often turned out to be related to the lenders. With their solvency in jeopardy, the S&Ls unloaded their mortgage portfolios to raise cash. Fannie Mae, the biggest customer, kept mortgages for the interest payments, or packaged them and sold them for a profit. Either way, Fannie Mae prospered.

The decade of the 1980s was also propitious for insurance stocks. The property-casualty index, which had dropped from 150 to 60 in 1974, jumped all the way to 400. The life and health index rose off its 140 bottom to touch 1,000. These were heady moves. Profit margins were chronically low, as usual. In some years, there was no profit in the industry as a whole.

Two names from the nineteenth century, Home and USF&G, continued to struggle. USF&G racked up huge losses in its bond portfolio and made no money selling new policies, either. In a frantic search for a more rewarding line of work, the company diversified into timber, farmland, natural gas, oil, and real estate. It sponsored the Sugar Bowl football game and showcased its pluses via nationwide TV commercials. These fixes were more harmful than beneficial. By the end of the 1980s, USF&G was earning an annual $1.50 per share, $3.50 less than it had earned at the end of the 1970s. The stock had sunk to 5⅜, the same price it had fetched 38 years earlier.

GEICO, on the other hand, had conjured up its old magic: lower costs and fewer claims than its competitors. Tougher penalties for drunk driving, improved headlights and taillights, reduced speed limits, and an aging population were pluses for auto insurers. But after the stock hit $194 in 1990 (a long way from its $2 low in the 1970s), the company frittered its advantage. Instead of sticking with car policies, GEICO dabbled in homeowners' insurance, aviation insurance, and consumer finance. It lost big when Hurricane Andrew hit Florida and neighboring areas.

GEICO's largest shareholder, Buffett, refused to sit by and watch this costly stumble into unfamiliar territory. At his urging, the CEO was dismissed. In 1994, Buffett bought all of GEICO's remaining shares for cash. The company he'd visited one weekend in 1951 was now 100 percent his.

This time, it was Shelby's turn to be unhappy with a Buffett maneuver. Shelby owned GEICO in his Venture Fund and opposed the cash deal, which was taxable. He preferred a tax-free stock deal in which Buffett would pay for GEICO with shares in his holding company, Berkshire Hathaway. Shelby thought about objecting to Buffett's acquisition, but decided against exercising his "dissenter's rights." A scuffle with Buffett wasn't worth the trouble.

With GEICO—and later, General Re—Buffett continued to add to his insurance holdings, even though he had little good to say about the industry. His droll annual reports, read by thousands of fans for entertainment as well as elucidation, were filled with disparaging barbs. Here are some samples:[1]

—"[Insurance] is cursed with a set of dismal economic characteristics that make for a poor long-term outlook: hundreds of competitors, ease of entry, and a product that cannot be differentiated in any meaningful way."[2]

—"You should be very suspicious of any earnings figures reported by insurers (including our own). The record of the last decade shows that a great many of our best-known insurers have reported earnings to shareholders that later proved to be wildly erroneous."[3]

—"If you want to be loved, it's clearly better to sell high-priced corn flakes than low-priced auto insurance."[4]

—"The [insurance] business has the potential for really terrible results in a single specific year."[5]

—"In most businesses, insolvent companies run out of cash. Insurance is different; you can be broke but flush. Since cash comes in at the inception of an insurance policy and losses are paid much later, insolvent insurers don't run out of cash until long after they have run out of net worth. In fact, these 'walking dead' often redouble their efforts to write business . . . simply to keep the cash flowing in."[6]

—"In such a commodity-like business, only a very low-cost operator or someone operating in a protected and unusual small niche can sustain high profitability levels."[7]

By all accounts, investment capital planted in this sorry industry had produced a meager harvest. Overhead was high, growth slow, morale low, return on equity sub par, imagination lacking. David Schiff, editor of a sassy and informative newsletter (Schiff's Insurance Observer—formerly Emerson, Reid's Insurance Observer) echoed Buffett's assessment: "Our industry is populated by an assortment of buffoons, jobbernowls, and chuckleheads. . . . The graduates of top business schools wouldn't be caught dead in the insurance business, and who can blame them? It has negative prestige, the pay is low, and the job security isn't good anymore. Walk into any of the plush new cigar 'clubs' in Manhattan and you'll see a slew of folks who don't work in the insurance business."

Yet if you picked the right stocks, insurance could be highly rewarding. In fact, big money was often made in sluggish industries, as Buffett, Davis, and Peter Lynch had proved. Smart, aggressive, resourceful companies distinguish themselves in sluggish industries. They can run mediocre competitors out of business or buy them out. In trendy industries (computers, the Internet, biotechnology), everybody's smart, aggressive, and resourceful, so those qualities can threaten an investment. When your favorite company makes an ingenious product, there's always a rival working overtime to make it better or sell it cheaper.

The way investors win in this inferior business is to buy the low-cost operators. That was the Buffett/Davis modus operandi all along. Both sought high-profit, well-managed insurers with minimal overhead, like GEICO and AIG. Inspired leadership was paramount. "You can get a lot of surprises in insurance," Buffett wrote. "[This business] tends to magnify, to an unusual degree, human managerial talent—or the lack of it . . . ."[8]

Early on, Davis had identified the most critical factor: the proliferation of assets inside insurance company portfolios. The industry's bottom line was disappointing, but income from bonds, stocks, and mortgages increased from $330 million in 1951 to $38.8 billion in 1999. This remarkable increase made insurance investing worthwhile.

CHAPTER 16

THE GRANDSONS
GET IN THE GAME

BORN IN THE 1960s, SHELBY'S THREE CHILDREN— Andrew, Chris, and Victoria ("Tory")—were introduced to stocks about the time the market began its tentative recovery from the 1973 to 1974 debacle. Between their father and grandfather, the young trio got a double dose of stock talk.

Andrew's enthusiasm was apparent in elementary school. When his teacher asked the class to write a report about the Pilgrims, he wrote about Memorex instead. The teacher told Shelby she'd never received an analyst's report from a fourth grader. Meanwhile, at Shelby's urging, the children opened savings accounts at the local bank in Tuxedo. Each deposited $25, one of their Christmas presents, in the Empire Savings Bank. This was their first lesson in the magic of compounding. Six years later—this was a period of high interest rates—they were astounded to discover their $25 had more than doubled.

Andrew doesn't remember being taught the Rule of 72, but he devised his own simplified version: "Going from $1 to $2 to $4 is okay, but going from $4 to $8 to $16 is terrific. Wait long enough, and the next double starts to make you wealthy."

By age 8, Andrew had learned that a savings deposit was a poor substitute for owning shares. Shelby encouraged the children to compound with their odd-job proceeds. To teach them the power of leverage, he matched their investment dollar for dollar.

After Andrew bought $800 worth of United Jersey Bank, Shelby set up a phone chat between the grade-school shareholder and the bank's investor relations officer. Andrew posed the questions and wrote down the answers. He wasn't sure what the answers meant, but the stock did well. He sold it at $12 and watched it rise to over $30—an early lesson in the annoyance of selling too soon. Still, he was impressed with his profit.

At age 10, Chris was already hip to the *great manager* theory of investing. He took a stake in an insurer, Associated Madison, after he found out Gerry Tsai was running that company. From hearing Shelby talk about the ex-go-go fund jockey, Chris figured Tsai was a high-powered celebrity. After he bought shares, Chris met a kid from Madison, Wisconsin, at a summer camp. "Does that Madison have anything to do with Associated Madison?" he asked the kid.

Both Chris and Andrew lost track of their early investments and don't recall what happened to their childhood assets. Chris figures the money is still out there, compounding in some forgotten brokerage account. In any event, they never complained about not touching their profit. They'd learned from Shelby and from their grandfather that spending, especially idle spending, was a regrettable habit.

Early on, the children lived in more expensive digs than Shelby had in his childhood (a midtown Manhattan apartment versus the antiquated homestead in Tarrytown), and their mother, Wendy, never paid much heed to the Davis austerity program. She was no Imelda Marcos, but her purchases rankled her father-in-law. She bought handmade

231

ornaments for the Christmas tree. She redecorated the apartment. During Davis's ambassadorial absence, she embellished the Tuxedo Park estate by adding a formal garden. She embellished her husband as well; Shelby was well supplied with new shirts and suits, high-end shoes, and snazzy cufflinks.

Though his family lived comfortably, Andrew got the sense there was no cash around the house. He grew up hearing and hating the Davis frugality mantra, "Use it up, wear it out, make do or do without." The bus was his main form of transportation. He rarely saw the inside of a cab.

Shelby and Wendy divorced in 1975. Shelby took up with Gale Lansing, a portfolio assistant in his office. A tall, slim, no-nonsense type with a subtle sense of humor, Gale came from modest circumstances in a small town in upstate New York. On her first visit to Northeast Harbor, Gale was subjected to the Davis mountaineering test. Shelby took her up the Precipice, a 1,000-foot cliff studded with handholds and ladders. This was tougher than Wendy's climb, but Gale was as cheery at the top as she'd been at the bottom, so she passed. Even better, she passed the frugality test.

Shelby and Gale had three children together, bringing Shelby's total to six. (The younger trio hadn't reached adulthood as of this writing, so I omitted them from this narrative.)

Without Wendy's Martha Stewartship, Shelby let the Tuxedo property fall into disrepair. He scrapped the formal garden—gardeners were too expensive. He heated with wood stoves to save energy, and he stopped heating unoccupied rooms. The money he saved on heating bills, he invested in his mutual fund. When he traveled in the summertime, he rented the house for extra income.

As a father, Shelby was a slightly mellower version of Davis—a stern and occasionally fun-loving taskmaster, generally absorbed in his work. After the divorce, he saw the children on weekends, and otherwise made other sporadic contact. Andrew had the hardest time coping with the new arrangement. He carried his anger into high school; then his stepfather, Tom McCain, forced him to have dinner with Shelby once a week for an entire summer. The time together drew them closer, and they established a basic rapport, which Andrew credits his stepfather for orchestrating.

Shelby's overriding concern was that his children not be "spoiled." Whether they spent the night in a shack or a mansion, they were taught to appreciate the experience. They never dug a swimming pool, but they raked a lot of leaves and shoveled a lot of snow. One summer, they cleared enough milkweed from around the Tuxedo house to fill a grain silo. Recreation was far from leisurely. If they were hobbled with blisters on a hike, or took a header on a bike ride, they didn't complain.

On ski trips to Europe or Colorado, the vacationing family rose before dawn, ate a quick breakfast, and hit the slopes as early as possible, to take full advantage of the all-day lift ticket. They didn't stop skiing until the lifts closed in late afternoon. Any Davis who quit the slopes for a leisurely lunch or a stroll around town was subjected to family heckling: "What's wrong with you? Your muscles went on strike?"

On the deck of the swimming pool at the Tuxedo house, Chris once saw his father flapping around like a stranded fish. Shelby appeared to be in pain.

"Are you okay?" Chris asked.

"Sure I'm okay. I'm doing my exercises."

"That's an exercise? Where did you learn it?"

"I made it up myself."

"How do you know it's good for you?"

"If it hurts, it must be good for you."

In family jaunts around their Tuxedo neighborhood, Shelby singled out two spoiled kids as examples to be avoided.

Being spoiled was closely related to spending, and "spender" continued to be the worst put-down in the family lexicon. "When Andrew and I were in high school," Chris recalls, "the first question Shelby asked about our girlfriends was 'Is she a spender?'"

Though he hadn't planned to become a distant father, Shelby later persuaded himself that his approach gave the children room to pursue their own interests without parental meddling or coddling. Whether or not they ended up on Wall Street, he hoped they'd share his passion for whatever career they chose. He expressed preferences, but not often. When Tory worked on trail maintenance in a national park, he thought a career maintaining trails was a misuse of her talent. Later, he applauded her decision to go to medical school, while secretly harboring a fantasy that someday she'd manage a Davis health-care fund. In the 1980s, he advised Andrew and Chris to avoid the short-term trading frenzy that attracted a young crowd to Wall Street. Speculating on gyrations in the market went against everything the family stood for.

"The most important thing I taught them about the investment business," Shelby recalls, "is how I loved being in it, even in the lean years of the 1970s. I was convinced picking stocks was something any kid could do, and I tried to make it fun and keep it simple. The math part—accounting and spreadsheets—I figured they could learn later. I got them involved in the detective work, sniffing out clues about a company's prospects. Sometimes, I took them along on company visits, just like my father had taken me."

Shelby had grown up on big-band jazz and the stock market; his children grew up on rock and roll and the stock market. When they reached junior high, Shelby paid them $100 a pop to analyze companies. Andrew was the math whiz; he multiplied and divided large numbers in his head—a skill he inherited from Shelby. But of the three budding analysts, Shelby thought Tory showed the most promise. She combined Chris's panoramic approach to a company's prospects with Andrew's precision and attention to detail. Tory churned out twice as many reports as her brothers did and was earning $500 to $600 a week at one point. After hearing the president of MCI make a persuasive case, she bought shares for her own account and put a family "buy" recommendation on the stock. Shelby ignored her tip, then took her advice and invested at double the $3 price Tory had paid.

On a typical Saturday morning in Tuxedo, Shelby could be found perched in a basement cubicle, reading the contents of his briefcase. Every Friday night, he and the children watched Lou Rukeyser's show, *Wall Street Week*, on the black-and-white TV that sat on a kitchen countertop. *Wall Street Week* was followed by *Washington Week*, a second obligatory event. "We never talked about baseball, hockey, or Hollywood," Andrew recalls. "Just stocks and politics." He remembers hiking down a steep trail with Shelby in Acadia National Park in Maine, discussing earnings versus cash flow. "Although you might want to talk about other things with Dad, this was it."

On the school front, grades weren't as important to Shelby as where the grades were headed. He tracked academic progress the way he tracked corporate profits: he looked for an up trend. A student who started the year with straight As and ended with straight As didn't impress him as much as one who started with Cs and moved up to As. Chris, Andrew, and Tory tried to give him an advancing trend line.

Though all three children were immersed in Wall Street (they got an extra dose from their stepfather, who worked at a Manhattan brokerage house), they were sick of the subject by the end of high school. The most prolific analyst, Tory, studied literature at Harvard, then medicine at Stanford. Andrew enrolled at Colby College in Maine, intending to major in psychology. The *Wall Street Journal* began to appear in his mailbox, but he hadn't ordered the paper, and assumed all students received a free subscription. In fact, Shelby had sent it incognito.

The steady supply of *Journals* helped rekindle Andrew's interest in the money game. He was always a hard worker. He split his summers between camps and jobs, including a two-month gig at a small investment house, arranged by his stepfather. After his first year at Colby, he changed his major to economics and business. He and Shelby were so far out of touch that Andrew was in his junior year when his father discovered he'd made the switch. He'd earned enough college credits to graduate early. Shelby offered to reward his effort with a check that equaled a year's tuition, but Andrew opted to stick around, slow the pace, and attend commencement with his class.

He and his college buddies shared a distaste for working with their successful fathers, so Andrew never considered applying for work with Shelby or with Davis. The family, he'd been told many times, was not an automatic employer, even as a last resort. Though his father was a minor factor in his life, Andrew followed in his footsteps and repeated Shelby's pattern. Shelby was hired out of college by the Bank of New York; Andrew was hired by Shawmut Bank in Boston. Shelby had apprenticed as an analyst in aluminum, rubber, steel, and other basic industries; Andrew apprenticed with PaineWebber's "commissioner" of steel.

In 1986, Andrew left Boston and Shawmut for New York and PaineWebber. He soon became the in-house expert in bond/stock hybrids known as "convertible securities"—or, in Wall Street parlance, "converts." A convert pays interest like a bond but offers its owner the possibility of capital gain if the company's common stock advances. A high-quality convert can capture 75 to 80 percent of the upside in a stock, while the bond feature limits its downside. Andrew created a 10-point rating system to aid comparison shopping in the group.

During a seven-year hitch at PaineWebber, Andrew moved quickly through the ranks to vice president. He became a star performer at the "shout downs"—daily briefings with 14,000 PaineWebber brokers listening to market advisories via a worldwide phone hookup.

Chris came to Wall Street by a more circuitous route. His grandfather was the primary inspiration. What Shelby disliked in Davis (snobbery disguised by a genial façade, plus a tendency to pontificate), Chris accepted with bemused fascination. At age 15, he signed on as the Davis summer cook at the Maine house. The next summer, when he turned 16 and got his driver's license, Chris became the family chauffeur and drove the patriarch back and forth to the Bar Harbor airport.

During the school year, he worked weekends in Davis's office at 70 Pine Street, stuffing envelopes, typing the insurance letter, and sending messages on the Telex system that Davis never learned to operate. Grandson and grandfather developed a warm and easy give-and-take—quite the opposite of the distant detente between grandfather and father. They took walks together. They discussed politics, Wall Street, and why a frankfurter was an unnecessary extravagance.

"One day, we were passing by the vacant lot next to the office," says Chris. Later, J.P. Morgan built its new world headquarters on that lot, but at the time, it was a popular location for pushcart food vendors. "I asked my grandfather for a dollar to buy a hot dog. He said, 'Do you realize if you invest that dollar wisely it will double every five years? By the time you reach my age, in 50 years, your dollar will be worth $1,024. Are you so hungry you need to eat a $1,000 hot dog?' I guessed not. In one swoop, he taught me three lessons: the value of a dollar, the value of compound interest, and the importance of always carrying my own money."

Around this time, Chris defected to the communists. He wore a Lenin pin, touted Karl Marx, and quoted Chairman

Mao instead of Warren Buffett. He called his father "a running dog of capitalism." Shelby called this rebellion the "big tweak."

A picture of Ché Guevara hung on Chris's bedroom wall—the political antidote to photos of Hoover, Dewey, Nixon, Ford, Kissinger, Reagan, Bush, and other GOP notables hanging on his grandfather's office wall, alongside numerous commendations and proclamations in parchment.

Chris loved animals. On summer vacations from high school, he worked at the Bronx Zoo, pro bono. He cleaned cages at the Humane Society clinic. Being an animal lover, he thought he'd make a good veterinarian. He attended prevet classes at Cornell University and planned to enroll as a full-time student, but a campus adviser suggested he take a year off and try something different. The University of St. Andrews in Scotland was recruiting Americans. Chris applied and was accepted. He'd planned to stay one year and ended up staying four. The tuition was cheap and he was beyond the parental gaze. "Scotland," he said, "was love at first sight."

In Scotland, he discovered another type of love when he and a girlfriend lived together in a cottage on a sheep farm near the university. He managed to subsist on $8 a week: $4 for groceries, $4 for the occasional beer. He graduated with a master's degree in philosophy and theology, and found himself attracted to the priesthood.

After graduation, Chris worked as a pastoral assistant at the American Cathedral in Paris. A family friend from a church in Tuxedo Park, Father Leo (the very Reverend James Leo or Dean James Leo), was in charge of the cathedral. Chris slept on the floor of one of the cathedral's lofts. He leaned over the edge to answer the telephone, perched on a table a few feet below. Once he fell off, answering a call. No date could visit his "room" without walking past a huge crucifix.

Chris saw his grandfather when the latter came to Scotland to visit life insurance companies (the Scots' term is "life assurance"). The country was well supplied with flinty savers, dogged investors, and some of the earliest mutual funds on record. Various institutions, including the life assurers, had listened to Davis's advice and bought shares through his office.

That his grandson was pro-Mao, anti-Wall Street, and studying for the priesthood didn't ruffle Davis. He made jokes about it. "Philosophy and theology give you the perfect background for investing," he said. "To succeed at investing, you need a philosophy. Then you've got to pray like hell." On another occasion, Chris traveled to London to meet his grandfather for dinner. Davis was lodged in a reputable hotel; Chris stayed in a slummy flat where some of his radical friends had squatted. The dress code was a problem. Chris couldn't don his jacket and tie in front of his squat mates, and he couldn't enter the dining room at Davis's hotel in his radical rags. To avoid embarrassment in both places, he exited the slummy flat wearing the rags and hiding his capitalist uniform in a plastic trash bag. He planned to change outfits in the hotel's public bathroom, but a doorman refused to let him into the lobby. He sneaked around the building and came in through a side door.

Chris related the story during the meal. Davis was amused. He admired Chris's buddies for figuring out how to live rent-free in London. On the virtues of not spending money, the GOP tycoon and the Marxist sympathizer could agree.

The pair hiked together in Switzerland, and Chris sat in on meetings between Davis and Swiss insurance executives. It was Davis and Shelby all over again, one generation removed. In fact, Chris saw a lot more of Davis than he saw of Shelby during this period. Shelby helped check Chris into St. Andrews and didn't visit Scotland again until Chris's graduation four years later. As mentioned above, Shelby had lost touch with Andrew, and his contact with Tory was sporadic. He was behind the curve on her latest romances. Once, he tried to reach her at her Harvard dorm several nights in a row with no luck. Her roommate answered each phone call, and told him Tory was in class, at the library, taking a shower, and so on. Later, he found out she'd flown to England to mend a relationship.

Chris exited St. Andrews with a master's degree in theology, but Father Leo helped him realize he wasn't cut out for the priesthood. He'd already decided he wasn't cut out for veterinary work, so he moved back to the United States and took up residence in Boston. His mother's family was well-known in the city and his brother Andrew had apprenticed there.

With his master's degree and his experience abroad, Chris considered various careers in politics and international affairs. He approached the CIA, figuring his early training in how to analyze companies could be useful in spy work, but he withdrew his application after the CIA asked him "nosy questions." He then decided to try education. He applied for teaching jobs at public schools in Boston, but his lack of a teaching certificate foiled him.

Several rejections later, he applied for a job at Putnam, the Boston investment house, but couldn't land an interview. He schmoozed a secretary who told him if he showed up at 8:30 A.M., she'd arrange a chat with the boss, George Putnam. Chris got the chat, but not the job. He never mentioned he was Davis's grandson, even though he knew Davis and Putnam were old friends.

Shelby provided all three children a $500-a-month stipend, payable after they left college. This family "safety net" was enough to cover part of Chris's rent, but he couldn't live on $500 without employment. Hitting his grandfather for a loan was inconceivable—a man who refused to finance a $1 hot dog and lose $1,000 compounded over 50 years wasn't about to spring for a grocery allowance or a down payment on a car. Davis had always insisted: "You're getting nothing from me. That way, you won't be robbed of the pleasure of earning it yourself."

Desperate for work by now, Chris scanned the classifieds in the *Boston Globe,* and found a training program at State Street Bank. Shelby advised that State Street's mutual fund business was exploding and the bank was in a hiring mode. Chris reminded himself that his father, his brother, and his stepfather all had trained at banks. Banking ran in the family.

State Street accepted him after he claimed he had minored in accounting in college. He erased this fib by taking night courses in accounting and economics—two subjects he'd avoided in the past. By day, he attended training sessions at State Street's IBM-type campus in a Boston suburb. Once he finished training, the bank put him to work calculating the net asset value of an array of mutual funds at the end of each day's trading.

After a few months of crunching the fund data, Chris was hired away by a small Wall Street boutique, owned and operated by Graham Tanaka. Before starting his own company, Tanaka had knocked around at J.P. Morgan and at Fiduciary Trust, where he'd worked with Shelby. Tanaka sought young talent; Shelby encouraged his son to apply. Chris got the job and moved to New York. By day, he worked for Tanaka as an analyst; by night, he took classes at the College of Insurance near the World Trade Center. One evening, when he was studying in the college library, he looked up from whatever he was reading and saw his grandfather's face on the wall. He quizzed the librarian and learned he was sitting in the Shelby Cullom Davis library. Davis had endowed it.

As Tanaka's insurance specialist, Chris attended meetings, visited companies, interviewed CEOs, and separated the doers from the bluffers. In late 1990, he ran into his father and his grandfather at a breakfast sponsored by the global insurer, Chubb. This was a momentous reunion: Three generations of Davises were attending the same meeting to get the latest details on the same company. None had a clue the others would be there.

During a coffee break in the hallway, Davis made his grandson an offer Chris couldn't refuse: "Come work for me," he said, "and keep an eye on things." Chris left Tanaka and moved to Davis headquarters on Pine Street. Davis hadn't offered Andrew a job, but because Chris had a chummier relationship with his grandfather, Andrew wasn't offended by the slight.

"Could my father have planned my reentry this way, knowing the three of us would meet at the Chubb conference and that my grandfather would make the first overture?" Chris wondered. "An alarming thought."

CHAPTER 17

THE FAMILY JOINS FORCES

ITH DAVIS SLOWING DOWN AND SHELBY considering his own retirement, the third generation was preparing a friendly takeover. They'd proven themselves at other firms (Andrew at PaineWebber; Chris at Tanaka), and now they were moving into the family financial fold.

Chris had quit Tanaka to work full time in his grandfather's office. (Their desks were just a few feet apart.) He noticed an old seersucker jacket draped over the back of Davis's chair. The blue stripes had faded; the white stripes had yellowed. Since Davis wore a newer jacket to work and never took it off, Chris wondered at the purpose of the sartorial relic. One day, he popped the question: "What's with that rag on the chair?"

"It's for the bank credit officers," Davis replied. "They come around to check on their margin loans. They arrive unannounced. If I'm not around to greet them, they'll suspect the boss is playing hooky and nobody's in charge. When they see the coat hanging on my chair, they think I just stepped out for coffee."

"How long has the coat been in that spot?"

"Twenty years."

When grandfather and grandson left the office for an analysts' meeting, Davis always jogged the distance, holding his suit jacket so it wouldn't flap in the breeze. An octogenarian jogger in a business suit was an entertaining sight. "If a customer sees me on the street, it's good for him to know I'm not lazying around," Davis explained.

Chris wrote a sample paragraph for Davis's weekly insurance bulletin. To his surprise, it appeared verbatim in the next edition. One paragraph became two, and soon Chris was writing the entire text. "I could tell my grandfather was relieved to be done with it," Chris said. Over a two-year period, he produced at least 50 letters. He changed the layout and omitted much of the industry data his grandfather had continued to print even after the latest numbers were accessible to any investor with a computer. He used the extra space to report on specific companies. The revamped format didn't generate reader response, any more than the old format had.

"Why do we bother with this?" he asked Davis, "when nobody reads it?"

"It's not for the readers," Davis said. "It's for us. We write it for ourselves. Putting ideas on paper forces you to think things through."

Chris learned, from his grandfather, not to take earnings at face value. Davis taught him how new life insurance sales built future prosperity while resulting in continuously reporting short-term losses, because commissions and marketing costs were deducted from earnings up front. An insurance policy that brought income to the company for the next 30 to 40 years went on the books as a debit.

Davis still commuted on the early train from Tarrytown, but he'd lost some pep. Little by little, the old man relinquished responsibility that Chris eagerly took on. After he got full control of the newsletter, Chris turned his attention to the few remaining "house accounts" that belonged to Davis's last remaining clients. He convinced his grandfather to charge a fee for managing these portfolios, as opposed to taking a commission on the rare occasion a stock was sold. Davis liked the idea and installed Chris as manager.

When his clients discovered that Davis had tapped his 25-year-old grandson (with no MBA) to handle their investments, they were politely unimpressed. "Why shouldn't they be wary?" Chris said. "I was untested, young, and related to the boss. But after a while, the results convinced them I wasn't just a nepotism hire. As for my lack of an MBA, neither my father nor my grandfather believed that degree was necessary, or even useful, in the investment business.

"The more responsibility my grandfather handed down, the more relaxed he became. I could see it on his face. Burdens were lifted."

The summer after Chris took this more prominent role, Davis, Kathryn, and a couple who were family friends got lost on a lobster picnic in Maine. They'd driven to a pullout, then carried their heavy supplies a mile down a familiar trail through the woods that led to a rocky beach. They took the obligatory cold swim, fanned the charcoal, drank bourbon-laced consomme, downed the lobsters, and cleaned the pot. As daylight turned to darkness. Davis couldn't find the trail in the woods he'd taken many times before. He stumbled around in the underbrush and gashed his leg on a branch. When they didn't return, the housekeeper called the Coast Guard, the Coast Guard referred the case to the local police, and a rescue squad reached them at sunrise. The two couples had spent a frosty night in the woods.

This navigational lapse was the first hint of a Davis decline. He spent less time at the office, leaving Chris underutilized. Not much was happening at the Davis headquarters, anyway. Davis's underwriting business was defunct, his regional offices had been disbanded, and his phone was often silent. Shelby, at one point years earlier, had suggested that his father should sell the firm to E.F. Hutton. But Hutton investigated and concluded that, beyond Davis himself, there was no firm. No offer materialized.

One day in 1992, Davis approached Chris's desk carrying a blue binder big enough to hold oversized maps. Inside was a thick computer printout. Chris thumbed through the top pages and realized he was staring at his grandfather's career. Here were the gains and losses from a half-century of investing, alphabetized by company and displayed on green-and-white-striped paper. Chris had never seen the printout; he knew Shelby hadn't either. He felt it was equivalent to being invited into the studio of an artistic recluse who'd never shown his work in public.

"Look this over and make some recommendations about what to sell and what to keep," Davis said, matter-of-factly. "I'll go through it," Chris promised. He was amazed that his grandfather would seek an outside opinion, flattered to be asked, and uneasy that Davis hadn't asked Shelby instead. He wondered whether Davis wanted him to show the portfolio to Shelby. Perhaps this was his grandfather's backhanded attempt to seek his estranged son's advice, or admiration, using Chris as a conduit.

After hours, Chris biked to his apartment with the printout stashed in his daypack. He decided to share it with Shelby, no matter what his grandfather's intent. That evening, he took the train to Tuxedo Park, where he and Shelby sat at the dining room table reviewing Davis's holdings, page by page. Shelby noticed more than a dozen stocks he'd owned and recommended.

Fiduciary Trust was there—Davis had bought shares after Fiduciary acquired his son's firm—Davis, Palmer and Biggs.

Fannie Mae was there—a stock Shelby had owned and recommended since the early 1980s. New York Venture was there, so Davis had bought Shelby's mutual fund without have mentioned it. Intel was there—as a rule, Shelby avoided tech stocks, but this one impressed him so much Shelby had made it a top ten holding in the Venture fund. He'd once touted Intel to his father and was rebuffed. "I don't trust technology," Davis had said.

Shelby didn't say so, but Chris could see he was touched by the evidence that Davis had secretly been taking Shelby's advice and investing in Shelby's favorite stocks—and in Shelby's fund. "Intel, Fannie Mae, and New York Venture" said Chris, "were the words of praise my father had waited all his adult life to hear, and my grandfather had never uttered."

"I was convinced my father and grandfather wanted to reach one another," Chris continued, "but they both were stubborn. Each wanted the other to make the first move. I was in the middle of this, so my role was to reunite them through the portfolio."

Shelby and Chris spent the rest of the evening sifting through the pluses and minuses in this stockpicker's grab bag. Three-quarters of Davis's assets were riding on 100 insurers worldwide; the rest were scattered among 1,500 companies of all stripes and sizes. Most were highly ranked by Value Line. Why had he acquired so many names? Shelby explained that his father had never kicked the habit of buying in 1,000-share lots. "Charlie, get me 1,000," he'd say to his trader, even after his portfolio had grown beyond $100 million. With that much money involved, and to stay fully invested, he ended up owning 1,000 shares in enough companies to fill a small-town phone book.

Shelby dealt in 10,000-share lots at the Venture fund. When Chris took over in 1997, Venture was so big that Chris was dealing in 500,000-share lots. "A half-million Hewlett-Packard?

Aren't you going overboard?" Shelby would ask. What looked to Shelby like a jumbo purchase was only 0.5 percent of the fund, but Shelby, too, had trouble adjusting to the latest order of magnitude.

The printout left no doubt what had put Davis on the *Forbes* list. It wasn't his phone book of stocks; it was a few names in the phone book. These were oldies from the 1960s that he had faithfully held—his financial Wyeths, Rauschenbergs, Warhols. With the typical mutual fund turning over 100 percent of its inventory every year, and the public trading in and out of stocks and funds just as readily, Davis remained loyal. Names he owned in 1950 still occupied his portfolio in 1990.

His million shares of Hank Greenberg's American International Group (AIG) were worth $72 million. Tokio Marine & Fire, the Japanese masterpiece that cost him $641,000 in 1962, was worth $33 million. Three other Japanese insurance holdings—Mitsui, Sumitomo Marine & Fire, and Yasuda Fire and Marine—were worth a combined $42 million.

Domestically, his second best investment, after Greenberg, was with Buffett. A 3,000-share purchase of Buffett's flagship company, Berkshire Hathaway, had grown into $27 million. He'd also parlayed five other U.S.-based insurers (Torchmark, AON, Chubb, Capital Holdings, and Progressive) into another $76 million. An additional $11 million had come his way (thanks to Shelby) via the mortgage packager, Fannie Mae.

This was the Davis Dozen—12 stocks worth $261 million, or, by today's accounting, at least two, and possibly three PowerBall jackpots. He won this prize on the original cash outlay of $150,000. The prize required a 50-year waiting period to accumulate, but Davis lived comfortably on small, anticipatory withdrawals along the way. Once he'd bought winning companies, his best decisions were never to sell. He sat on his insurance stocks through daily, weekly, monthly gyrations. He sat through mild bear markets and severe bear markets, crashes, and corrections. He sat through scores of analysts' upgrades and downgrades, technical sell signals, and fundamental blips. As long as he believed in the strength of the leadership and the company's continual ability to compound, he held.

Counting Buffett's company as an insurance play (Berkshire Hathaway was heavily invested in the sector), 11 of Davis's biggest winners were insurers. The lone outsider, Fannie Mae, resembled an insurer in that it was both a borrower and a lender, and it trafficked in mortgages and bonds.

Davis's intermediate winners (stocks that made him $4 to $9 million) were insurers as well. This list included St. Paul, CNA Financial, Hanover, Hartford Steam Boiler (which sold insurance policies for industrial furnaces); Kemper, Primerica, Safeco, 20th Century, U.S. Life, Conseco, and other names. The bottom line on this portfolio is: A few big winners are what count in a lifetime of investing, and these winners need many years to appreciate. All of the Davis Dozen had been parked in his portfolio since the mid-1970s. Any young, inexperienced investor has a built-in advantage over a mature, sophisticated investor: Time.

On the minus side of the ledger, Shelby and Chris found an ample assortment of flops, bombs, and wealth busters—or whatever other name fits stocks investors wish they'd never met. Among hundreds of losers, Davis's most expensive flop was First Executive, a persistent reverse compounder that turned his $2.5 million outlay into goose eggs. Not only had he refused to part with First Executive during its death spiral, he'd kept the corpse on the books.

In the final analysis, Davis's mistakes hindered his prosperity the way a gnat flusters a buffalo. His portfolio proved once again that, over a lifetime of investing, a handful of high achievers' ideas can support a multitude of ne'er-do-wells.

Curiously, the sworn enemy of bonds had acquired a $23 million bond portfolio to complement his stock collection. Given the magnitude of the latter, the former was a token commitment, and thankfully so. As interest rates fell and most bonds rose in value, Davis lost money on his bond holdings. What explained this subpar result? He'd bypassed reliable U.S. Treasuries in favor of high-yielding junk. Moreover, he'd bought the wrong junk, overlooking the fatal flaws that caused Long Island Lighting, Eastern Airlines, and several prominent savings and loans to renege on their debts. The dogged researcher in the equity department was less dogged in the bond department; and Davis's poor showing reminds us that dumb bond picks can be just as costly as dumb stock picks.

After they'd finished admiring the printout, Shelby and Chris discussed how they might prepare for the time when Davis was no longer capable of handling his affairs. There was no definite plan, but the general idea was to funnel Davis's assets into Shelby's Venture portfolio, along with an array of new funds he soon would launch or acquire. Chris and Andrew, meanwhile, would be tapped to manage some of these newer portfolios, and if they performed well, they'd be qualified to run the expanded Davis operation. The accumulated wealth of two generations would now be left in the hands of the third, along with considerable assets from public shareholders.

In 1990, Saddam Hussein and his Keystone Kops army sacked Kuwait. The invasion that led to the Gulf War was bullish for oil prices but bearish for stocks. After breaking 3,000 for the first time, the Dow dropped 20 percent. The Tokyo market collapsed. Japan's Dow (the Nikkei) fell 48 percent. The Gulf war turned to rout, the U.S. economy went into short recession; the Fed cut rates, and stocks resumed their climb on a surge in corporate profits. Russia staged its second revolution of the century. Communism and Mikhail Gorbachev were ousted in 70 hours.

Hoping their portfolios would bring them a carefree retirement, U.S. baby boomers tossed billions into mutual funds. Their vigorous buying helped make the 1990s the best decade for stocks since the 1950s.

The 1991 recession was brief and relatively mild, but it strained the banking system. Banks were still enfeebled by the permissive lending of the late 1980s, when they'd financed too many malls, high rises, and fanciful corporate takeovers. Among the brand-name banks in distress, Citicorp was technically bankrupt. At least 40 other U.S. banks were in or close to the same fix.

Citicorp had been a bank that couldn't say "no." It said "yes" to Canadian laughingstock Robert Campeau and financed Campeau's Mittyesque takeover of the largest department store chains in America. It said "yes" to real estate speculators in overbuilt markets, at a time when the bank hadn't fully recovered from its earlier yeses to corrupt and debt-ridden Latin American regimes.

Toward the end of the 1980s, a glut in commercial real estate pushed this once-proud multinational into technical bankrupcy as "nonperforming assets"—a bankers' euphemism for loans-we-wish-we-hadn't made—reached 6 percent of total assets. Citicorp's insufficient loss reserves didn't begin to cover its bad loans. The stock fell from above $35 to below $10.

At that point, the bank was operating on "trace amounts" of capital. Had regulators played by the book, Citicorp would have faced government seizure and possible liquidation. Luckily for shareholders, Citicorp was put in the "too big to fail category."[1] Regulators allowed it to stay in business, with federal oversight. In a "memorandum of understanding," the bank promised to consult with the Federal Reserve and the Office of the Comptroller of the Currency on all consequential decisions.

Citicorp's pestiferous chairman, John Reed, didn't appreciate the unsolicited advice, but at least his bank was spared dismemberment. Soon, a Kuwaiti oil sheik came to the rescue with a huge bailout loan. The Gulf War, fought to protect Kuwaiti oilfields, also helped keep the biggest U.S. bank afloat.

Banking problems and Saddam's bear market gave Shelby his latest chance to prospect in familiar territory. Like everyone else who read the business section and watched financial TV, he'd heard influential alarmists predict the demise of Citibank and escalating real estate loan losses for Wells Fargo. The prices of both Citi's and Wells's stock reflected their predicaments. Refusing to take somebody else's word for it, and convinced that the Fed wouldn't allow a top-notch bank to fail (already, Fed chairman Alan Greenspan had cut short-term rates), Shelby quizzed the horses, as usual.

The answers reassured him. Insiders at Wells Fargo told Shelby their loan problems weren't as problematic as headlines suggested. The bank had moved into Southern California, hoping to benefit from that state's fast growth. It beat many competitors into supermarkets with ATM machines. In Wells Fargo's chairman, Carl Reichardt, he found the kind of no-nonsense leader that had inspired Davis to make his best investments. "Shelby, I've got $50 million of my own money in this institution," Reichardt told him. "I won't let you down." When Wells merged with Norwest, it inherited two more top managers, Dick Korvasovich and Les Biller.

With slight trepidation, Shelby loaded up on shares of Wells. So he wouldn't be caught off guard by unpleasant surprises, he kept close tabs on the latest developments. "At night, I'd wake up worrying about some detail, and the next day, I'd call to check. I talked to them at least twenty times in six months. Gradually, I was more convinced they had their problems under control."

Here's another tidbit from the Great Investors Think Alike department: Warren Buffett was also buying Wells. Just as Buffett and Davis had owned the same insurance companies, Buffett and Shelby favored the same bank.

That two great investors were bullish didn't faze the short-selling Feshbach brothers. Wall Street's most famous pessimists bet heavily against Wells. Miscalculations on the short side cost them their Lear jet and their billion dollars under management.

Citi was in worse shape than Wells, but Shelby was impressed with its global franchise. On a family trip to the Far East, when Shelby was a teenager, he'd met the head of Citi's Burmese branch. He likened the bank to an embassy, with operatives in every country. Now, 40 years later, he favored globetrotting companies, and Citi's crisis gave him a chance to steal one. Though its foolish lending habit, especially in the Third World, had nearly cost Citi its corporate life (doing business abroad was no cinch), Shelby figured U.S. banking authorities wouldn't allow it to fail. In an effort to cut back on costly generosity, Citi's bosses had tightened the purse strings in the lending department. Also, they'd hired a "brand promoter" to help Citicorp—renamed Citigroup—capitalize on its fame.

By the end of the decade, Shelby's Citi investment had advanced twentyfold, and he'd acquired more shares after the merger with Travelers. (The Venture Fund already owned Travelers.) The new Citigroup entity was run by Sandy Weill, Travelers CEO and another Davis-style leader. Weill was one more example of how a great leader can take a company farther than any data cruncher could fathom. Like Greenberg at AIG, Weill's mission was to "acquire, grow, and cut costs." He accomplished all three and kept his promise of doubling Citigroup's earnings every five years.

Impressed with Chris's success with the house accounts, Shelby installed Chris as manager of the new Davis Financial Fund in 1991. With the banking crisis still in the news and the entire sector irresistibly cheap, Chris could apply his stock-picking skills to the sector. Moreover, financial services already had begun to benefit from baby boomers' squirreling for retirement, just as insurance companies benefited when the baby boomers' parents bought policies after World War II.

"A general fund couldn't have owned 90 percent financials," Chris said. "I wanted to be able to concentrate. If I made a good showing, it might put me in line to manage Venture after my father retired. The Davis board of directors handles such decisions, and I wanted to prove myself to the board."

Using the family's invest-in-great-leaders technique, Chris picked a winner in Eli Broad's insurance company, SunAmerica. Thirty years earlier, Shelby's partner, Jeremy Biggs, had lent venture capital to Broad's home-building operation, Kaufman & Broad. Broad and his associates put 2,000 residential developments on the map, selling mostly to baby boomers. Broad was now selling financial products to the same people who had bought his houses. SunAmerica proceeded to capture $50 billion in retirement assets. Based on Chris's analysis, Shelby made SunAmerica one of Venture's top picks, and the stock proceeded to rise twentyfold.

The life of a mutual fund isn't as dull as it might sound. A $1 billion fund with an average turnover (100 percent) buys and sells $1 billion worth of inventory each year. Managers with average longevity have owned enough companies to fill a small town's phone book. Some companies are acquired once and then dumped for good; others are owned, disowned, and acquired again. The managers regret having sold some companies, and they regret having bought others. Writers may balk at rereading their earliest work; actors may prefer not to watch their old movies; and fund managers may avoid contemplating their mistakes.

Chris's biggest rookie mistake was to urge his father to kick Fannie Mae out of Venture. Shelby took his son's advice and Fannie Mae proceeded to mock the decision by quadrupling in price. "I concocted a compelling story about why not to own it," Chris recalled. "The company had thrived on the S&L crisis, packaging and reselling mortgages. As my story went, the one-time bonanza was over, and, without that, Fannie was a lackluster prospect. As it turned out, Fannie was a continuously exciting prospect. Since my regrettable misjudgment, I've tried not to analyze companies by telling a story and then finding data to support it."

In their off hours, Shelby and Chris planned the gradual liquidation of Davis's holdings. Shelby wanted to sell some of the duds first, to create tax losses that would offset gains from the sale of winners. "Spring housecleaning," Shelby called it. Chris broached the subject with Davis. "I mentioned housecleaning one day," Chris said, "emphasizing the part about the tax breaks to play on my grandfather's loathing of taxes. I didn't mention that my father thought some of these stock picks were misguided to begin with. To bring that up was like squirting charcoal starter on a grass fire.

"Screwing up my courage, I asked my grandfather point-blank how he wanted us to handle his portfolio when he died. His answer surprised me. 'I want my money invested in the Davis funds,' he announced. He'd already concluded that leaving his portfolio intact with Shelby in charge was a foolhardy strategy because, in that case, poor performance might go unpunished. With the money in the funds, a board of directors would safeguard the assets. If Shelby failed to deliver, or his successors failed to deliver, the directors could find new managers."

Chris relayed this conversation to his father, and, soon after, the three generations openly conferred on the transfer of assets. Duds were unloaded immediately, and the bulk of the portfolio was slated for sale after Davis's death.

Meanwhile, Venture continued to outperform its rivals and outdistance the market, and Shelby's roster of funds expanded. He took control of three funds purchased from a subsidiary of Lincoln National Life, and renamed them Davis Growth Opportunity, Davis High Income, and Davis Tax-Free Income. He hired a new manager for each. Later, two additional funds—Selected American and Selected Special Shares—fell into his lap. After an in-house squabble over fees and commissions, the powers-that-be at Selected sacked the former management group (Kemper) and switched to Shelby. Shelby wasted no time replacing unproductive consumer stocks with banks, insurance, and brokerage names.

When he'd finished the remodeling job, Selected American was an identical twin to New York Venture. That the latter charged customers a commission, and the former was "no load" was the only difference between the two.

Among other powers-that-be, Martin Proyect had owned a 55 percent stake in Venture's management company, Venture Advisers, since he'd created the fund in the late 1960s. With his controlling interest, Proyect was a threat to Davis hegemony, so Shelby offered to buy him out. While he was at it, he bought his friend Biggs out as well. With money he'd saved by living in a Greenwich Village walk-up, Chris invested in the buyout as well. Venture Advisers became Davis Selected Advisers, and the family was now in full control; Shelby operated from the World Trade Center, and Chris from his new location on Fifth Avenue. Following the migration of Morgan Stanley, PaineWebber, and other financial gorillas, Chris closed his grandfather's Pine Street office and moved uptown. To keep the Davis tradition intact, Chris brought along his grandfather's furniture, VIP photographs, and citations, and installed them in the conference room at the modest new digs.

By 1993, Chris's brother Andrew had quit PaineWebber, frustrated that younger employees had trouble rising through the old-boy network. Before the Venture Advisers buyout, Andrew had flown to Santa Fe, where Proyect had set up Venture headquarters, to interview for a job. Proyect hired him to work in marketing and administration, but Andrew soon discovered that he preferred to crunch numbers and analyze companies, like a typical Davis. Impressed with Andrew's success in the convertible bond department at PaineWebber, Shelby decided to start a convertible fund to showcase Andrew's talent, just as he'd done with Chris and the financial fund. While he was at it, Shelby also put Andrew in charge of a new real estate fund, since a major slump in commercial property made real estate stocks attractive.

In their new managerial roles, Chris and Andrew were picking stocks in a market that wasn't the cheap, down rodden variety that Davis had encountered in 1947, nor the extravagant, hyperbolic variety that Shelby had encountered in 1969, though it was closer to the latter than to the former.

Soon, Andrew was absorbed in getting the scoop on scores of real estate companies, many of which had recently gone public. He moved his family to Santa Fe, where he tended both portfolios and also kept tabs on administrative matters. Andrew was two time zones away from Chris, who managed the more prestigious financial fund, worked more closely with his father, was chummier with his grandfather, and stood first in line to replace Shelby at Venture. One weekend in 1993, he and Chris met at a Colorado ski resort to talk through this apparently unequal distribution of responsibility, notoriety, and clout.

Andrew told Chris he wasn't bothered that Chris had landed the higher-profile assignment. Andrew preferred a low profile, and he felt his personality was too similar to Shelby's for peaceable collaboration in close proximity to his father. The brothers promised each other they'd maintain an honest dialogue to ward off future misunderstandings.

On a ski trip to Switzerland in the spring of 1993, Davis refused to ski. There was a strange hitch in his walk. Alarmed at these developments (Davis never missed a chance to ski), Kathryn sent him to a doctor when they returned to the States. The doctor found nothing wrong. Then, at a Society of Cincinnati luncheon held in Tarrytown, Davis stood up to make a toast, bungled the words, and slumped back into his seat. He tried to raise himself but couldn't walk. Two table-mates helped shuffle him to an exit.

Kathryn retrieved her stricken husband and drove him straight to Columbia-Presbyterian Medical Center on Riverside Drive in Manhattan. An emergency room doctor said Davis had suffered a stroke and admitted him for observation. Kathryn booked a room in the luxury wing, which provided live chamber music and afternoon tea served in the garden. Davis was confined to a bed and a wheelchair. He must have felt very ill; he accepted the first-class accommodations. After two weeks of rehab, he limped out of the hospital against doctor's orders to attend a Value Line board meeting.

The family handled the stroke with its usual gritty aplomb. The Davis approach to injury, infirmity, or disability was "Don't give in to it." After Diana's husband, John Spencer, was stricken with multiple sclerosis, his in-laws continued to invite him on ski trips. He stumbled and tumbled down the slopes, taking bad spills along the way, while the family cheered and egged him on. Dad was always very empathetic to John about the plight of his M.S. He had a very caring side.

Now it was Davis's turn to travel incapacitated. He took short walks but needed the wheelchair as a backup when he got tired. His doctors suggested more rehab, but Kathryn insisted on taking him and the wheelchair to Russia. The Davises had signed up for a boat trip up the Volga River on Boris Yeltsin's yacht, and, stroke or no stroke, Kathryn was sticking to the plan although she asked Chris to come along as well.

Upon their return from the Volga, Davis was transported to the Maine house for the summer. His old friend, Richard Murray, came to visit, and the pair sat on the porch, looked out at the coastline, and reminisced. "I could tell the stroke had done some brain damage," Murray recalled. "He couldn't tell me who Truman was, and he'd worked for Truman's opponent."

By summer's end, Davis wobbled more and remembered less. He was readmitted to Columbia-Presbyterian—weakened, disturbed, mentally confused, and angry at his condition and the fuss it was causing. In the hallway outside his grandfather's room, Chris watched his grandmother cry. It was the first time he'd ever seen her break down. "I'm afraid," she said, "our best days are behind us." Chris took it as a positive she'd come to this conclusion at age 84. "If that's the first time you've noticed your best days are behind you," he said, "then you've had a wonderful life." Kathryn installed an elevator in the Tarrytown house and hired nurses to keep her husband fed, clothed, and medicated, and to wheel him around. Davis chafed at his confinement and yelled at the nurses: "Get them away from me."

With Davis incapacitated, Kathryn took over the Davis seat on the New York Stock Exchange. She was (and, as of this writing, still is) the oldest woman member of the exchange. When he bought the seat in 1940, Davis needed a partner for legal reasons. He tapped his wife because he knew she wouldn't meddle, second-guess, or otherwise get in his way. Kathryn didn't mind being listed as Davis's spousal stamp and serving in name only. She had no more interest in the NYSE than she had in the NFL. She hadn't visited the exchange in 40 years.

In early 1994, a family doctor advised Kathryn to transfer her husband to a warm climate. Shelby had bought a vacation home on Florida's Hobe Sound, a low-key millionaires' rookery north of Palm Beach, and he urged his mother to rent a place near his. Davis had always disliked the flat topography of Florida, but Kathryn agreed that the sunshine might be beneficial, so she followed Shelby's suggestion.

Davis suffered more strokes. His mind deserted him. One doctor diagnosed Alzheimer's; another tagged him with dementia. This once fearless swimmer in cold harbors and choppy seas was afraid to wade in the backyard pool. Walking with a cane one day, outside the rental house, he stumbled and broke his hip. He was confined to the wheelchair and never escaped it again. His spirits got a lift when Shelby showed him the latest investment results. It had taken Davis 42 years to make the first $400 million. Shelby's mutual funds helped him make the next $500 million in four years. Had Davis switched his assets to the Venture Fund earlier, he'd have made a lot more.

The family lingered in Florida through the spring. Kathryn had flown to Massachusetts to attend a trustees' meeting at Wellesley College when she got word that Davis was close to death. She flew back with her daughter Diana to keep vigil at his bedside; other family members drifted in and out. When Chris arrived, he walked through the door and saw Shelby sitting on the bed, patting Davis's hand in reassurance, telling him everything would be okay. "I was touched by this scene," Chris said. "It was the most tender physical contact I'd ever witnessed between my father and grandfather." Davis died on May 24, 1994, at age 85.

The family struggled with funeral plans, given Davis's oft-stated opinion that funerals were a waste of time. When asked what sort of send-off he'd want, Davis always said: "None. My friends are much too busy for such nonsense." Kathryn and Shelby figured a way to finesse his objection (not that Davis

261

was in any condition to object) by staging the ceremony in downtown New York at lunch time, so the mourners could pay their respects without taking time off from work.

St. Paul's Chapel, close to Wall Street, was the obvious choice, but it was booked for a lunch concert. After a spirited negotiation, St. Paul's agreed to cancel the concert, and the Davises arranged to make up the lost revenue. (Davis wouldn't have approved of this "waste" of money.)

The patriotic societies he loved and supported paid tribute by sending 75 flag bearers into the chapel. Sad strains from a lone bagpiper could be heard all the way down Wall Street. Chris gave a moving speech, quoting from his grandfather. Kathryn had written an eight-word eulogy: "He was my closest friend for 65 years." Diana spoke of her father citing examples of how he instilled her with a work ethic. A reception was held at the Downtown Association, Davis's favorite club.

Davis left a widow, two children, eight grandchildren, and $900 million, later to become more than $2 billion. He was cremated in Florida and his ashes were shipped to Maine. The family buried the urn in a glade at the edge of the property and installed a memorial bench.

Since the Davis estate was earmarked for charity, the remains of the portfolio could be liquidated free of capital gains taxes. The assets now belonged to the Davis charitable trust, controlled by a family board that included Kathryn, Shelby, and Diana. The trust income belonged to Kathryn until her death. The principal and the future income would then become the property of the foundation.

Davis left nothing to Shelby. Diana did receive $5 million—in today's dollars, far less than the $4 million her father snatched away in 1963. Shelby's firm got more assets to manage in their mutual funds, but he got nothing directly. Following his father's lead, Shelby warned his six children not to expect any windfall from him. Entering his "return" phase,

Shelby made a $45 million donation to the United World College scholarship program and set up a $150 million foundation. He supported the programs on their own merits, but these endeavors were also a "message to my offspring. Don't plan to coast through life on the family fortune."

With no tax bill to worry about, Shelby accelerated the selling from his father's portfolio. He diverted the cash into the various Davis funds, including the Selected group that had been transferred from Kemper. Selected's board had hoped the switch to Davis would attract more investors to their product, but they never imagined Shelby would invest so much of his father's wealth that two-thirds of Selected's assets came from the family. Shelby, who'd worked hard to make money for thousands of small investors, was now making it for his father's favorite causes.

"Having so much Davis money in the Davis funds helped us keep priorities straight," Chris said. "We cared less about bringing in more investors and more about doing well for existing investors. That's not because we were altruistic. It's because we were the biggest existing investors, by far. If stocks in the fund rose 1 percent, the Davis family and our related charities benefited far more than we'd benefit by attracting another $10 million in clients' money."

In a bold and unsentimental maneuver, Shelby unloaded his father's beloved Japanese insurers. What went around came around: Shelby saw a striking resemblance between Japan in the 1990s and the United States in the 1930s. Both economies had stalled, and consumers were short on funds and afraid to spend money. Interest rates dropped to record lows—in Japan's case, below 2 percent. Low rates bedeviled insurers. Their bond portfolios didn't throw off enough cash to pay claims and/or benefits to policyholders.

The Japanese Dow (the Nikkei) already had declined 40 percent when Shelby began selling Tokio Fire and Marine, and others. Chris disputed the sale. "Grandpa never would have let his favorites go," he argued. "Anyway, Japan has had its bear market. Stocks have hit bottom. From here, they have nowhere to go but up."

Shelby agreed that Japan was due for a bounce, but doubted it was bouncing any time soon. The 1930s—and, to a slightly lesser extent, the 1970s—had shown that it often takes years, perhaps decades, for a market to recover from a devastating loss. So far, there was no hint of Japan's economic recovery, and waiting for a comeback, Shelby concluded, was a futile exercise. Seeing better opportunities at home in 1994 (just as his father had seen better opportunities abroad in 1963), Shelby said *sayonara* to Japan and sank the proceeds into U.S. stocks, just in time to catch Wall Street's latest 300 percent rise.

After guiding Davis Financial through four years of above-average returns, Chris was elevated, in 1995, to comanager of Venture and its twin, Selected American. He put in long days doing research. A reporter described him as "having the glassy eyes of the sleep-deprived." Learning of Chris's promotion, *Forbes* magazine dropped Venture from its honor roll. Shelby had made the list five years in a row, but the editors noted that Shelby's admirable past performance no longer qualified him for the award, because he was sharing the job with his son. The editors noted that Chris would be eligible at some point in the future, after he met "our tough test for continuity."

Andrew's real estate fund had distinguished itself from 1994 to 1997. Then an apparent glut in office space and shopping malls caused investors to retreat from the sector, in anticipation of a bust. Much of the retreating cash was deployed in a hotter sector: technology. Demoralized and doubting his commitment, Andrew sought his father's counsel, expecting Shelby to pass along some profound advice about coping with bear markets, such as the one Shelby had survived in 1973 to 1974. Hc got three words: "Hang in there." It wasn't the message Andrew had expected, but later he realized it was the only sensible response a veteran could give. In the first year of the twenty-first century, real estate rebounded with double-digit gains, providing a rewarding alternative to double-digit losses in tech stocks.

CHAPTER 18

CHRIS INHERITS VENTURE

CHRIS DAVIS TOOK OVER VENTURE'S ASSETS IN 1997, the sixteenth year of the latest bull market. Over this remarkable stretch, Mr. Market's earnings—the E in the P/E calculation—were up fourfold. The price (P) had done even better, up more than eightfold. Investors in the Dow who paid a 7 multiple at the dawn of the advance—reluctantly, in many cases—now eagerly paid a 20 multiple in the twilight.

Shelby exited on a remarkable winning streak. Not only had his fund beaten the S&P 500 in 16 out of 20 years, he'd beaten the index by an annual 4.7 percent throughout this period. An original $10,000 investment had become $379,000.

Shelby gave himself a new title: Chief Investment Officer (CIO). "Chris is the quarterback," he said. "I'm the coach." To underscore this change of roles, Chris gave him a jacket that read "Coach." Chris was the same age as Shelby was when Venture was launched. He had proven himself and had earned his place at the helm. Father and son met every week or so, and they talked constantly on the phone. Before Shelby moved to the sidelines, Venture attracted a torrent of new money. This $3 billion fund in 1991 became a $25 billion fund in 1997.

The backdrop for Chris's soloing with Venture bore an unsettling resemblance to the backdrop in 1969, when Shelby took charge. Then, fewer than 400 stock funds were operating in the United States. Now, with no birth control practiced in mutual funds, Wall Street's incubators had created 5,000 alternatives on the equity side alone. A record 45 percent of U.S. households had cash riding on this bull into the thin air of valuation. Stock ownership had never been higher, and Americans' personal savings had never been lower.

The hoopla in 1969 was directed toward computer peripherals, mainframes, or companies with names ending in "-ionics." Now, it was directed at dot-coms, B to B, C to C, chip makers, networking, and connectivity. Yesterday's go-go operatives (Gerry Tsai, Fred Mates, and similar headliners) were now replaced by "momentum" managers and thirty something Internet wonders like Ryan Jacobs. As described in the *New York Observer,* Jacobs was catapulted into the driver's seat of the nation's first mutual fund for Internet stocks. Prior to this unexpected job offer, Jacobs had worked as a reporter for a relatively obscure newsletter: *IPO Value Monitor.* In a hot market, people, as well as stocks, can be elevated to improbable heights.

This opportunistic fund, a home-grown concoction with 20 shareholders and $200,000 in assets, was launched by a brother of one of Jacobs' friends. Jacobs' hand was on the *Buy* button just in time to satisfy the Internet mania, and, in 1998, he wowed the Street with a 196 percent return. This result caused a buying scramble and a torrent of paperwork as new money poured into the fund's headquarters—a house in Babylon, Long Island. Jacobs made the cover of *Kiplinger's* magazine and was the subject of numerous adulatory articles (the *Observer* described him as "a Slim-Fast version of Matthew Broderick").

By 1999, the Internet fund had swelled to $500 million. Like Gerry Tsai during an earlier era, Jacobs decided he'd attracted enough of a following to bolt the parent company. He quit his friend's brother's shop and set up his own: the Jacobs Fund. Investors laid a quick $150 million on the tyro, and higher stock prices and more investors quickly doubled those assets. Then, in the Internet crash of Y2K—seers had predicted that computers would break down, but computer stocks broke down instead—the Jacobs Fund lost a third of its former self, and the earlier client rush to join became a rush to resign.

The *Observer* reported late in 2000, that Jacobs believed his Internet picks would rally. What he couldn't quite believe was how, with no prior experience, he got his own mutual fund at age 30.

The same unconditional love that was delivered to "data" and "-ionic" stocks in the late 1960s was applied to dot-coms and Silicon Valley start-ups in the late 1990s. In the late 1960s, value guru Ben Graham issued warnings about market excess and was dismissed as a hoary crank; in the late 1990s, Graham's student, Warren Buffett, issued similar warnings and got the same brush-off. In 1965, Fed chairman William McChesney Martin chided the zealots for proclaiming the "new era" when recessions were passe and stock market fundamentals no longer applied. The last new era, Martin reminded, was the 1920s.

A quarter century later, Martin's cryptic, rumple-suited successor, Alan Greenspan, cried "Irrational exuberance," as did Warren Buffett at the Berkshire Hathaway annual meeting that year. After a reflex lapse, the Dow proceeded to add 2,000-plus points to its already bloated self. In sum, the late 1960s and the late 1990s were the best of times for cockeyed optimists and the worst of times for wary shoppers. Value-oriented funds (Venture among them) fell behind as hell-bent growth funds raced ahead. Several notable old-school managers, including

Bob Sanborn at Oakmark and Julian Robertson at Tiger Management, quit the business outright. In 1999, Buffett's company had its worst year on record. The fogy himself, celebrated as money's Merlin as recently as 1995, was sent to the metaphoric nursing home by journalist Michael Lewis, author of the *New New Thing*, a book about a Silicon Valley instant billionaire. Lewis penned a *New York Times* column that chided some Old, Old Things, namely financial has-beens such as Buffett, Robertson, and George Soros.

In these Soaring '90s, a standard household routine was to pay bills with debt (maxing out on credit cards and home equity loans), then funnel extra cash into the can't-lose tech sector. This was an anti-Davis maneuver—instead of saving to invest more, people invested to save less. Wishful thinking convinced them that their borrow-and-plunge strategy would finance a comfortable retirement *and* give them instant gratification along the way. In 2000, Mr. Market destroyed this illusion. Stocks had gotten far ahead of their 10 to 11 percent average annual reward, and the tech sector underwent a quick and violent regression to the mean. Belatedly, losers realized that the best investment they could have made was paying off their unpaid credit card balances.

Chris was six years older and considerably more experienced than Jacobs, but his debut at Venture was less enriching. Venture held its own and then some against its value-oriented peers in 1997 to 1999, but Mr. Market outran the value crowd, and tech was the booster. Having company didn't allay the misery among cautious investors. As money cascaded into funds like Jacobs', the inflow into Davis funds was reduced to a trickle. The board of directors at Davis Advisers had left well enough alone when well enough meant beating Mr. Market, but now it showed its impatience. Board members quizzed Chris on his mistakes. They suggested that he should hire more analysts. They wanted to know why he hadn't added more tech to the fund, even though tech companies rarely appeared on the Davis value screen.

"We're running a marathon, not a sprint," Chris said. "So it was a bit unnerving to be second-guessed on short-term performance. The whole money management business was fixated on the short term. Consultants, magazines, rating systems were geared to what you did this week, this month, this quarter. If you underperformed for six months—or, God forbid—two years, you were in trouble."

"Following in the family tradition," says Chris, "I'm in business to defeat the S&P 500 index over time." So was every other fund manager on the planet, although for two decades this goal had eluded 75 percent of the managerial population. The question became: Why did millions of investors continue to pay proven losers to deploy their capital with below-average results? Under Shelby, Venture consistently beat the average, but in 1998 and 1999, Chris and the value crowd had no chance against reckless euphoria.

During this turmoil, Chris promoted in-house analyst Ken Feinberg to share the hot seat as Venture co-manager. Ken was the detail man, the micro to Chris's macro. "I never cared about building my own empire," Chris says. "I'd always admired Ken's work. I liked having somebody to bounce ideas off of, somebody who could share the research. My grandfather ran a one-man show, and so did my father, after Biggs backed away. I wanted a two-man show, with an assist from Shelby. Ken and I agreed we'd never buy anything without talking to him. My father's a tremendous filter. He's known many of these companies for decades."

Chris can't chat with CEOs on the phone any time he feels like it, the way Shelby and Davis did. Companies are cautious about what they say, when they say it, and to whom they say it. What an executive might once have mentioned off the cuff is now filtered through lawyers and public relations departments. Because the Davis funds are bigger and better known than they were in the Shelby era, Chris enjoys better access than average managers.

Before he took the Venture job, Chris had noticed that popular performance ratings didn't necessarily tell a useful story. "Everybody in the business is accustomed to keeping score with one-, three-, and five-year results," he said, "but the scoring system implies a consistency that isn't really there. For instance, let's say I lagged the market four years in a row, and then, in the fifth year, I was up 200 percent. I'd get a great five-year score, even though the fund had only one great stretch.

"Fund rankings can also mislead. Let's say a fund's return puts it in the top 10 percent for ten years, top 25 percent for five years, and top 50 percent for one year. This progression makes it look like the manager lost his touch. While his portfolio may be out of favor temporarily, the strategy that put him in the top ten for ten years is still intact. But the data don't show that.

"In the same vein, a fund could rank thirtieth out of 100 similar competing funds every year for three decades, and still end up number one for the entire period. As other short-term wonders move down in the rankings, a consistent performer moves up."

To Chris, the truest test of stockpicking talent is the "rolling return," which tracks a fund over a succession of five- or ten-year periods. Obviously, this only applies to a portfolio with some history behind it, like Venture. Someone following Venture's rolling return, for instance, would look at results from 1969 to 1979, then 1970 to 1980, then 1971 to 1981, and so on.

At the start of the long bull market, investors could buy Mr. Market for 10 to 15 times earnings, so thousands of stocks were in the Davis ballpark. When Chris got involved, Mr. Market was selling for 25 to 30 times earnings, and the Davis ballpark was far less crowded. It was harder to find a proven high achiever with a promising future and a reasonable price tag, unless some bad press or a disappointing quarterly result caused the Street to ditch the stock. Chris and Ken took advantage of the fact that, late in this bull phase, Mr. Market had gotten the shakes, or in brokers' lingo, "increased volatility."

"In a recent stretch," Chris recalled, "the stock prices of 32 of our top 40 holdings moved up and down more than 50 percent between their lowest low and their highest high. And 15 of these stocks vacillated 100 percent." The shakes were disconcerting to an owner, but inviting to a potential buyer. Companies that Chris and Ken liked, except for their prices, suddenly became buys. An analyst at Morningstar, a mutual fund research service, called Venture "a rehab center for fallen growth stocks."

During the Fen-Phen crisis, drug maker American Home Products faced a multibillion-dollar liability over allegedly fatal side effects from the diet pill. Believing that "the stock price more than discounted the likely outcome" of the lawsuits, the duo brought American Home at a relatively safe and sane price. They also bought a high-flying conglomerate, Tyco, after SEC sleuths launched an investigation of accounting "irregularities." Along with associate Adam Seessel, Ken did a thorough number crunch and convinced himself (and Chris) that the SEC was on a snipe hunt.

In Venture's semiannual report, Chris and Ken told their shareholders that American Home and Tyco were "illustrative of our willingness to purchase companies opportunistically while others are anxiously selling." They picked up Costco and Tellabs during similar sell-offs.

Their crisis surfing didn't always gratify. Chris and Ken resisted buying $80 Lucent until Mr. Market gave them the chance to own it at $60. The new owners watched Lucent drop into the $20s. "We thought we paid a reasonable amount, but the company used some creative accounting to fluff up the earnings." Waste Management, the world's biggest trash hauler, had pulled a Lucent. So had Bank One. Still, Chris and Ken saw less risk in buying disparaged and fundamentally attractive companies after a markdown than in overpaying for celebrated and fundamentally attractive companies.

Creative accounting wasn't limited to Lucent and Waste Management. Chris discovered that many companies were fluffing their books to meet Street expectations and create an illusion of predictable success. Earnings were less and less what they appeared to be, so the most important measure of corporate merit was no longer reliable. The same fluffery had occurred near the top of the rise in Bull II, when Shelby was making his managerial debut. Shareholders didn't complain and regulators didn't investigate until after the market imploded. "I expect the same will happen after the next bear market," said Chris, "when the accountants' bag of tricks will be exposed."

A typical fund manager moved in and out of stocks at a frenzied pace—trading away every year, the portfolio's entire value and then some. The Davises remained boringly steadfast. Still the biggest clients of their own products, they minimized taxes by keeping a lid on the selling. Then, in 2000, the market momentum caused Chris and Ken to do a lot of uncharacteristic selling. Instead of waiting for companies to earn their way into higher valuations, investors bid them up in advance. Many stocks left the range of fair value and reached target prices the comanagers hadn't expected to see until 2005. Why wait for a prosperous hereafter if the hereafter has prematurely arrived? With that question in mind, they reduced their holdings in Texas Instruments and Applied Materials.

They also cut back on the banking sector, keeping their favorites (Wells Fargo, Fifth Third), but scuttling the Bank of America. Across the industry, profits were squeezed by higher interest rates. Delinquent loans were up; revenues were flat. In the insurance sector, they sold Chubb and Allstate. In the brokerage sector, they kept DLJ and Morgan Stanley Dean Witter. They held onto Wells Fargo, Citicorp, J.P. Morgan, Morgan Stanley, and AIG, all companies that Shelby had installed in the fund. They improvised with McDonald's and Nike and played on, using Shelby's multinational theme. Shelby was never partial to retailers.

To Chris's grandfather, a stock was forever. Davis sold a few companies along the way, but his biggest winners were eternal holds. Shelby held onto AIG through most of his career, but he owned relatively few forever stocks. Though only time will tell the outcome, Chris picked American Express, McDonald's, Wells Fargo, AIG, and Buffett's Berkshire Hathaway as possible forever candidates.

Berkshire Hathaway was a Davis eternal hold, but Shelby never bought it for Venture. It got into the portfolio indirectly when Buffett acquired insurer General Re. Shelby owned General Re shares and received Berkshire stock in the deal. As GEICO and General Re had proven, if you owned a great insurance company, there was a good chance you'd end up working for Warren Buffett or for Hank Greenberg at AIG. Greenberg had snapped up numerous small insurers in the Davis portfolio. In the 1990s, he acquired Eli Broad's SunAmerica.

Chris sees promise in multinational companies that can allocate capital around the world, wherever the best return can be earned. In the German, Japanese, and other foreign markets, he sees opportunity as more businesses follow America's lead and streamline their operations. Though he avoids Internet investments per se, he looks for the beneficiaries of Internet shopping and banking. American Express and Citicorp are two obvious examples.

"There's no investor who argues what he's buying is overvalued," Chris told a reporter, wading into the endless growth–value debate. "That's what investing is—trying to realize value." The two sides differ. Value investors seek to buy earnings at a reasonable price (although "reasonable" is open to interpretation). Growth investors will pay an apparently exorbitant price for a future earnings bonanza. Embryonic growth companies with zero earnings are bid up in anticipation of spectacular results ahead. In every promising start-up, investors hope to find the next Microsoft, Wal-Mart, Cisco, or Home Depot.

Given the fortunes that fast-growing companies like Microsoft have made for their founders, you'd think the high-priced, fast-growth camp would have landed a few stock pickers on the Forbes 400 richest Americans list. Yet no billionaires or near-billionaires have materialized from that group. Davis and Buffett got to ten figures from the value camp. They bought growth at modest prices.

The Nifty Fifty is a case study in the perils of high-priced growth. After the bears mauled the tech sector in 1969 to 70, investors fled to the presumed safety of America's most esteemed enterprises. From Coca-Cola to Pfizer, Merck to McDonald's, Disney to American Express, the fleeing horde paid top dollar for quality. Most Nifties are far bigger and more profitable today than they were in 1970, so as growth companies they succeeded. But as top-dollar investments, they didn't live up to the price tag.

Wharton Professor Jeremy Siegel put a positive spin on the Nifties in his book, *Stocks for the Long Run*. According to Siegel, if you bought all 50 at peak prices in 1970, ignored your huge paper losses, and stuck with the portfolio, your loyalty was rewarded by 30 years later. At that point, the patient Nifties investor had caught up to the S&P 500.

Siegel's argument cheered up the growth camp because it vindicated the pricetag-be-damned growth stock strategy. Then astute reporters at *Barron's* magazine poked two big holes in Siegel's contention:

1. What investor was stubborn enough to ignore the initial 70 to 80 percent decline in his or her holdings and carry the Nifties through seven Presidential administrations? Families could raise kids and see them graduate from college before the Nifties paid off.
2. To get Siegel's result, you had to "rebalance" the portfolio every year by subtracting money from the winners and adding it to the losers. If you held the shares you bought in the first place, the Nifties returned about 2 percent a year. A passbook savings account was more rewarding.

Thus, owning some of the finest companies in the world was a lousy deal if you overpaid and a worse deal if you bought the most expensive Nifties. Companies with lower P/E ratios, such as Gillette and Disney, did better than those with higher ratios, such as Polaroid and Xerox, which never reached their former lofty prices again.

"Owning slower growth (8 to 14 percent) can be tremendously profitable if you don't overpay for it," Chris said. "But the Street aims for faster growth. Piles of analysts' reports land on my desk, and no matter what company is being analyzed or what product it sells, the conclusion is almost always the same: The long-term growth rate will equal or exceed 15 percent. With that in mind, I give friends, analysts, and other fund managers the following quiz: How many of the great Nifty Fifty companies grew their earnings at 15 percent, or better, from then to now?

"Knowing the Nifty list included Coke, Merck, IBM, Disney, and other outstanding performers, most people answer: '20 or 30 companies.' Or, if they try to give a low-ball response, they say: '10 or 15.' The real answer is three: Philip Morris, McDonald's, and Merck. This trio is the exception that proves an important point. It's unrealistic to expect companies to grow at 15 percent for extended periods. Most great companies can't do it. People who pay high prices for stocks, based on high growth assumptions, are asking for trouble up the line."

That's why the Davises, Peter Lynch, and Warren Buffett generally have avoided tech stocks. They've all made jokes about being technophobic, and Lynch admitted he was all thumbs with anything more sophisticated than a push-button phone. But the real cause of their avoidance is: Tech businesses aren't predictable. "Who could tell," Shelby said, "which of the dot-com companies would thrive, or even survive, over time? In other industries that transformed the country, from autos to airplanes, most of the pioneering companies' industries are no longer in business today."

In 1999, Chris heard Warren Buffett tell an audience he expected stocks to return 6 percent a year for the next 17 years—less than half the payoff during the prior 17 years. Buffett based this sobering forecast on simple math: In 1999, the entire lineup of Fortune 500 companies was selling for $10 trillion, supported by $300 billion in annual earnings. When the annual fees shareholders paid to own those assets—roughly, 1 percent of $10 trillion, or $100 million—were subtracted the actual payoff from their investing was $200 million. Contemporary investors were buying Mr. Market for 50 times earnings. Because an entire economy can't justify a multiple, of 50, Buffett surmised, stock prices would have to give. They might give slowly or give quickly, or meander until the nation's earnings caught up to them, but they couldn't rise at their former pace without violating the laws of financial gravity. A $3 trillion price tag on a market with $200 billion earnings might be reasonable—but $10 trillion? No way.

High valuations in the turn-of-the-century market caused Shelby to turn cautious as well. "Worst case, we go into a depression," he'd said, in his usual cheerful tone in the summer of 1998. He worried about the Asian financial mess in general, and Japanese bank failures in particular. His sidekick, Jeremy Biggs, had sighted a huge flock of construction cranes in Shanghai on a trip to the Far East. "Cranes on the skyline are a sign of a market top," Shelby said. He worried that the Japanese public would lose its life savings because Japan lacks deposit insurance. He fretted over unsold merchandise piling up in Chinese warehouses. "You sort of wonder if China will be forced to devalue its currency, hurting our exports and overwhelming us with imports." He wondered if his father's description of the 1930s, "a scary 10 years," would fit the 2000s.

He suspected the U.S. economic handlers—Treasury Secretary Rubin and Fed Chairman Greenspan—were putting a happy face on a grim situation. Though the Fed had proven it could quell inflation, he doubted it could foil deflation, the flip side of inflation (lower prices) and potentially just as dangerous. Already, deflation was spreading across Asia. Was the United States the next stop? "Deflation is tough to fight," Shelby said. "Lower interest rates won't do the trick, because banks aren't lending and companies aren't borrowing. Normally, companies borrow to expand, but now they're not expanding. In a deflationary crisis, they have no reason to expand because people aren't buying their products. People aren't buying because they're out of money."

Turning to the bright side, Shelby reminded himself that the Asian bear market offered U.S. multinationals a chance to go shopping with spare cash. When valuable assets went on the block in Japan, Korea, or Thailand, Citigroup and its ilk were there to snap them up. He thought the Japanese banking crisis wasn't as bad as the press made it out to be. "In some ways, the U.S. savings-and-loan crisis of the late 1980s was worse," he said. "Japan can borrow its way out of trouble with single-digit interest rates, while the U.S. government paid 9 percent on its S&L bailout bonds. Also, the Japanese consumer isn't saddled with bank and credit card debt the way U.S. consumers are."

Whatever happens, Shelby expected stocks to stop racing ahead and revert to their customary canter. "If the Dow continued to rise at the same pace it's risen over the past two decades, it would stand at roughly 100,000 two decades from now," he said. "But we're certain that won't happen. Even if the rise slows to 7 or 8 percent a year, the Dow could reach 40,000 to 50,000. So a lot more wealth can still be created long-term. On the other hand, the surge in corporate profits and P/E ratios that created the 1990s bonanza isn't likely to continue. It won't surprise me if the market is stuck in a trading range for the next five to ten years. Good stock pickers will make money, but the averages may not show much movement."

In the next comeuppance, whenever it occurs, Chris expects the growth-at-prudent-prices (GAPP) stocks will suffer less than growth-at-silly-prices (GASP) stocks. "One scenario has Mr. Market shedding 30 percent and Venture shedding 15," he said. "But there's no guarantee of that, and, anyway, if our fund is down with the rest, nobody will congratulate the managers on losing less than the dart board. If a modern Cassandra tipped me off to the exact arrival date of the next bear, I'd raise cash to invest after the onslaught. But without a Cassandra, there's no way of timing calamity. If I prepare for the worst and stocks rise another 15 percent, I don't want my fund to rise zero.

"Our best bear protection is buying companies with strong balance sheets, low debt, real earnings, and powerful franchises. These companies can survive bad times and eventually become more dominant as weaker competitors are forced to cut back or shut down."

In the early phase of the Chris–Ken collaboration, Venture has had its occasional midyear slump, but the comanagers ended the millennium on an upbeat note. According to Morningstar, Venture recorded its sixth consecutive year of superior performance in its category, and Davis Financial had led its category for five straight years. Venture gained 10 percent in 2000 while the average stock lost that amount and the Nasdaq was having its 50-percent-off sale.

Chris sees making good investments as only part of Venture's job. Just as important is persuading clients to park their cash in the fund long enough to reap the benefit. As reported in *Mutual Funds* magazine (March 2000), typical investors stay with a typical fund less than three years. Then they're lured away by more exciting funds, just at the point when these others falter. This frequent switching has been costly. The average fund gained more than 500 percent between 1984 and 1998; the average owner gained only 186 percent. The rest was lost to the dating game. Lackluster funds were routinely dropped and replaced by more exciting funds, just at the point where the exciting funds lost their luster and the duller, spurned funds regained theirs.

In bad times, Chris hopes his customers will stick around for the inevitable rebound. "Our firm is devoted to educating customers to stay the course. We try not to be too positive about short-term successes, or too negative about short-term setbacks."

CHAPTER 19

INVESTING À LA DAVIS

N THE FAST-GROWTH LANE, A FEW RELIABLE winners (the Microsofts and Wal-Marts) race ahead of the wanna-bes in every decade. Invest four figures in the next reliable winner and, 20 years later, you can retire with a seven-figure portfolio. Take Microsoft—and what investors don't wish they had? The stock looked extravagant at almost any time. It has continued to sell at a pricey 30 to 40 times earnings throughout its lucrative history. Yet, with the earnings doubling every 24 months, Microsoft buyers always found themselves holding a bargain two years after their "undisciplined" purchase. Their patience was well rewarded. A modest investment during Microsoft's infancy was as good as winning the lottery. What's the catch? Finding another Microsoft among the hopeful enterprises that annually go public in growing numbers. Picking the survivors, let alone the winners, is as hard as figuring out which turtle eggs hatched in the sand will become the giant turtles of the future. It's curious how few great fortunes have been made by fast-growth technology enthusiasts. Founders and other insiders have become wealthy on high-tech, but where are the outsiders' yachts? No high-tech stockpicker has made the Forbes 400 list, perhaps because successful trendy investing demands contradictory abilities: the ability to see the next New New Thing and the courage to take a chance on it, plus the skepticism and the flexibility needed to abandon the New New Thing before it succumbs to the New New New Thing. People who stick too long with a technology play find their paper profits quickly vaporize, as they did in 1970 and can be expected to do in the future. Every trendy industry in one decade has a habit of destroying its backers in the next.

On the flip side of fast-growth investing is *value*. Value investors ignore the wanna-bes and concentrate on the has-beens. According to Benjamin Graham, the father of value investing, a perfect value play occurs when a company's tangible assets (cash in the bank, buildings, machines, and so on) will fetch more in a going-out-of-business sale than can be realized in the current market. This affords investors some margin of safety. If all goes badly, the company can be liquidated and they will get back more than they paid for their shares. The catch is: Value companies tend to have problems, and a stock that looks cheap today continues to get cheaper.

Between the fast growers that flame out and the value companies that limp along, there's a middle ground where companies offer steady profit growth at a reasonable price. Generally, reasonable prices don't exist in hot industries, so middle-ground investing automatically keeps adherents away from fanciful and dangerous territory like the Internet.

The Davises occupy this middle ground. They started with insurance stocks, and then, after a period of unfortunate fast-growth experimentation, Shelby applied his father's method to other industries, especially finance.

The math is instructive because the middle ground requires a longer wait for a big payday. Davis stayed with the middle ground for more than 40 years, but 40 years is exactly what a 30-year-old investor is looking at when he or she begins to prepare for retirement. "Investing isn't as complex as some people make it out to be," Chris volunteered. "You're deploying cash today, hoping to get more cash back in the future. That's all investing is. For us, the whole process hinges on two questions: What kind of businesses to buy, and how much to pay for them? To answer question one: A company worth buying makes more money than it spends. Its profit is recycled for maximum shareholder benefit. The second question, the price tag, is often ignored."

In the distant past, people bought stocks for their dividends, but dividends have gone the way of the manual toothbrush. Today, profit is paramount, and before Chris can determine whether the price tag is excessive, irresistible, or reasonable, he turns a skeptic's eye toward the earnings.

"We ask ourselves," said Chris, "if we owned the company outright, how much reward [would] we pocket at the end of the year, after reinvesting enough cash to maintain the status quo, and before reinvesting for growth? The result is called 'owner earnings.' This isn't a snap to calculate. We adjust for stock options, the depreciation rate, deferred taxes, and other subtle factors. Owner earnings are almost always lower than the earnings reported by the company.

"We also take a hard look at debt. Two businesses may have identical earnings and sell for the same price, so apparently they're valued the same. However, if one is saddled with a large debt and the other is debt-free, they're not the same at all."

Once Chris translates the often fanciful "reported" earnings into "owner earnings," he compares the expected future payoff from holding the stock to the payoff from holding a government bond. Bondholders receive predictable payments; a stock's benefits are potentially superior but often less reliable.

[For purposes of comparison, Chris translates owner earnings into an "earnings yield" by dividing the earnings by the stock price—the inverse of the P/E ratio. Thus, a $30 stock that earns $2 (a P/E of 15) "yields" 6.6 percent, or more than a contemporary bond. But when a $60 stock earns $2 (a P/E of 30), it yields 3.3 percent, much less than a bond.]

"You'd be crazy to own a business that yields 3.3 percent instead of a 6 percent bond, unless the business can increase its earnings yield in the future," Chris says. "In other words, it must be able to grow."

"The challenge is to project that growth out eight or ten years. For any projection to be close to the mark, the business must be relatively predictable. You can't pin a ten-year forecast on the typical tech company. Even if you buy tech at a relatively cheap price (we picked up Hewlett-Packard at 15 times earnings), it can take years before the return on the stock matches the return on a bond." The Davis strategy—the result of five decades of trial, error, and refinement—worked its way through father, son, and grandsons, and each generation tweaked it and tuned it to fit the era. The 10 basic tenets remain the same:

1. *Avoid cheap stocks.* Shelby learned from experience, in the 1980s, that most cheap stocks deserve to be cheap because they're attached to dud companies. Chances are, a dud company will stay that way. Its CEO will predict better times ahead, as CEOs always do. The company may put itself in rehab, but rehab is an iffy proposition. "Even when it works," says Shelby, "it usually takes a company longer to turn around than anybody expects. You have to be a masochist to like this kind of investing."

2. *Avoid expensive stocks.* Stocks may deserve to be expensive because they're attached to great companies, but Shelby refuses to buy them unless they carry a sensible price tag,

relative to their earnings. "No business is attractive at any price," says Shelby. The Davises never overpaid for clothes, houses, or vacations. Why should investors overpay for earnings, which after all, are what they're buying whenever they invest in a company?

Chris describes the fictional epitome of what's wrong with hot issues that fizzle: "Microscape Casino and Steakhouse." The stock symbol for this imaginary enterprise is GOGO. Is this an Internet café with slot machines? Who cares! Whatever it does, GOGO has a boffo debut. Buyers pay 30 times earnings for the shares, and, over a four-year stretch, GOGO grows its earnings at a gratifying 30 percent annual clip. In the fifth year, GOGO loses some pep; earnings are up "only" 15 percent. For most companies, 15 percent is a fine result, but GOGO investors expect more. Now, they're balking at the shares and paying half the prior multiple—15 times earnings. This results in a 50 percent "correction" in the price.

At this point, the paper profits vaporize, and any early buyer who held GOGO through its brief heyday is left with a paltry 6 percent annual return—hardly a fair compensation for the risk. U.S. Government bonds paid 6 percent, and those were much less risky.

Once a fast grower disappoints, investors fall prey to cruel mathematics: a stock that's down 50 percent must rise 100 percent before it returns to the break-even point.

3. *Buy moderately priced stocks in companies that grow moderately fast.* Shelby's idea of a superior investment was a company that had a growth rate faster than the "multiple." He avoided GOGO and looked for companies like SOSO, an imaginary regional bank. SOSO, an unspectacular 13 percent earner, was selling for a modest 10 times its earnings. If SOSO continued to perform as advertised for five years, causing investors to pay 15 times earnings for the stock, the patient shareholder

bagged a 20 percent annual return, as opposed to the 6 percent that would have been received from GOGO.

Occasionally, the Davis clan discovered a "stealth grower" with a SOSO reputation and Microsoft's knack for profit. Spectacular returns for a bleacher price is an irresistible combination, and Davis found it in AIG and numerous others.

Had AIG sold pacemakers or genetically altered seeds, investors surely would have awarded it a higher multiple. As a boring insurance company, it never attracted much exuberance—irrational or otherwise. That the stock was chronically undervalued kept the downside risk to a minimum.

4. *Wait until the price is right.* When Shelby liked a company but not the price tag, he waited for a chance to pay less. Analysts who changed their opinions three or four times a year created chances to buy IBM, Intel, and Hewlett-Packard. The occasional bear market also became the careful shopper's best friend. As Davis used to say, "Bear markets make people a lot of money, they just don't know it at the time."

Sometimes, an industry has its own bear market. The real estate bear of the 1980s spread into banking and gave Shelby a chance to buy Citicorp and Wells Fargo. The Clinton Administration's misguided health care reform package, in the early 1990s, sicced the bears on drug stocks, and first-rate pharmaceutical manufacturers (Merck, Pfizer, Lilly, etc.) were marked down 40 to 50 percent. Shelby and Chris built positions in all three.

An individual company can have its own bear market when bad news (an oil spill, a class action lawsuit, a product recall, and so on) sinks the stock. This is a buying opportunity, as long as the calamity is short-lived and doesn't hinder the company's long-term prospects.

"When you buy a battered stock in a solid company," Shelby says, "you take some risk out of the purchase. Investors have low expectations."

Through the 1980s, Shelby could choose from an ample selection of growth companies selling at 10 to 12 times earnings. These all but disappeared in the Roaring '90s. More than ever before, Chris and Ken were forced to wait for a markdown.

5. *Don't fight progress.* Shelby chose his tech stocks carefully, but he didn't avoid them entirely, as two well-known technophobes, Buffett and Peter Lynch, had done.

As long as he could find reasonably priced companies with real earnings and established franchises, he was eager to invite technology into his portfolio. Otherwise, he'd miss the liveliest part of the economy. He bought Intel early and rode it to a fantastic gain. He owned IBM since the mid-1980s. He bought Applied Materials, a modern "pick-and-shovel play." In the Gold Rush of the nineteenth century, merchants who sold picks and shovels made ample profit, but their prospecting customers went broke. In similar fashion, Applied Materials sold equipment to prospectors in the semiconductor industry.

6. *Invest in a theme.* "Bottoms-up" stockpickers invest in companies that have favorable attributes. They'll buy an oil driller as readily as a fast-food chain, if the story is promising. A "top-down" stockpicker surveys the economic climate, finds industries that are likely to thrive in current conditions, and chooses companies from those industries. Shelby is "top down" and "bottoms up." Before he puts new cash to work, he looks for "themes." Most of the time, themes are obvious.

In the 1970s, the obvious theme was rampant inflation. Shelby filled Venture's portfolio with oil, natural gas, aluminum, and other commodity-based companies that stood to profit from higher prices. In the 1980s, there were signs the Fed was winning its war against inflation. Shelby found a new theme: lower prices and lower interest rates. He cut back on the hard assets and bought financial assets: banks, brokerage houses, and insurance companies. A financial group benefits from falling interest rates. Shelby sank 40 percent of his fund's assets into financials, just in time for their great leap forward. These "stealth growth stocks" didn't increase profits as fast as Microsoft or Home Depot, but they delivered happy returns nonetheless.

In the 1990s, Shelby and Chris acted on another obvious theme: aging baby boomers. As the wealthiest generation in U.S. history approached geezerdom, drug companies, health care, and nursing homes were beneficiaries. After a big run-up in drug stocks, Shelby waited to buy at the next markdown.

7. *Let your winners ride.* The typical growth-stock mutual fund sells 90 percent of its holdings every year and replaces them with other, presumably more promising merchandise. The turnover rate at New York Venture hovers around 15 percent. The Davises prefer to buy and hold, primarily because they avoid paying the huge capital gains taxes on their long-term gains. The buy-and-hold approach keeps transaction costs low and eliminates mistakes that happen with frequent trading. Frequent traders are just as likely to trade a winner for a loser and vice versa.

Throughout Shelby's childhood, Davis harped on the futility of market timing. Shelby passed the message along to Chris and Andrew.

"We buy at a bargain price we can live with for a long time," Shelby says. "Eventually, we hope to see the stock sell at 'fair value,' and once it reaches that point, we tend to keep it as long as earnings continue to rise. We like to buy at a value price but we want to end up with growth companies.

"I was comfortable owning a stock through two or three recessions, or market cycles. That way, I learned how the company handled bad times, as well as good times."

8. *Bet on superior management.* Davis invested in great managers like Hank Greenberg at AIG. Shelby did the same with Andy Grove at Intel and Eli Broad at SunAmerica. If a great leader left one company for another, Shelby moved money

into the new enterprise, buying the manager's talent again. When Jack Grundhoffer switched from Wells Fargo to First Bank Systems, Shelby bought First Bank. He bought American Express when Harvey Golub surfaced there.

"It's a Wall Street truism that good management is important to any company's success, but the typical analyst's report ignores the subject," says Chris. "Analysts prefer to discuss the latest numbers, but we never buy anything without assessing the leadership."

9. *Ignore the rear-view mirror.* "Computers and their endless databases cause investors to focus on the past," says Shelby. "More than ever before, people are looking backward into the future." The most valuable lesson to learn from history on Wall Street is that history doesn't exactly repeat itself. For 25 years after the 1929 Crash, hordes of investors avoided stocks on the false premise that a 1929 rerun was imminent. After World War II, they avoided stocks because they'd learned wars are always followed by recessions. In the second half of the 1970s, they avoided stocks and prepared for a repeat of the 1973 to 1974 bear market. As Shelby wrote in 1979, "The majority of investors today are spending an inordinate amount of time defensing against what we believe is an improbable if not almost impossible decline of similar magnitude." From 1988 to 1989, they avoided stocks and prepared for a repeat of the 1987 Crash. In all cases, they wished they hadn't. Numerous fallacious lessons have been learned from Wall Street experience. For example:

- "Stocks only rise when corporate profits rise." Actually, stocks often do well when profits sag.
- "Stocks are hurt by high inflation." They weren't hurt during the early 1950s.
- "Stocks are a perfect hedge against high inflation." Not in the early 1970s.

10. *Stay the course*. "Stocks may be risky for one, three, or even five years, but not 10 or 15 years," says Chris. "My father got in at a market top and, 20 years later, his bad start was irrelevant. In our messages to shareholders, we keep repeating ourselves: We're running in a marathon."

The Davis Checklist

As Shelby noted in a memo he wrote on May 22, 1997, every company he installed in Venture's portfolio exhibited most, if not all, of the following characteristics:

- First-class management with a proven record of keeping its word.
- Does innovative research and uses technology to maximum advantage.
- Operates abroad as well as at home. Overseas markets have given mature U.S. companies a second chance at fast growth. Some Wall Street analysts dubbed Coca-Cola a has-been in the early 1980s, but Coke went abroad and proved them wrong. The story was the same for AIG, McDonald's, and Philip Morris.
- Sells products or services that don't become obsolete.
- Insiders own a large chunk of shares and have a personal stake in the company's success.
- Company deliver strong returns on investors' capital, and managers are committed to rewarding investors.
- Expenses are kept to a minimum, which makes the company a low-cost producer.
- Company enjoys a dominant or a growing share in a growing market.
- Company is adept at acquiring competitors and making them more profitable.
- Company has a strong balance sheet.

In the months this book went through the editing gaunt-
let, owners of tech stocks or tech mutual funds saw for themselves the perils of growth at any price, in the collapse of the
Nasdaq market. Cheerleaders of the new-era concept gained
a retroactive respect for old-era concepts—crusty truisms
about overheated markets always finding a way to cool
down. Whether we've found the bottom of this latest bear
market, or whether the bottom is yet to be reached is anybody's guess, but already the decline of 2000/2001 has cost
investors trillions and demoralized the stock-hungry public.
It also has brought the market closer to the Davis comfort
zone, where money can be made buying companies at less
than 15 times earnings and investing in the 7 to 15 percent
annual earnings growth that has been the norm for many
decades.

Figure 19.1 Davis New York Venture Fund Class A Shares (February
17, 1969 to December 31, 2000). Fund performance includes 4.75
percent maximum sales chare and reflects reinvested distributions and
changes in net asset value for Class A shares.

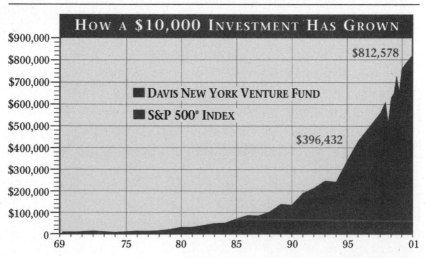

Confronted with high expectations and valuations to match, Chris and his partner Ken Feinberg have struggled to find opportunities that would have made sense to Chris's grandfather and to Shelby. They've made their rookie mistakes: just has Shelby had his Memorex—a trendy pick on the way up, when buyers thought no price was too high, and a wealth wrecker on the way down, when sellers learned no price was too low. Chris and Ken have had Lucent Technologies, a similar disapointment to date. But generally, they've stuck to more reliable growth at a reasonable price, as did their predecessors. They'll rely on the Davis Double Play, and not on risky bets on high flyers, to give their returns a boost.

Through difficult times, the Davis family has found solace in the Rule of 72, realizing that if you can manage to compound your money at 10 percent per year, you'll be well rewarded, and if you can compound at 15 percent or better (as Davis did with his own portfolio and as Shelby did with the Venture portfolio), you'll enjoy an enormous return that will make the recent setback seem as a trivial feint. Patience, long-term thinking, and a generational time frame make up the Davis dynasty's recipe for successful investing.

Source Notes

Introduction

1. Buffett's ownership of a public company gave him more capital on which to capitalize than Davis had gathered from his spousal till. Davis, for his part, augmented his returns by investing "on margin." He borrowed money from banks and used the cash to buy more stock. While it artificially enhanced his return, margin also left him small margin for error. During bear markets, many less adept margin investors were forced to liquidate their portfolios to repay their lenders. Davis always managed to keep his portfolio intact.

    In the bullish 1990s, many shareholders learned to take 20 percent annual returns for granted, along with Social Security and the cable box, but over the market's longer haul, 20 percent is such a rarity that Peter Lynch bagged 20 percent for 16 years and became a celebrity. So rare that 23 percent compounded put Davis on the *Forbes* list and made Warren Buffett the first- or second-richest American, depending on how well Bill Gates was doing at the time.

2. The Rule of 72 tells you how many years it will take to double your money in any investment—based on the rate of return. With bonds, the return is predictable; with stocks, you can only make an educated guess. Once you've got the rate (10 percent, 20 percent, and so on), you divide it into 72. With a 10 percent return, you'll double your money in 7.2 years (72 divided by 10). With a 20 percent return, you'll double your money in 3.6 years.

    A quick crunch of the numbers shows that Davis's annual return on investment was 23 percent over four decades. In case you want to try this at home, here's how 18 years' worth of 20 percent annual gains can fatten a bankroll, via the magic of "compounding": $100,000 becomes $3.2 million; $250,000 becomes $8 million.

2. From the Great Depression to the Hitler Crisis

1. Marquis James, *The Metropolitan Life: A Study in Business Growth,* 1947.
2. James Grant, *The Trouble with Prosperity,* Times Books, Random House, 1996, p. 69.
3. Ibid., pp. 69–73.

4. A Last Hurrah for Bonds

1. Shelby Cullom Davis, *America Faces the Forties,* Dorrance & Company, 1940.

5. A Crib Course in Coverage

1. Robin Willis, "Taking a Risk, an Historical and Hysterical Look at the Purveyors of Dream, Doom, and Destruction," Pamphlet, Witherby, London,

1988. Donald Armstrong, "History of Property Insurance Business in the U.S. Prior to 1890," PhD diss., New York University, 1971. "Early History of Insurance," published by The Society of Chartered Property and Casualty Underwriters, 1966.
2. "Milestones in Insurance History," Booklet, The American Mutual Reinsurance Company. Alwin E. Bulau, "Footprints of Assurance," MacMillan, 1953.
3. Marquis James, *Biography of a Business: Insurance Company of North America,* Bobbs-Merrill, 1942.

6. From Bureaucrat to Investor

1. James Grant, *The Trouble with Prosperity,* p. 89.

8. Davis Shops Abroad

1. John Brooks, *The Go-Go Years,* Wiley, 1999, p. 27.
2. Material on the successful entry of AIU, AIG, and AFLAC in Japan comes from Michael Lewis, *Pacific Rift,* Norton, 1993, a short book about U.S.-Japanese business relations.

9. Wall Street a Go-Go

1. John Brooks, *The Go-Go Years,* Wiley, 1999, pp. 12, 279, 305, 353.
2. National Association of Securities Dealers Automated Quotations (Nasdaq).

13. The Worst Decline Since 1929

1. Roger Lowenstein, *Buffett: The Making of an American Capitalist,* Random House, 1995, p. 195.

15. Shelby Buys Banks; Davis Buys Everything

1. David Schiff published a compilation of the Buffett quotes on insurance in *Emerson Reid's Insurance Observer,* November 1995, and cited Buffett in subsequent issues of *Schiff's Insurance Observer.*
2. Berkshire Hathaway annual report, 1988.
3. Ibid.
4. Ibid.
5. Berkshire Hathaway annual report, 1980.
6. Berkshire Hathaway annual report, 1985.
7. Ibid.
8. See note 5.

17. The Family Joins Forces

1. James Grant, *The Trouble with Prosperity,* Times Books, Random House, 1996, p. 175.

Index

Adams, Wendy, 142, 231–232
Adams, Weston, 143
Alger, Fred, 120
Aluminum industry, 147–149, 177
America Firsters (isolationists), 52
Art Loom, 20, 21, 25, 35, 36, 54
Associated Madison, 231

Bank(s)/banking, 28, 32, 47, 77,
  149–150, 216–220, 241, 252,
  275
Bank of New York, 9, 143–150, 162,
  187, 191, 217, 236
Batterson, James, 72
Beck, Harry, 88
Berkshire Hathaway, 129, 225, 249,
  250, 276
Biggs, Jeremy, 132, 162–163, 165,
  166–171, 180, 186, 190, 191,
  255, 257, 272, 280
Biller, Les, 253
Blue chips, 119, 171. *See also* Nifty
  Fifty
Bonds (*vs.* stocks), 15–16, 40, 56, 57,
  64, 76–77, 95, 102–103, 135, 251
British *vs.* U.S. compared, Great
  Depression era, 41–42
Broad, Eli, 255, 276, 291
Brokaw, Frank, 28, 83
Brooks, John (*The Go-Go Years*), 123,
  124, 126
Buffett, Warren, 81, 87, 122, 152,
  182, 183, 203, 206, 210, 211,
  238, 254, 270, 271, 276, 277,
  279

Davis compared with, 4–5, 17, 254
Davis investment in, 249, 250
GEICO, 195, 198–199, 200, 201,
  225–226, 227
and zero population growth, 210
Bullock, Hugh, 166, 183, 190
Bundy, McGeorge, 122
Bush, Julian, 156
Byrne, Jack, 200, 201

Campeau, Robert, 216, 252
Carr, Fred, 120–121, 125
Chase, Stuart, 43
Cohen, Manuel F., 118
Compounding, power of, 37, 152,
  230, 231
Cullom, Julia, 16
Cullom, Shelby, 14–15

Data processing stocks, 123, 124, 168
Davis, Andrew, 10, 213, 229, 242,
  244, 258–259, 264–265
Davis, Chris, 10–11, 183, 208, 209,
  213, 229–242, 243–265,
  267–282, 286, 287
Davis, Diana. *See* Spencer, Diana
  Davis
Davis, George Henry ("the judge"),
  16–17, 18, 153
Davis, Kathryn Wasserman, 5–6
America Firsters (joined in
  support of husband), 52
article, "Household Servants Are
  Gone Forever," 55
childhood, 21

civic affairs, 38, 50, 52
daughter-in-law compared to, 142
on daughter's inheritance flap,
    154, 158
death of third child, 52
house hunting, 55–56
eulogy for husband, 262
jobs, 22, 30, 35, 83
League of Women Voters, 38, 52
meeting husband, 19–20
oldest woman member of NYSE
    (taking over Davis seat at age
    84), 260
on paper wealth, 139
Planned Parenthood, 38
politics, 52, 211
schools/colleges, 24, 25–26,
    29–30
source of Davis's initial Wall Street
    investment, 3, 5–6, 51
wartime (walking not driving), 53
"Waterman" (in Who's Who in
    America), 35
wearing gold ambassador's wife
    pin, 202–203
Davis, Palmer, and Biggs, 161–173,
    189–190, 247
Davis, Shelby (first), 3–4
aging/decline, 10–11, 245, 246,
    259, 260, 261, 262–263
ambassadorial appointment to
    Switzerland, 9, 132, 133–134,
    176, 194, 195, 200, 202, 232
and anti-Semitism, 36
bad eyesight keeping out of
    military, 51–52
birth (1909), 14
from bureaucrat to investor, 75–89
childhood/youth/schools, 6–7, 15,
    16–17, 18, 20, 24, 25–26, 29
children's births (Shelby and
    Diana), 50
comparison to Buffett, 4–5, 17,
    254

contrarian crusade (antibond
    maverick; pro-stocks), 56–61
Davis Dozen, 249
day trading (dabbled in), 207
"dean of American insurance," 99
death/funeral (1994), 5, 11,
    261–262
depression era/postmortem, 23–38,
    39–47
estate planning, 210–211, 241,
    256, 257, 262
favorite CEOs, 8
foreign investing, 105–115 (see also
    Japanese holdings)
genealogical interest, 141, 212
on inherited wealth, 153
isolationism, 29, 36, 51–52
jobs, 29–38, 50, 55
journalism/freelancing, 30, 38, 50
lifetime investment record (ledger),
    247–251
margin investing, 56, 86, 96, 107,
    202, 244
marriage/newlywed, 19–22, 25–26,
    28–29
net worth, 5, 9–10, 22, 89, 95, 101,
    107, 138, 146, 194, 209, 216,
    223
old coat anecdote, 244–245
organizations, 81, 88, 98, 141,
    262
philanthropy, 209
Princeton donation ("inheritance
    flap"), 151–160
relationship with son Shelby, 7,
    136, 163, 248
seat on New York Stock Exchange,
    51, 56, 189
work/career milestones, 3–4,
    29–38, 50, 55, 75–89, 188,
    193–203
wrote America Faces the Forties, 38,
    40, 41
wrote Your Job in Defense, 50

INDEX

Davis, Shelby (second), 3
  birth (in 1937), 6, 35, 38, 50
  and Buffett, 254
  childhood/youth/schools, 6–7,
    52–53, 134–143, 254
  children, 213, 230, 232–233, 234,
    235, 240
    Andrew working for, 258
    Chris working for, 10–11, 255,
      268
  on *Forbes* honor roll (1988), 223
  and Graham, 183, 184
  relationship with father, 10,
    142–143, 149, 160, 163, 176,
    209, 212–213, 237, 248, 261
    rejected job offer, 10, 143
    similarity to, 6–7
  style (both top down and bottoms
    up), 290
  wife 1 (Wendy), 142, 143, 232
  wife 2 (Gale), 213
  work/career milestones, 9, 143–150,
    161–173, 175–191, 272
Davis, Victoria (Tory), 213, 234,
  235, 240
Davis, Wendy Adams, 142,
  231–232
Davis Advisers, 257, 271
Davis Double Play, 95–96, 107, 165,
  170, 186, 216, 295
Davis family:
  accidental meeting of three
    generations, 241–242
  checklist, company characteristics,
    293
  frugality of, 8–9, 18, 22, 30, 51,
    83–84, 102, 138, 139, 213,
    232
  funds, 11, 248, 255, 257, 282
    (*see also* Venture Fund)
  investing tenets, 283–295
  joining forces, 243–265
Day trading, 207
Delaware Fund, 34, 37, 38

Depression era/postmortem, 18,
  23–38, 39–47
Dewey, Thomas E., 38, 50, 55, 64,
  82, 132, 137

Ebbitt, Ken, 99, 134, 194
Ecker, Frederick, 59
Enterprise Fund, 120, 125

Fannie Mae, 168, 223–224, 247–248,
  249, 250, 256
Federal Deposit Insurance
  Corporation (FDIC), 57–58
Federal Reserve, 37, 41, 93, 95, 214,
  215, 217, 252, 253
Feinberg, Ken, 272, 274, 275, 281,
  290, 295
Fiduciary Trust, 189–190, 212, 241,
  247
Foreign investing, 105–115, 276,
  293
Free trade, 44
Funston, G. Keith, 93–94, 107, 118,
  137
Futures, 207–208

Galbraith, John Kenneth (*The Affluent
  Society*), 140
Gay Nineties bond rush, 95
Go-go investors, 119, 120, 122, 126,
  168, 186
Goheen, Robert, 154
Golub, Harvey, 292
Goodwin, Leo, 198
Grace, Oliver, 114
Graham, Benjamin, 81, 86, 87, 89,
  183–184, 195, 198, 199–200,
  201, 270, 285
Graham, Key, 200
Grant, James (*The Trouble with
  Prosperity*), 54, 95, 104, 171
Greenberg, Maurice ("Hank"), 8,
  200, 202, 219, 249, 254, 276,
  291

Greenspan, Alan, 253, 270, 280
Grove, Andy, 219, 291
Grundhoffer, Jack, 292

Haidt, Francis, 110
Halley, Edmund, 66
Hamilton, Alexander, 68, 149, 217
Hancock, John, 68
Havemann, Ernest, 103
Hazen, Paul, 253
Hedge fund split, 208
Heritage Foundation, 211, 223
Hettinger, Al, 114
Hillary, Sir Edmund, 100
Hoover, Herbert, 45
Howe, George, 33
Hull, Cordell, 44

Income *vs.* stock portfolio, 210. *See also* Bonds (*vs.* stocks)
Inflation, 47, 59, 77, 95, 104, 189, 214, 215
Insurance industry, 63–73
    automobile, 71–72
    Davis as government bureaucrat, and, 55, 64
    Davis investments in, 79–89, 195, 219, 224–227, 275
    earnings study (Plotkin), 126–129
    history of, 27–28, 59, 60, 64–73, 195–203
    as interstate commerce, 72
    mutual *vs.* stock companies, 70
    regulation, 27–28, 59, 60, 70, 71, 72, 127
    stock market performance charts, 196, 197
Internet fund, first, 269–270
Investing:
    bonds *vs.* stocks, 15–16, 40, 56, 57, 64, 76–77, 95, 102–103, 135, 251
    checklist for company characteristics, 293

"cruel joke" (most popular asset of each era will impoverish its owners), 60–61
long-term (Davis dynasty as 50-year case study), 11–12
margin, 56, 86, 96, 107, 202, 244
middle ground (growth *vs.* value), 285–286
power of compounding, and Rule of 72, 6, 10, 37, 135–136, 152, 230, 231, 295
vs. speculators, 81
summary of market changes over 50 years, 11–12
tenets of stockpicking (Davis strategy), 287–293
    avoiding cheap stocks, 287
    avoiding expensive stocks, 287–288
    betting on superior management, 291–292
    buying moderately priced stocks in companies that grow moderately fast, 288–289
    ignoring rear-view mirror, 292–293
    letting winners ride, 291
    not fighting progress, 290
    staying the course, 293
    theme investing, 290–291
    waiting until price is right, 289
    top down and bottoms up, 290
Isolationism, 29, 36, 51–52

Jacobs, Ryan, 269–271
Japanese holdings, 109–114, 176, 177, 178, 202, 216, 249, 263–264, 280
Jones, Alfred, 208
Jones, Paul Tudor, 221
Junk bonds, 216

Keynes, John Maynard, 42, 43, 58
Kline, Sidney, 158

Korvasovich, Dick, 253
Kroeger, Keith, 142

Labor unions/strikes, 34–35, 43, 54, 177
Lansing, Gale, 232
LeBay, Peter, 144
Lehman Brothers mutual fund, 103
Leo, James, 238
Leveraged buyout heyday, 216
Levy, Louis, 33, 37
Lewis, Michael, 271
Lloyd, Edward, 67
Lloyd's of London, 67, 73, 129
Loeb, Gerald (*The Battle for Investment Survival*), 31–32, 220
Lovett, Robert, 37
Lowenstein, Roger, 4, 5, 152
Lynch, Peter, 79, 187–188, 223, 227, 279

Main, Jeremy, 127, 128
Manager/management importance, 231, 291–292
Manhattan Fund, 120, 124–125
Margin, 56, 86, 96, 107, 202, 223, 244–245
Market-timing, 220, 291
Marshall, John, 68
Martin, Truman, 71
Martin, William McChesney, 118, 270
Massachusetts Investors' Trust, 19
Mates, Fred, 121, 125–126, 269
McCain, Tom, 233
Memorex, 168, 169–170, 186, 219, 230, 295
Merrill, Charles, 85
Merrill Lynch, 119, 122, 223
Milken, Michael, 216, 224
Money market fund, 183
Municipal bonds, 42–43
Murray, Richard, 101–102, 108–109, 111, 114–115, 150, 260

Mutual funds, 77–78, 119–120, 121, 252, 255, 273
 Davis family, 11, 248, 255, 257, 282 (*see also* Venture Fund)
 first for Internet stocks, 269
 misleading rankings, 273
 pioneers, 19

Nasdaq, 124, 171, 293, 294
National Board of Fire Underwriters, 71
New York Society of Security Analysts (NYSSA), 87–89
New York Stock Exchange:
 membership seat, 51, 56, 189, 260
 post-Crash solvency test, 223
 S&P 500 performance *vs.* New York Venture Fund, 294
 value of shares (1943), 57
New York Venture Fund. *See* Venture Fund
Nifty Fifty, 171, 172–173, 180, 181–182, 184, 187–188, 277, 278

PaineWebber, 236, 237, 244, 257
Palmer, Guy, 162, 163, 167, 168, 190
Parkinson, Thomas, 54, 60
Peck, Ralph, 199, 200
Peltz, Nelson, 216
Perot, H. Ross, 124, 180
Pike, Sumner, 60
Plotkin, Irving, 126
Politics, 22, 25, 211, 238
Portfolio insurance (sophisticated hedging system), 221
Proyect, Martin, 166, 171, 190, 221, 257, 258
Putnam, George, 240

Railroad industry, 15–16, 19, 27, 46, 60, 124
Real estate, 265, 289

"Rear-view mirror," 39–47, 61, 292–293

Reed, John, 231, 253

Reinsurance, 101–102, 109

Robertson, Julian, 271

Rockefeller, John D., 139

Rogers, Jim, 221–222

Rogers, William, 132

Rohm & Haas, 165–166

Rolling return, 273

Roosevelt, Eleanor, 31

Roosevelt, Franklin D., 32, 42, 43, 45, 47, 54, 60

Rosenwald, James, 110, 111, 113, 114, 176, 177, 178

Rule of 72, 6, 10, 37, 135–136, 152, 230, 231, 295

Samuelson, Paul, 120

Sanborn, Bob, 271

Schiff, David, 226–227

Schumpeter, Joseph, 54, 56

Scott, Howard, 46

Security Equity Fund, 120

Seessel, Adam, 274

Selected group (funds), 257, 263, 264

Shawmut Bank in Boston, 236

Short sellers, 208, 254

Siegel, Jeremy (*Stocks for the Long Run*), 277

Smith, Edgar Lawrence (*Common Stocks As Long-Term Investments*), 18–19, 31, 37, 45

Soros, George, 271

Spencer, Diana Davis, 7, 8, 50, 52–53, 135, 139, 152, 153, 154, 158, 209, 211, 259

Spencer, John, 154, 158, 159, 259

Stagflation, 123, 183

State Street Bank, 241

State Street Investing Company, 19

Stix, Edith. *See* Wasserman, Edith Stix

Stock-lending program (launch of Davis's), 207–208

Stocks *vs.* bonds, 15–16, 40, 56, 57, 64, 76–77, 95, 102–103, 135, 251

Strikes/labor unions, 34–35, 43, 54, 177

Tanaka, Graham, 241, 242, 244

Tariffs, 46

Taxes, 42–43, 76–77, 86, 93, 210, 211, 256, 263

Technocrats, 46

Technology stocks, 170, 271, 279, 285

Templeton, John, 91, 114

Themes in investing, 290–291

Tontine, Lorenzo, 66, 68

Top-down stockpickers, 290

Treasuries, 58, 59, 251

Truman, Harry S., 85, 137, 260

Trusts (income producing *vs.* wealth building), 209–210

Tsai, Gerry, 120, 124–125, 231, 270

Twentieth Century Fund, 123

U.S. Treasuries, 40–41

Value investors/funds, 270, 277, 285

Value Line, 206–207, 209, 248, 259

Van Der Starr, Cornelius, 113

Venture Advisers, 257

Venture Fund, 9, 132, 166–169, 180, 212, 215, 216, 219, 251, 254, 255, 261, 264, 270, 273, 274

Davis's investments in, 248

Fiduciary Trust deal and ("orphan in this merger"), 190

flops in, 183

Forbes magazine dropping from honor roll (Chris promoted to comanager), 264

launched, 166–169

INDEX

Venture Fund *(Continued)*
  performance, 2, 9, 183, 187, 189, 214, 220, 222, 257, 294
  "rehab center for fallen growth stocks," 274
  rolling return, 273
  Shelby taking control of, 9, 132
  vs. S&P 500 index (graph), 294
  value-orientation of, 270
Volcker, Paul, 189, 214, 215

War debts ("triple swindle"), 57–58
War rationing, 52–53, 54
Wasserman, Bill ("Wild Bill"), 30–31, 32–33, 35, 36, 37–38, 44, 51, 60, 100, 170
Wasserman, Edith Stix, 21, 22, 99–100

Wasserman, Howard, 21
Wasserman, Isaac, 20–21
Wasserman, Joseph, 20–21, 22, 24, 25, 35, 36
Wasserman, Kathryn. *See* Davis, Kathryn Wasserman
Wasserman, Steven, 100
Wasserman family trusts, 41, 170, 209
Weill, Sandy, 254
Widlitz, Arnie, 222, 223
Wile, Frederick William, 29
Wilkinson, E. C., 28

Zulauf, Felix, 221